FUNDING EXTENDED CONFLICTS

FUNDING EXTENDED CONFLICTS

Korea, Vietnam, and the War on Terror

RICHARD M. MILLER, JR.

Foreword by Dr. Dov Zakheim

PRAEGER SECURITY INTERNATIONAL
Westport, Connecticut • London

Library of Congress Cataloging-in-Publication Data

Miller, Richard M., 1967–
   Funding extended conflicts : Korea, Vietnam, and the War on Terror / Richard M. Miller, Jr. ;
   foreword by Dov Zakheim.
      p.   cm.
   Includes bibliographical references and index.
   ISBN 978–0–275–99896–7 (alk. paper)
      1. War—Economic aspects—United States.   2. Korean War, 1950–1953—Economic
aspects—United States.   3. Vietnam War, 1961–1975—Economic aspects—United States.
4. War on Terrorism, 2001—Economic aspects.   I. Title
   HC110.D4M55   2007
   355.6′220973—dc22   2007016120

British Library Cataloguing in Publication Data is available.

Library of Congress Catalog Card Number: 2007016120
ISBN-13: 978–0–275–99896–7
ISBN-10: 0–275–99896–7

First published in 2007

Praeger Security International, 88 Post Road West, Westport, CT 06881
An imprint of Greenwood Publishing Group, Inc.
www.praeger.com

Printed in the United States of America

The paper used in this book complies with the
Permanent Paper Standard issued by the National
Information Standards Organization (Z39.48–1984).

10 9 8 7 6 5 4 3 2 1

To Lily Victoria,
In hopes that my generation
Can produce solutions to these problems
So your generation does not have to;

And to
The Men and Women of the United States
Who have given the last full measure of their devotion
In the War on Terrorism;

For while we study financial costs and consequences herein,
Let us never forget the bills they and their families have paid
In blood, sweat, and tears.

Contents

Foreword

Richard Miller offers a pathbreaking study of the interplay between budgets and policy, and specifically, the role that the Congressional power of the purse has played in funding past limited but lengthy wars in Korea, Vietnam, and the current ongoing Global War on Terror (GWOT). Miller provides the reader with a clear understanding of the otherwise arcane defense budget process. He demonstrates that a common set of issues has arisen in all three wartime contexts under review, lessons learned and re-learned, called "Resourcing Considerations."

A key consideration is that initial estimates of war costs have invariably fallen short of actual expenditures. Congress and the Executive Branch have repeatedly clashed over the use of supplemental appropriations to fund America's limited conflicts. These appropriations, which are not calculated against the total annual budget, have been a source of especially sharp debate in the current conflict because they mask the actual size of annual budget deficits.

Wars eventually do transition from supplemental budgeting to annual "baseline budgets." Ironically, however, and contrary to popular opinion, and that of many in the Congress, the research shows that supplemental appropriations actually provide greater visibility into wartime spending. Thus, they actually can help the Congress to monitor the nature of wartime expenditures. Moreover, supplemental appropriations, by their very nature, are requested and approved much closer to the time they are needed. Accordingly, projections and estimates that underlie the requests are more accurate than they would be if used to support a "baseline" budget that would only come into force some 18 months after it is initially prepared.

On the other hand, supplemental appropriations run afoul of Congressional authorization committees, whose jurisdiction does not traditionally extend to them.

Moreover, supplementals have at times become a vehicle for adding "pork," both those Congressional projects irrelevant to the wars in question, and, indeed, Executive Branch projects that might not otherwise survive intensive Congressional scrutiny.

This work illustrates that supplemental appropriations offer the Executive Branch a great degree of flexibility in moving funds to where they are most needed. Such flexibility, of course, flies in the face of those in Congress, and particularly on Congressional staffs, who are prone to engage in budget micromanagement and prefer that all reallocation of budgeted funds from one account to another receive prior Congressional approval. More than descriptions and analyses, Miller also offers solutions. In particular, he suggests some creative approaches that might help reconcile the conflicting attitudes to supplementals held by the Executive and Legislative Branches, and addresses many of the valid concerns held on both sides of that heated debate.

This book provides the most detailed history to date of the Defense Department's supplemental requests after 9/11. Further demonstrated are that war costs are not, and cannot be, simply those attributed to the Department of Defense (DoD), whether in its baseline or supplemental budgets. These costs are spread throughout government agencies, but rarely receive the prominence that is attached to DoD budget requests.

Some in the Congress have argued during the current debate over supplemental funding of the Iraq and Afghan wars that the Vietnam War was fully on budget by Fiscal Year 1970, that is, by July 1969. They therefore assert that the current conflict likewise should be fully funded in the DoD budget. In fact, this study reveals the DoD required an additional $2.3 billion to cover higher pay and related personnel costs, while non-DoD agencies required an additional $800 million. In today's terms, of course, that combined figure would exceed $15 billion. The Korea and Vietnam experiences also showed that war funding generally runs out before war bills are fully paid. Similarly, with respect to the current ongoing conflicts, there are legitimate fears that future modernization plans will be delayed and disrupted as the Nation finds it must continue to fund exploding personnel—especially healthcarem—and operations and maintenance accounts generated by the Iraq and Afghan wars.

Miller also draws attention to the reality that outlays resulting from a given conflict continue years, even decades, after that conflict has drawn to a close. There is already widespread public and Congressional recognition of the need to repair and replace weapons and systems employed in the current GWOT. The cost of "reset" is already estimated in the billions, and the end of the conflict is not even in sight. Moreover, since the current war has essentially been financed by debt, interest payments on that debt will be another expense that the Nation must bear for years to come.

Finally, we are reminded that the government continues to pay benefits to veterans of the Vietnam War, and will do so for decades, or even a century, until all those eligible as survivors and beneficiaries have been fully compensated. The

Nation therefore faces the prospect of paying veterans of the Global War on Terror for many years, even as it also pays veterans and others eligible as a result of the Vietnam, Balkan, and even Korean Wars.

The foregoing are only some of the nuggets the reader will mine in this immensely valuable volume. As the United States confronts the challenges of a new century, of which the Global War on Terror is the first, but most certainly not the last, its leaders need to understand, and cope with, the fiscal consequences that will accompany them. For those leaders, and for the informed public, this volume will no doubt prove an invaluable tool.

Dr. Dov Zakheim
Under Secretary of Defense (Comptroller) 2001–2004

Preface

An often overlooked aspect of war is addressed in this book—how much it costs and how to pay for it. When the topic is discussed today, especially in relation to the current Global War on Terror (GWOT), comparisons to past conflicts are often drawn. In listening to these debates, I was always frustrated by the misinformation surrounding historical examples and flawed presumptions based on lack of knowledge. This book provides a similar baseline comparison of the direct federal costs in America's two major extended conflicts during the Cold War, Korea and Vietnam, and today's GWOT. There are too many issues regarding war financing and budgeting to give them all appropriate coverage. I have limited the field of examination, as outlined in the first two chapters, to provide an overview of these three conflicts and enable a reasonable set of comparisons in the space of a few hundred pages.

The aim in content and message is "the middle." Considerations examined are below the level of grand strategy, yet largely above the finite details of the federal budgeting process and individual resourcing initiatives. To that end, for the professional reader, I have attempted to include enough detail for those involved in programming and budgeting resources to provide lessons learned and useful examinations of past methods. At the same time, for those strictly involved in the policy realm, I have attempted to limit technical budget jargon and details to illuminate valuable overall insights when examining funding options for extended conflict and long-term war. For the general reader, hopefully the overview of these past and current conflicts are sufficient to enable a more informed citizenry in this important aspect of the debates on war and security. As a guide to reading, whether going cover to cover, looking at individual case study chapters, or simply reviewing the final two chapters for enduring lessons learned (and relearned), any approach will hopefully leave the reader with something of value.

I am deeply indebted to my family for the completion of this book. My eternal gratitude goes to my wife for her love and support as always, but especially this time for her patience and late nights tending to a new baby so that I could find the necessary hours to bang on the computer keyboard some more. To my in-laws, Ignacio and Lidia; many thanks for all the support at home, supply of strong coffee to keep me going, and most of all, their unique understanding and appreciation for the price of freedom.

Professional thanks also go to many. My first debt of gratitude is to Dr. Mark Clodfelter, of the National War College. Clod's humor and patience made an arduous research task on this project bearable. More importantly, his tremendous insights and suggestions have improved the end result immeasurably and I am most grateful. Thanks also to the staff at the Pentagon Library for their cheerful assistance and occasional refreshments—they provided welcome relief from many hours spent in the Law stacks, and to Dr. Michael Hussey at the National Archives and Records Administration (NARA II), College Park, for skillfully navigating me through the index of voluminous records boxes to find the necessary nuggets of truth.

Finally, thanks to the staff at Praeger Security International, especially Senior Editor Robert Silano for his belief and enthusiasm for this project, and Adam Kane and the rest of the staff for their dedicated support in the publication process.

Everyone's advice and assistance has made this book better—any shortcomings or errors clearly remain my responsibility.

Abbreviations

9/11	September 11th, 2001
APPN	Appropriation
ASFF	Afghan Security Forces Fund
AVF	All-Volunteer Force
BCT	Brigade Combat Team
BoB	Bureau of the Budget
CBO	Congressional Budget Office
CEA	Council of Economic Advisors
CERP	Commanders Emergency Response Program
CIF	Commanders-in-Chief Initiative Fund
CJCS	Chairman of the Joint Chiefs of Staff
COST	Contingency Operations Support Tool
CPA	Coalition Provisional Authority
CRS	Congressional Research Service
CY$	Constant Year Dollars
DERF	Defense Emergency Response Fund
DFAS	Defense Financial Accounting Service
DoD	Department of Defense
DPA	Defense Production Act
EEE	Emergencies and Extraordinary Expenses (Authority)
E/S	End Strength
FSA	Family Separation Allowance
FY	Fiscal Year
FYDP	Future Years Defense Plan
GAO	Government Accountability Office

GDP	Gross Domestic Product
GNP	Gross National Product
GWOT	Global War on Terror
HAC	House Appropriations Committee
HR	House Resolution
IDP	Imminent Danger Pay
IFF	Iraq Freedom Fund
IRRF	Iraq Relief and Reconstruction Fund
ISFF	Iraqi Security Forces Fund
JCS	Joint Chiefs of Staff
L&S	Lift and Sustain (Authority)
MEU	Marine Expeditionary Unit
MILCON	Military Construction
NRRRF	National Resources Risk Remediation Fund
NSC	National Security Council
O&M	Operations and Maintenance
OCTF	Overseas Combating Terrorism Fund
OEF	Operation ENDURING FREEDOM
OIF	Operation IRAQI FREEDOM
OMB	Office of Management and Budget
ONE	Operation NOBLE EAGLE
OPTEMPO	Operations Tempo
ORHA	Office of Reconstruction and Humanitarian Assistance
OSD	Office of the Secretary of Defense
PAYGO	Pay as You Go
PL	Public Law
POTUS	President of the United States
PPS	Policy Planning Staff
PROC	Procurement
RDT&E	Research, Development, Test and Evaluation
SAC	Senate Appropriations Committee
SEA	Southeast Asia
SEAEF	Southeast Asia Emergency Fund
SECDEF	Secretary of Defense
SGLI	Serviceman's Group Life Insurance
SUPP	Supplemental
T&E	Train and Equip
TOA	Total Obligation Authority
TY$	Then Year Dollars
UN	United Nations
U.S.	United States
USAID	United States Agency for International Development
USCG	United States Coast Guard
USSR	Union of Soviet Socialist Republics
VA	Veterans Administration

1 ——————————————————————————

Introduction

The spirit of a people, its cultural level, its social structure, the deeds its policy may prepare—all this and more is written in its fiscal history, stripped of all phrases. He who knows how to listen to its message here discerns the thunder of world history more clearly than anywhere else.

> —Joseph A. Schumpeter, Economist

History is always written wrong, and so always needs to be rewritten.

> —George Santayana, Philosopher

THE PROBLEMS FACED TODAY

America's so-called Global War on Terror (GWOT) has created controversy on many fronts. Besides a rash of conflicting views over how best to fight the current conflict, equally contentious opinions have arisen over how best to fund it. Components of the government's Executive Branch, the Services, the Chairman of the Joint Chiefs of Staff (CJCS), the Office of the Secretary of Defense (OSD), and the Office of Management and Budget (OMB), have on occasion locked horns with each other and with Congress, regarding how much money is necessary, the appropriate manner to provide it, and where it should come from. In making those arguments, many debaters have turned to history—and often their use of history has suffered from misinformation or a high degree of selectivity. America's actual record of how it funded long-term conflicts since World War II offers intriguing insights for those who must now grapple with GWOT-spawned conflicts while also addressing significantly increasing budget deficits, constrained domestic spending priorities and uncertain tax policy, particularly if the GWOT truly becomes a generational or decades-long challenge as some predict. As the following account will show, similar contradictory concerns have also existed during America's long-term wars in its recent past.[1]

How America dealt with such funding difficulties during the Korean and Vietnam conflicts—two examples of extended "hot" conflicts during the Cold War era—should provide useful insights for comparing how America has dealt with similar "hot" conflicts during the current GWOT. The examination of Korea and Vietnam will establish a comparable baseline as to the actual direct United States federal government cost of these wars and how the nation budgeted for those costs. The analysis will further provide baselines for reviewing how the United States has funded conflicts in the aftermath of 9/11—specifically, the wars in Afghanistan and Iraq. The collective analysis will in turn provide a basis for examining useful insights and comparisons from the three major conflict cases where appropriate lessons may be drawn for future consideration, and conclude with a discussion of the future economic environment facing the United States and the implications that portend against the backdrop of long-term warfare that may be with us for many years to come.

Cost of War: A Frame of Reference

Events are the ephemera of history; they pass across its stage like fireflies, hardly glimpsed before they settle back into darkness and as often as not into oblivion. Every event, however brief, has to be sure a contribution to make, lights up some dark corner or even some wide vista of history. Not is it only political history which benefits most, for every historical landscape—political, economic, social, even geographical—is illumined by the intermittent flare of the event.

—Fernand Braudel, Historian

Money is but the Fat of the Body-politick [sic]. . . .

—William Petty, Economist

It is useful to address several background questions before delving into the case studies.

WHY LOOK AT KOREA AND VIETNAM?

In his seminal work, *The American Way of War*, Russell Weigley presented the American experience of war through World War II as a study in the development of annihilation warfare.

In the Indian wars, the Civil War, and then climactically in World War II, American strategists sought in actuality the object that Clausewitz saw as that of the ideal type of war, of war in the abstract: " . . . the destruction of the enemy's armed forces, amongst all the objects which can be pursued in War, appears always as the one which overrules all others."

> .... Throughout American history until that time, the United States usually possessed no national strategy for the employment of force or the threat of force to attain political ends, except as the nation used force in wartime openly and directly in pursuit of military victories as complete as was desired or possible. The only kind of American strategy employing the armed forces tended to be the most direct kind of military strategy, applied in war.
>
> During the Cold War and especially after the Korean War, the belief that the United States was involved in a protracted conflict with international Communism led to a departure from historic habits and to an effort to form a national strategy for the employment of American power in defense and promotion of the country's political values and interests. The new national strategy would be not merely a military strategy but an all-inclusive planning for the use of the nation's total resources to defend and advance the national interests, encompassing military strategy and Clausewitz's use of combats along with other means.[1]

Korea and Vietnam are considered not only because they were both long-term conflicts, but also because they were limited "hot" wars fought on the backdrop of the grander strategic struggle of the Cold War. These conflicts ushered in the era of limited wars for the United States where simple military victory was not necessarily the ultimate end. The nuanced mix of grand strategy, political ends, and military strategy became interwoven into complex policies in pursuit of American security and interests. Similarly, if today's limited war engagements the United States has undertaken in Iraq, Afghanistan, the Horn of Africa, the Philippines, and even in the U.S. homeland are overlaid on a still evolving yet larger-scale struggle known as the GWOT, it makes sense to examine circumstances of the past to look for potential insights for the future.

FUNDAMENTALS OF FINANCING WAR

The political economist A.C. Pigou, described a country's resources as follows:

> The real resources possessed by any country consist of the mental and manual power of its people, of its land and mineral deposits, of its material capital of buildings, plant, railways, ships and stores of goods, of its immaterial capital of "organization," and of the legal rights of its citizens to payments from foreigners.[2]

He further described how in peacetime, these various resources are engaged in regular patterns of activity that produce the national dividend or income. Furthermore, in peacetime, some of this dividend is reinvested in capital to allow for future growth in production. Due to leisure desires and demand changes in the market, the country's resources will never work at the "maximum imaginable intensity." In wartime, Pigou states these resources are reapplied as society's interests change. The populace focuses on the maximum amount these resources can produce for immediate use to achieve victory in the actual process of war. He then describes the four principal sources from which the income-producing power of a country—the "real war fund" as he calls it—can be drawn: (1) augmented production, (2) reduced personal consumption, (3) reduced investment in new forms of capital, and (4) depletion of existing capital.[3] In context, as a British citizen writing before the onset of World War II, he envisioned the economic performance anticipated through the lens of total war mobilization. While these fundamental principals are still true, the U.S. financing of limited war has taken on slightly different forms. In recent practice, the United States has financed war through four main methods: raising taxes, offsetting costs from other government spending, creating more money, and government borrowing.[4] Some combination of these methods is an option that has also been used in past war financing efforts. A fifth way, done only recently and once to a considerable extent, was direct foreign subsidy of U.S. combat operations as seen in Operations Desert Shield/Storm.

The first option, increased taxation, is straightforward in concept; however, it can be very complex in execution depending politically on how the tax burden is distributed. Taxes can be levied against individuals, property, business profits, commodities, etc.—the burden falls upon those who have their taxes raised. Taxation also has the consequence of placing the burden on the current generation conducting the war. The economic impacts of taxation are generally easier to measure in the near term than the impacts of either creating or borrowing money. This greater transparency and immediacy of the burden are the two main reasons many politicians shy away from using heavy taxation to finance conflict.[5]

Offsetting other government spending is another option, albeit a less utilized means to defray war costs. The evolved composition of the total federal budget is a significant reason for this decline. Broken into six broad categories over time, it tells the story in Figure 2.1. Financing costs on the national debt is the first category shown at the top. The government is obligated to make these interest payments when due and is provided little discretion other than rolling over that debt into further deficit borrowing and therefore delaying, but increasing, the outlays required. The next two categories are mandatory spending. Often called "entitlement programs," these include such items as Social Security, Medicare, and other benefit programs. They are entitlements because the governing criterion determining the structure of their expenditures is written into law by Congress. As such, without subsequent legislation changing these programs, the government is obligated to make these payments. The final three categories are discretionary funding, with number four being domestic spending, and five and six representing international programs and defense respectively. Figure 2.1 clearly reveals the dominating position mandatory spending has taken from less than half of all federal spending in the time of the Korean War to approximately 65 percent today— and the trend is increasing. Entitlements are incredibly popular with the public, often considered untouchable by politicians and are written into law. Decreasing

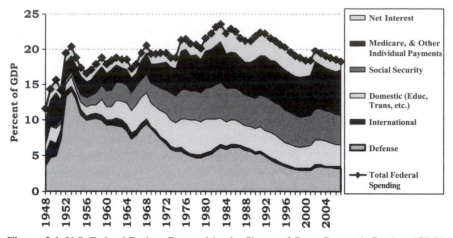

Figure 2.1 U.S. Federal Budget Composition by Shares of Gross Domestic Product (GDP)
Source: Congressional Budget Office, *The Budget and Economic Outlook: An Update* (Washington, DC: GPO, August 2002), 1–19, and Office of Management and Budget, *Historical Tables of the Fiscal Year 2007 Budget* (Washington, DC: GPO, 2006), 3.1, 6.1, 9.1.

spending here would shift economic burden onto those whom the spending was previously directed.

The politics involved with this today makes flexibility for offsetting expenditures from entitlements significantly limited. In this breakdown, defense and international programs are the centerpieces of national security and foreign affairs. Therefore, in general, increases in these categories are assumed to occur in wartime. If entitlement laws remain the same, that leaves only the discretionary, nondefense domestic spending available to help finance the war effort—clearly a very small portion of the overall spending picture to absorb any significant and sustained wartime spending—and an unlikely mechanism for wartime financing.

The third option, simply printing more money, has an inherent disincentive for conflict financing due to the resulting dramatic inflation that usually occurs. Under this option, only the paper supply of money is increased and not the supply of real resources in the economy. The new money supply can be exchanged for fewer real resources, whose demand also generally increases in wartime. This resulting form of government financing has often been characterized as an "inflation tax."[6] Rapidly rising prices can also lead to hoarding of goods, further generating a hyperinflationary tendency.[7] Likewise, significant and extended inflation can distort public perceptions about future price changes, thereby altering economic behavior. Over time, this option places a greater burden on those who have a higher percentage of income spending required for subsistence, and often ultimately results in significant consumer backlash against the political decisions perceived to have caused the inflation. The government may attempt to mitigate the inflationary impacts in wartime with various control mechanisms on prices, wages, etc., but depending upon implementation, these controls come with their own discriminating effects on the economy and can generate further discontent.

The last of the methods is deficit spending—when the government borrows funds by selling bonds. This burden shifting mechanism places the onus on future generations to liquidate the deficits accrued today and their added finance costs. Furthermore, when debt financing leads to reduction in private capital formation, future generations can also suffer from future lower growth rates.[8] In today's context, another concern recently highlighted in the press and other venues is the identity of the holders of these growing numbers of U.S. treasury bills. In conflicts of old, war bonds and other bond measures were sold largely to domestic individuals, banks, or other institutions. Today, foreign holdings of U.S. debts are significant and growing. Taken in isolation, this situation is not necessarily a national security threat. However, it is a situation worth monitoring for the implications of potential leverage against the U.S. dollar and economy by foreign powers with competing interests and motives.

FUNDAMENTALS OF BUDGETING FOR WAR

A related but separate topic from the financing of war is war budgeting—the intergovernmental process by which funds are planned, requested, authorized, appropriated, apportioned, obligated, and executed to pay for war. In this sense, budgeting is the process and the mechanics of getting the war bills paid, not raising the money to make the payments, which is finance. Basically, the cost of war may be included as part of the regular annual budget submission to Congress, or through supplemental appropriation submissions during the fiscal year in progress, or through a combination of the two methods. Regardless of which budgeting method is used, there is also a decision whether to keep the spending "on-budget," that is, within the total spending limits established, or "off-budget," normally done by declaring the spending as an emergency measure and thereby not subject to limit enforcement.[9]

Likewise, in both regular or supplemental budget submissions and appropriations, the actual war costs can be broken out and distinguished as distinct line items, or they can be "rolled-up" within larger appropriations that cover similar expenditures for other functions as well. As a matter of practice, when incorporated in regular appropriations, war costs are usually included within the larger appropriations requested and not clearly broken out into specific line items attributable to the war effort. Politically, this tactic in budgeting is obvious—if it is easier to identify true costs, it is easier for critics to have a clear target to aim at. Because of this practice, it is often difficult historically to determine clearly what the specific cost of war entailed.

PROBLEMS IN DEFINING WAR COSTS

The fundamental problem in determining war costs is to understand what is included and, perhaps more importantly, what is excluded. The most common dollar measurement is the direct military cost. In recent history, this figure is often reported for the United States as Department of Defense (DoD) spending during the conflict. However, to incorporate all DoD spending as war costs can be misleading, as the Department spends money on a variety of other functions and missions even during times of conflict. Yet even determining what is spent directly on combat operations is still difficult. The reason for this difficulty is the difference between total costs and incremental costs.

In total cost estimation, all expenditures that can be attributed to the conflict are counted. In an incremental costing figure, only the additional costs accrued as a result of the conflict are considered. For example, assume a hypothetical military, consisting of 100 personnel total that recruited no additional personnel specifically for a conflict, and used 50 of those 100 personnel in fighting the war. In a total cost estimate, the full cost of those 50 personnel who fought would count toward war costs. An incremental estimate would only consider the additional costs for those 50 personnel resulting from the war effort, such as hazardous duty pay as a result of combat operations. Similarly, for equipment and weapons, incremental costing only counts what is used above and beyond normal peacetime expenditures as legitimate war costs.

Another problem in determining war costs is specifying the value of dollars being used. Dollars can be basically of two values; Then-Year (TY) dollars that reflect the actual value of the money in the time period being considered or Constant-Year (CY) dollars that are adjusted for inflation and "baselined" for a particular year. For example, $100 in 1950 taken with, say, a hypothetical inflation factor of 10 to equate value in 2006 would yield:

$100 (TY 1950 dollars) $\times$ 10 (inflation factor) = $1000 (CY 2006 dollars)

and likewise,

$100 (TY 2006 dollars)/10 (inflation factor) = $10 (TY 1950 dollars)

In the federal budgeting cycle, the monetary value reflected can change based on where the cost measurements are made. In the normal sequence, funds are requested, appropriated, apportioned, obligated, and executed. Funds are generally requested by the executive branch and then provided in some amount by Congress through an "appropriation." Following the appropriation, the Office of Management and Budget (OMB) "apportions" the appropriated funds out over time to the executive department or agency tasked with conducting the function for which the money is provided. That department or agency will then "obligate" funds, making commitments through various contractual measures and ultimately will "execute" the funds when the U.S. treasury actually makes a payment for goods or services rendered. Obviously, for any one program or function, depending on where in this process the cost measurement is taken will usually result in a different value of war cost.

For all the factors discussed above as related to direct DoD spending, the same considerations hold true for direct and indirect costs for other government agencies supporting the conflict. Other associated costs, such as foreign aid, military assistance spending, war production and mobilization, etc. are just some of the items that may or may not necessarily appear as monies provided to the DoD but can be considered legitimate war costs nonetheless. Additionally, long term, post-conflict costs like Veterans Administration benefits/pensions to war veterans and debt servicing (assuming the conflict was all or partially financed via deficit spending) can also be considered.

Beyond simply considering government expenditures, war costing may also consider the costs of second and third order effects that occur in the economy. What are the lost productivity and earning power over a lifetime of those killed in conflict? What are the impacts of adjusted tax burdens, new business costs, and inflationary conditions on both business and consumers? How are wealth and productivity redistributed within the economy? These are but a few examples. Finally, the toughest war costs to quantify are opportunity costs: what other economic activity is delayed, reduced, or foregone entirely to support the war efforts? All of these are legitimate, but often overlooked, aspects of considering the costs of war, especially when examining options for long-term conflict. Problems with determining these types of costs are the high dependency on assumptions and determining causal links to the war as the generating source of the incurred costs.

SUMMARY

Uniform criteria regarding methods of financing, budgeting, and the value—and types—of dollars being examined will be specified for each of the case studies that follow. By establishing these baselines, and clearly defining answers to many of the questions posed above, equitable costs of war will be better articulated allowing more accurate and meaningful comparisons across the cases reviewed. Definitions are provided to clarify and reference the unique terms used throughout in the Glossary.

Korean War: Fiscal Years 1951–1953

... We cannot count on native Korean forces to help us hold the line against Soviet expansion. Since the territory is not of decisive strategic importance to us, our main task is to extricate ourselves without too great a loss of prestige.

—George Kennan, U.S. Statesman/Strategist, in Policy Planning
Staff Report-13, November 6, 1947

... The attack was naked, deliberate, unprovoked aggression, without a shadow of justification.

The attack upon the Republic of Korea makes it plain beyond all doubt that the international Communist movement is prepared to use armed invasion to conquer independent nations. We must therefore recognize the possibility that armed aggression may take place in other areas.

The free world has made it clear, through the United Nations, that lawless aggression will be met with force. This is the significance of Korea—and it is a significance whose importance cannot be overestimated.

We are moving as rapidly as possible to bring to bear on the fighting front larger forces and heavier equipment, and to increase our naval and air superiority. But it will take time, men, and material to slow down the forces of aggression, bring those forces to a halt, and throw them back.

The increases in the size of the armed forces, and the additional supplies and equipment which will be needed, will require additional appropriations.

—Harry Truman, U.S. President, Excerpts from
Report to Congress, July 19, 1950

As often as not in history, it is the unintended consequences that really matter.

—Lawrence Stone, Historian

FISCAL BACKGROUND

How much did the Korean War cost the United States in monetary terms? The spending statistics recorded on this question are not consistent, nor conclusive. In actual 1950s dollar amounts, most estimates published vary in the $30 billion to $60 billion range and some even exceed the $100 billion mark.[1] The disparities arise from many of the reasons discussed in the preceding chapter on defining war costs. Another significant complicating factor in this specific case was the general defense build-up undertaken in concert with the prosecution of the Korean War. This additional spending is often generically termed the "NSC-68 Build-up" after the National Security Council (NSC) policy document that outlined the strategy and defense posture for communist containment. In mid-to-late 1950, with the commonly held view that Korea was but one stage, or the opening battle, in a coming world war of communist aggression, it is apparent why some cost estimates reconcile this additional spending as part of the Korean War cost. This argument's rationale is that if conflict in Korea had not started, final approval of NSC-68, the general build-up of U.S. and allied military forces, and the associated fiscal demands would likely not have been undertaken in the manner they ultimately developed. The underlying strategic perceptions and economic conditions prior to the start of Korean hostilities are a context worth reviewing to better understand and appreciate the economic magnitude of the Korean War response.

World War II had profound impacts on all aspects of social, economic, and political life in the United States. As a result, the Korean War financing story cannot be fully understood without the context of the environment resulting from the end of World War II. The evolving security strategy, surrounding economic conditions, and executive-legislative political interplay from 1946 until the outbreak of the Korean War on June 25, 1950, had significant ramifications on early war financing. The following summaries highlight these aspects that set the financial/economic stage for how the United States handled the Korean War.

Security Strategy and Fiscal Opinions—A Brief Developmental Review

The overarching factors driving U.S. security spending in the late 1940s were the pre-NSC-68 impressions of the American security posture and concern over heightened military costs. Because of these factors, American foreign and defense policies were often conflicted during this period, if not downright schizophrenic.[2] On one hand, there was a perception of an increasing threat from the Soviet Union that continued to build over time. On the other, the means developed to cope with the perceived increase in Soviet strength were inadequate in the minds of many senior leaders. The disconnect was partly due to an intellectual debate where differences of opinion and uncertainties resided as to the nature, degree, and timing of the Soviet threat and the types of forces necessary to meet this ill-defined challenge. It was also due to the political realm and climate of the late 1940s, with the persistent myth that the economy could not tolerate higher spending. Pressures for economizing were so great within the Truman Administration that appropriations for Fiscal Years (FYs) 1949, 1950, and 1951, as planned for DoD, declined in real terms, as did purchasing power under increasing inflation. These declines inhibited serious consideration of a new defense policy and made far-reaching changes all but impossible.[3]

A series of policy papers leading up to final approval of NSC-68 highlight these tensions. George Kennan, the head of the State Department's Policy Planning Staff (PPS), for then Secretary of State George Marshall, prepared the first paper in the series, known as document PPS-13. Kennan drafted it in November 1947, in preparation for a cabinet meeting on the world security situation. Entitled, "Résumé of World Situation," the first sentence was telling: "The danger of war is vastly exaggerated in many quarters."[4] The remainder of the next four paragraphs outlined a view of likely Soviet actions to consolidate a communist hold over Eastern Europe. The fifth paragraph implied that the United States could not afford to take on the Soviets alone: "Our best answer to this is to strengthen in every way local forces of resistance, and persuade others to bear a greater part of the burden of opposing communism. The present 'bi-polarity' will, in the long run, be beyond our resources."[5] In fact, at least 11 times, the very short document made direct or implied references to economic concerns regarding countering Soviet intentions and the desire to increase burden sharing of this task.

Shortly after Kennan prepared PPS-13, the NSC staff began work in December 1947 on a document eventually serialized as NSC-7. After interagency consultation with the military, intelligence community, State Department, and others, the NSC staff prepared the draft report in March 1948.[6] NSC-7 was vague on specifics regarding implementation. It recommended a general U.S. force build-up of unspecified size and a "world-wide counter-offensive" aimed at checking Soviet expansionism. The PPS at the State Department felt some recommendations were not sufficiently clear and Kennan himself had reservations before the NSC considered it. The Joint Chiefs concurred in part, but with many questions and qualifiers. As a result, the NSC returned the paper to the staff for revision and ultimately it was never approved; however, it did lay the groundwork for the NSC-20 series documents.

Out of NSC-7, Secretary of Defense James Forrestal pushed to clarify strategy to aid in budget development. In a letter to the President in July 1948, Forrestal requested "preparation of a statement which specifies and evaluates the risks of the future, states our objectives, and outlines measures to be followed in achieving them."[7] That letter circulated among the NSC staff as NSC 20 on July 12, 1948. The PPS at the State Department was already working a draft paper addressing similar concerns. The paper was further refined as NSC 20/3, which focused on the measures to achieve the directives, and then consolidated and approved by President Truman as NSC 20/4 in November 1948.

NSC 20/4, both in tone and substance, was a restrained and cautious assessment. It acknowledged the USSR posed a grave potential threat to U.S. security, but made no mention of any need for increased military preparedness. In fact, it warned against "excessive" armaments as a menace in itself to the country's economic stability, as well as the potential for misinterpretation by the USSR.[8] It assumed the United States could afford to accept some degree of risk as it estimated the USSR would not be ready for a general war offensive against the West until the mid-1950s.

The timing of NSC-20/4 also weighed heavily on its economic precautions. Inflation was on the rise, a tax-wary Congress sat on Capitol Hill, and it was a presidential election year with the outlook for Truman's reelection uncertain at best. He campaigned on a platform of striving for a sound economy, reducing inflation, limiting federal spending, and minimizing disputes with the USSR (although campaign rhetoric, it had carryover influence). Truman's come-from-behind victory likely emboldened his view of public support for those campaign policies and his economizing position on federal, and particularly defense, spending.

Another political-economic problem that lay within the suggested "foreign" framework of these NSC documents was the difficulty in rebuilding European economies. While the NSC called for burden sharing and allied rearmament, these governments were unlikely to increase their arms budgets. Additionally, countering a serious Soviet challenge on the continent would require German rearmament— something likely to trigger strong opposition from France and Britain. France was particularly not interested in German rearmament while heavily committed in Indochina.[9] American leaders had further committed themselves to German disarmament as stated formal policy.

Thus, the early history of NSC-68 was constrained, if not outright precluded, by fiscal concerns. When the NSC-68 draft was refined in early 1950, with a view toward a favorable review by the President, Truman continued to send it back for staff work based on costs. He did so despite the fact that the position of his Council of Economic Advisors (CEA) had significantly shifted. When NSC-7 had been prepared 2 years prior, the CEA warned that accelerating expenditures might require imposition of significant economic controls reminiscent of the World War II experience. At that time, Truman reacted very negatively to this idea and imposed tight restrictions on military spending.[10] Even in September 1949, the CEA chairman warned against an NSC staff recommendation which called for a modest $2 billion increase in defense spending, claiming resulting deficits would be a greater harm to national security than any gains the funds would provide.[11] Now, 2 years later, the incoming CEA Chairman, Leon Keyserling, advised the President on using Keynesian techniques for government stimulation aimed at economic recovery and increased growth rates.[12] While Keyserling initially thought the President's domestic program could spur spending, the proposed buildup called for in NSC-68 could trigger some of it as well. Yet, the inherent economizer in Truman, coupled with his perceptions of a tax-wary public and Congress, won out and not only prevented increased defense expenditures, but also delayed final approval of NSC-68 until after the outbreak of Korea. Despite the aggressive North Korean posturing prior to the invasion of the south, Truman held the line on spending, and "the pressures for economizing were so great that the administration's request for FY 1951—the budget Congress was contemplating in June 1950—was almost 15% below the appropriations for the year before."[13]

The vantage point of the Joint Chiefs of Staff (JCS) also revealed the magnitude of fiscal restraint. The JCS preliminary estimates the year before for the FY50 budget estimates had initially been approximately $30 billion. After several weeks of cajoling by Secretary of Defense Louis Johnson to reduce the Service requests, the Joint Chiefs resubmitted a total request of $23.6 billion—still more than 60 percent greater than the amount of $14.6 billion the administration would ultimately support. Further aggravating the Joint Chiefs, Secretary Johnson later imposed a ceiling on obligation of funds at $13 billion to match actual expenditures to the anticipated cap of $13 billion on DoD spending planned for the following year. This move followed campaign rhetoric that had even suggested defense spending at or below $10 billion. The JCS responded to the final budget figure with a statement that the proposed budget was "insufficient to implement national policy *in any probable war situation.*"[14]

Public opinion also largely reflected the schism that was apparent between ends and means in the government policymaking. The American public was clearly and consistently anti-Communist. This sentiment was so strong that two polls in late 1949 indicated that 68 percent, nationwide, thought the Communist Party should be banned by law in the United States, and another poll indicated 77 percent felt that one could not even be a good Christian if also a communist party member. The same percentage also favored requiring all Communist Party members to register with the Justice Department. A significant majority saw the Soviets as ultimately trying to build itself up to be the ruling power of the world.[15] Yet despite the threat perceived by the American people of an expansionist Soviet Union and communism in general, by and large there was little support to accept greater defense spending or the accompanying potential increased tax burden.

In fact, in March 1950, Truman's "minimalist" defense budgets, both in current year execution and next year planning, were supported as sufficient by nearly a three to one margin, with 44 percent saying "about right," another 15 percent saying "too much," and only 23 percent claiming "too little."[16] Despite the increased threat perception, surprisingly, the trend of opinion on the likelihood of war was declining. If the United States did need to go to war, nearly three quarters of those polled felt the U.S. Air Force would play the most important part in winning the war. This reflected a view consistent with the ideas of strategic bombing, nuclear weapons and "war on the cheap" that was popular at the time. Regarding taxes, in November 1949, a mere 7 months before the outbreak of Korean hostilities and the beginning of significant taxation to pay for the war, 68 percent of Americans were opposed to President Truman's call for a tax increase to address the budget deficits and only 14 percent approved of any increase.

The public's outlook for supporting American actions in Asia was even less encouraging. Few Americans seemed focused on the Far East, as reflected by their responses concerning China, the biggest Asian security issue of the day. Only roughly one-third of those polled had any knowledge of the U.S. government reports and assessments of the situation in China at the time, yet, nearly 60 percent of those were sure the communists would take over China and half of the overall population surveyed felt the same way.[17] Despite a general fear of communism and widespread belief of a Chinese Communist takeover, there was virtually no support for the United States to intervene and very little support for sending aid, whether economic or military.[18] Yet, when surveyed on the more generic question of providing aid (war materials and money) to governments opposing potential Russian aggression (at the time focused in Europe), there was a significantly larger margin of support with nearly half of those polled in favor (46 percent in favor to 40 percent opposed nationwide).[19] Comparing these numbers to the lack of support for aid to China indicated an American public bias toward Europe rather than Asia. If China were a lesser concern, Korea was essentially nonexistent as such. In summary, what was the American public's state of mind concerning Korea prior to the North Korean invasion in June 1950? As McCullough points out in his seminal biography of President Truman, it was " . . . a place most Americans still had trouble finding on a map."[20] For all the lack of clarity on security and defense issues, and lack of emphasis on foreign policy toward Asia during this time, the exact opposite could be said for domestic concerns over the economy.

Economic Considerations and Concerns

The U.S. economy before the Korean War is largely a story of demobilization, reconversion, and relaxation of controls from the total war experience of World War II. President Truman felt that too much of the war effort had been financed through borrowing and deficit spending. He was committed to balancing the budget and making progress on debt reduction from the war. Throughout the late 1940s, he tried to shift the focus of government spending from military and security needs to domestic priorities and consumer well-being. Inflation, deficits, tax rates, industry and labor adjustments, recessions and fear of another depression all weighed heavily on public opinion, politicians, and government policymaking.

The end of World War II brought about a rapid decline in government expenditures. Wage and price controls during the war artificially limited both wholesale and consumer price increases. The controls also restricted production of consumer goods and construction. Further, war production demands on resources resulted in numerous shortages. Likewise, the shortages resulted in greater consumer savings. In fact, individual financial assets increased nearly tenfold from 1939 to 1944 alone.[21] Additionally, the government printed extra currency during World War II to help finance the war effort. The combined effect of shortages, a rough doubling of the nation's money supply, pent up consumer demand and cash savings, and the relaxing of controls after the war all fed an initial inflationary response that took several years to dissipate.

Of course, World War II helped put an end to the depression of the 1930s and high unemployment. It also threatened prosperity, at least in the short term, as it came to an end. Cancellation of unneeded war contracts and rapid demobilization created the potential for high unemployment. Both President Truman and the Republican controlled 80th Congress seemed more concerned with the impact of tax relief, deficits, and the public debt than on ensuring maximum employment. As long as public reactions to unemployment remained below the "political boiling point," both parties appeared content to pursue deficit reduction policies through lower federal spending (significantly at the expense of the defense establishment) and tax reductions (although Truman consistently fought against significant tax reductions during the postwar period, he did acquiesce to significant reductions in 1945 and 1948).[22]

Beyond this focus, strikes and labor-management problems consistently appeared as a top problem facing the country in the opinion polls. While preventing war often ranked high, other economic concerns such as the cost of living, government spending, unemployment, taxes, rent control, etc., always seemed to dominate, or at least equal, foreign affairs-related issues (handling Russia, controlling the atomic bomb, communism). When polled in March 1950, anticipating the mid-term congressional elections in 8 months, the domestic agenda accounted for 74 percent of the responses on "the most important issues of the day," compared to only 15 percent for various foreign policy-related concerns.[23]

Summary

In the aftermath of World War II, perceptions were influenced by wartime experiences. President Truman was strongly influenced by the World War II debt financing, and a desire to approach future conflict in a "pay-as-you-go" manner with a balanced budget—and therefore likely higher taxation. Consumers, conditioned by the previous war's shortages and rationing, initially responded to Korean hostilities by hoarding civilian goods, resulting in artificially high inflation in the first few months of the war and causing the administration to impose anti-inflationary forms of control used before. Polling information on a variety of topics concerning interests, security, economy, communism, and war displayed an American mind-set in early 1950 focused on domestic economic concerns. The large tax increases Truman ultimately pursued to finance the Korean War and general force buildup for containment were not predisposed to public support.[24] While communism was a concern, as it related to Korea, there was an inherent focus on Europe rather than Asia, primacy of domestic concerns over economic matters, and an overall lessening of fear over the likelihood of conflict. These

Table 3.1 Department of Defense Total Obligation Authority

$Millions	FY48	FY49	FY50	FY51	FY52	FY53	FY54	FY55	FY56
TY	11,903	13,204	14,337	45,173	57,188	44,283	30,429	33,790	38,065
CY2006	154,205	164,274	164,938	397,349	518,217	422,093	316,452	325,690	340,251

Source: Office of the Under Secretary of Defense (Comptroller), *National Defense Budget Estimates for FY 2006*, (Washington D.C.: GPO, 2005).

factors combined to presuppose that the American public would not likely tolerate a costly war on the Korean peninsula. That supposition proved correct.

COST AND BUDGETING OVERVIEW

Tracking the costs of the Korean War in isolation is virtually an impossible task for several reasons. First, many of the government systems for accounting, documentation, and procedures in use today to identify and quantify costs were not in existence in the early 1950s. This void resulted in a lack of data for the Korean conflict when compared to the cost reporting systems for today's conflicts. Secondly, rearmament and mobilization for the Korean War was done simultaneously and concurrently with general rearmament and mobilization of the United States for the heightened Cold War threat that Korea represented. Over a year into the conflict, Secretary of Defense, George Marshall, succinctly stated the view of rearmament for Korea coupled with a worldwide threat. "Hostilities in Korea and the increased threat of communist aggression throughout the world clearly revealed to the American people the full menace of Soviet imperialism and made possible an upward adjustment of the [U.S.] armed forces to the realities of the world situation."[25] Finally, looking at just the Department of Defense spending (as is often done) likely yields an incomplete picture as to the true totality of economic impact.

A brief example illustrates the funding challenges highlighted by the war. Table 3.1 and Figure 3.1 depict Department of Defense Total Obligation Authority (TOA)[26] for the 3 fiscal years encompassing the Korean War (FY51–53) as well as each of the 3 fiscal years preceding and following the conflict.

An assumption could be made that the spending "hump" during FY's 51-52-53 represents the cost of the Korean War. But does it really? What assumptions should be made and how should comparisons be drawn? Simply summing the area under the TOA curve of the 3 war years suggests a war cost of $147 billion in 1950s dollar values ($1,338 billion in FY2006 dollars). This figure would be a total costing of all defense dollars, yet we know defense spending during this time served functions other than just the Korean War. An incremental cost comparison could be drawn if the 3-year average preceding the war (FY48–50) is assumed to represent normal defense spending. Totaling the increase over the prewar average in each of the war years (area below the TOA curve and above the lower dashed

TY $Millions

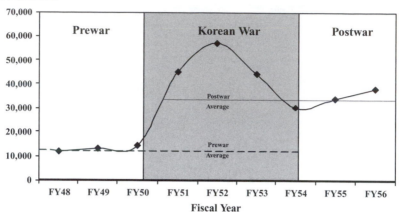

Figure 3.1 Department of Defense Total Obligation Authority
Source: Office of the Under Secretary of Defense (Comptroller), *National Defense Budget Estimates for FY 2006* (Washington D.C.: GPO, 2005).

prewar average line) yields a then-year war cost of $107 billion ($854 billion in FY2006 dollars). However, since increased defense spending in the war years also supported the general buildup called for in NSC-68, as well as for fighting in Korea, this incremental comparison seems inflated. Assuming the average of the 3 postwar years (FY54–56) reflects a better Cold-War baseline to compare against (higher overall defense spending), a similar calculation (area below the TOA curve and above the upper dotted postwar average line) reveals a then-year war cost of $44 billion ($355 billion in FY2006 dollars). The results of this example are not very useful; the then-year incremental cost estimates vary by $63 billion and the total cost estimate is roughly between 40 and 230 percent higher than the incremental estimates. Also, assuming that a significant conflict like Korea would involve other federal government entities, each with corresponding spending impacts beyond DoD, any analysis like the one above would disregard these costs entirely.

To improve the cost estimates, one must examine the spending measures, various official statements, and budget documents from the period and make reasonable estimations of items of government spending that can be attributable to the war in Korea. Because of the previously discussed lack of clearly defined war cost accounting, in addition to direct costs, the analysis will also define government war costs in two other categories: "mixed" and "indirect." Mixed costs are where funds obviously support both the Korean Theater and the general defense buildup, yet there is no clear way to identify the appropriate percentage to attribute to each endeavor. Indirect costs are those in support of national security in general, yet increased because of the heightened threat of communist expansionism typified and triggered by Korea. Finally, the analysis will try to capture the costs of other increased spending not attributable to Korea or national defense yet made possible by taking advantage of the spending measures Korea generated. In modern parlance, this equates to "pork" spending. Since the June 25, 1950, invasion by North Korea and the July 27, 1953, armistice align almost exactly day for day with the U.S. fiscal years 1951–1953, these are the focus of the examination. To define this effort, the costs examined will be federal government incremental costs, funds that were authorized and appropriated by the Congress, and will exclude nonmonetary costs.

Initial Response: The First FY51 Supplemental Request

The United States entered the Korean War just as unprepared in economic and budgetary terms as it was militarily. The June 25, 1950, North Korean invasion of the Republic of Korea was only five days before the end of U.S. Fiscal Year 1950. The FY51 budget had already been prepared several months prior and was finishing the appropriation process in Congress. Since those appropriations were not completed by the start of the new fiscal year, the government operated on a continuing resolution beginning on July 1. It was from these funds the Services "cash-flowed" or forward financed the initial budgetary response to Korean hostilities. Subsequent FY51 fiscal actions for Korea occurred through a series of supplemental appropriations—mainly four different supplemental spending bills. Work on the first supplemental began almost immediately. Truman submitted it to Congress in late July and it was enacted into law on September 27, 1950.

Even from this first supplemental, prepared only during the opening three weeks of conflict, the fiscal requirements requested were more than just supporting Korea. All the Services, the Joint Chiefs, and the political leaders in the administration viewed the outbreak of hostilities as a potential harbinger of greater conflict. They saw Korea as a dangerous feint, and the war enhanced the uniformed military's previous acute sense of "under financing" during the drive to economize after World War II. Likewise, administration leadership that had driven this economizing stance recognized the need to expand U.S. forces in general and began the process immediately with the first supplemental, in addition to financial support for Korean operations. Yet, despite recognizing the need to expand, Secretary of Defense Johnson still felt the need to defend his previous economy program and looked to constrain spending if possible, maintaining a ceiling between $10 and $11 billion on the supplemental request.[27]

The Army structured its supplemental request in three main increments: (1) to support the immediate force increase (end strength of troops in the Army's case), (2) to support the ongoing operations in Korea, and (3) to support the longer-term buildup of Army size. The second increment costs are directly attributable to the war in Korea. Funds for the first and third increments represent "mixed" costs in that some portion ultimately provided direct support for Korea, while the remainder provided for the general buildup in U.S. defense posture. Because the Army did the brunt of the ground fighting, a higher percentage of its request went toward direct support of Korean operations rather than the general buildup.[28] However, despite the larger share of funds dedicated to Korea, ultimately the Army expansion not only tapped into existing contractors and defense production facilities, but also required significant expansion of production capability in certain areas.

The Navy similarly structured its request around supporting Korea and an overall increase in fleet size and strength. Expanding from the baseline FY51 program, particularly in aircraft and ship numbers, the Navy made gains toward full wartime manning levels to support existing ships and air squadrons as well. In building the first FY51 supplemental budget submission, Admiral Forrest Sherman, the Chief of Naval Operations, stated the Navy approach was essentially in three increments: (1) to provide what was necessary for Korea, (2) to replace anything committed from existing resources under the first increment, and finally (3) to conduct the long-range buildup of increased strength.[29] He further stated that roughly $1 billion of the $2.6 billion Navy request was dedicated to support Korea while the remaining $1.6 billion would contribute to the overall buildup of forces.[30] In testimony to Congress, Navy witnesses admitted that they had spread their limited regular appropriations over the entire Navy industrial base so that supplemental dollars would essentially just increase production rates and amounts at the same set of suppliers. The Marine Corps request and testimony was done as part of the overall Department of the Navy plan. Korea was the Marines' justification for growth and essentially all of the requested funding, albeit small compared to the other Services, was attributable to the Korean effort.[31]

The Air Force approach was a simple two-part plan: support the current Korea efforts projected through the remainder of the year, and complete the buildup of the Air Force from 48 to 58 air groups. For the Air Force leadership, this program was hopefully a "way-point" en route to the long-desired goal of a 70-group Air Force overall. As with the Navy, the bulk of the funds requested by the Air Force (nearly 70 percent) were identified as supporting the general buildup and therefore are categorized as "mixed" costs, rather than direct cost, for Korean war accounting purposes.[32]

Following initial congressional testimony by DoD witnesses in late July 1950, some limitations in the supplemental submission became clear, particularly the disparity between aircraft modernization provided the Air Force and a lesser extent in the naval air forces. Navy officers testified that an additional $950 million was required to fully modernize the fleet air forces. Likewise, initial public works and military construction requirements were not yet presented to Congress. Immediate feedback from members of the House Appropriations Committee suggested the administration should request these funds. Following testimony, the DoD Comptroller, Wilfred McNeil informed the Secretary of Defense "... that Rep. Harry R. Sheppard thought Johnson [SECDEF] should 'fix them now or you'll regret it and be subject to a lot of criticism later.'"[33] Ultimately, the administration sent a smaller request to Congress in August for $1.156 billion to address these

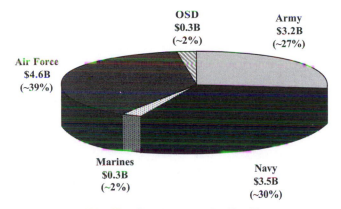

OSD
$0.3B
(~2%)

Army
$3.2B
(~27%)

Air Force
$4.6B
(~39%)

Marines
$0.3B
(~2%)

Navy
$3.5B
(~30%)

Figure 3.2 FY51—First Supplemental: Service Shares

concerns. Congress essentially treated these two requests as one and provided the funds in the first supplemental of FY51.

Concerns over funding the war effort were abundant on both ends of Pennsylvania Avenue. At such an early stage in the hostilities and uncertain of their outcome, President Truman was wary of putting too much into the defense program and initiating a costly, long-term buildup of forces. Congress, always jealously guarding its power of the purse, was willing to provide what was required for Korea and initiate the general buildup of American strength. However, many congressional members expressed concerns over waste and providing funds that could not be spent within constraints of the U.S. economy. Nevertheless, Truman requested significant funds for both Korea and general buildup efforts, and Congress provided virtually everything requested in the first FY51 supplemental.

The first supplemental appropriated more than $11 billion for DoD and more than $5 billion throughout the remainder of government for the Korean situation and the general force buildup.[34] Figure 3.2 shows the breakout by Service of the DoD appropriated funds. Despite heavy Army engagement on the Korean peninsula, the Air Force and Navy received significant funding (both with shares larger than the Army). The Air Force and Navy appropriations supported Korean operations, and contributed substantially to increasing overall U.S. fleet and air strength.

Figure 3.3 depicts appropriations that could be clearly identified in support of or resulting from Korea, those dedicated only toward the general force buildup, and the "mixed" category that clearly supported both efforts but where specific breakout details between the two was unclear. Also, like virtually any other spending bill moving through Congress, various members' interests and agendas enabled insertion of spending that did not support national security and did not make it through the regular appropriations process. Known today as "pork spending," these are shown as the "Unrelated Costs" in the chart.

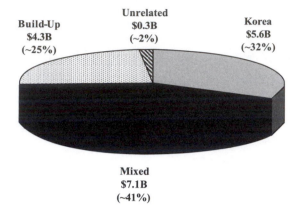

Figure 3.3 FY51—First Supplemental: Functional Shares

Another way to examine the funds is grouping the dozens of different appropriations into five simple categories for comparison: investment, operations, manpower, foreign aid, and the unrelated discretionary funds. "Investment" consists of the various procurement, research and development, and construction appropriations. "Operations" encompasses various accounts for conducting operations, maintenance, and support of day-to-day activities. The "Manpower" category contains all the pay, benefits, training, and other spending associated with supporting personnel. "Foreign Aid" are those funds used by any department for supporting foreign governments, militaries, or populations. Finally, the remaining discretionary funds are those described above as unrelated costs. Figure 3.4 represents the percentage breakdown of the supplemental in these categories. Interestingly, despite prosecuting an active "hot war," two of the supplemental's smallest percentages of funds were dedicated to operations and manpower. In fact, those two combined are approximately equal to the funds dedicated for foreign aid. Investment is by far the overwhelming percentage of funds, not only providing equipment for use in Korea, but clearly showing an early emphasis on the simultaneous general buildup as well.

Perhaps the final way to view the supplemental for quick comparisons is by its distribution to departments and agencies within the federal government. Figure 3.5 highlights the overwhelming majority of funds went to the Defense Department (69 percent) and the Executive Office of the President (29 percent), with the remaining 2 percent spread over multiple organizations. While the DoD figure might be expected, both the request and provision of almost 30 percent of the funds to the Executive Office of the President reveals the extent to which Truman desired to assert himself in the resourcing decisions for this conflict—and the early concurrence he received from the Congress to do so.

The Administration also received a significant grant of flexibility in authorities and funds. Approximately 26 percent of the appropriations provided broad latitude

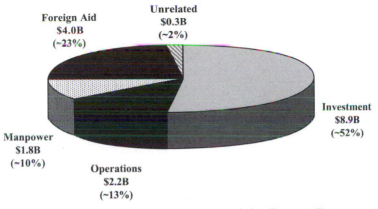

Figure 3.4 FY51—First Supplemental: Appropriation Category Shares

in reprogramming authority or flexibility in execution for the Executive branch with minimal-to-no congressional guidance or reporting requirements. Critics would argue it was too flexible in light of the uncertainties that existed at the time. Champions of this approach would argue those very uncertainties made it essential for the Executive to have the flexibility for timely and appropriate responses under wartime circumstances. The perpetual argument offers reasonable facts on both sides of the debate.

Given the regular FY51 federal budget was approved in early September (just a few days before the first supplemental was signed) as one large Omnibus bill, where it is generally easier for legislators to include pet projects or "pork" items,

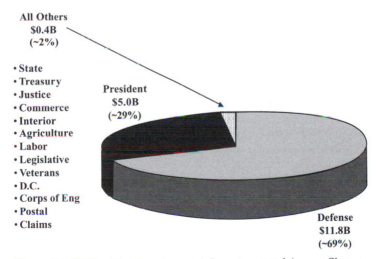

Figure 3.5 FY51—First Supplemental: Department and Agency Shares

the fact that more than $280 million (approximately $2.8 billion in FY06 dollars) in nondefense-related items made it into the bill indicates the extent these items were egregious "pork" spending. In no way did these appropriations support of the Korean War effort; nonetheless, they were spending that indirectly resulted from the opportunity presented by the war appropriations.

Further Developing the War and Buildup Programs: The Second FY51 Supplemental

Work on the second supplemental began in late summer 1950 when the first supplemental was being completed. In large part, the timing of submission was dictated by the mid-term congressional elections in November 1950. President Truman's policies received significant election season criticisms from the Republicans. The Korean War was a particularly potent issue, with the sharpest critics linking it to other perceived failures in the Administration's foreign policy.[35] Some critics went as far as saying the Korean War was, "an entirely unnecessary war."[36] At the least, Truman's economic and budgetary handling of the war was largely blamed for increased tax burdens and higher costs of living. Claims were also made of budget waste and extravagance in the war response.[37] With concerns mounting over war costs, inflation, mobilization, and the apparently increasing communist menace, the President was hesitant to roll out another large supplemental request just before the election.[38] This election concern regarding fiscal burdens was on top of the already enacted Revenue Act of 1950, a preelection tax hike of $4–5 billion to help finance the Korean War, and public discussion—and apparent congressional commitment—for tax increases on future excess profits.[39]

Nevertheless, the military continued to work throughout the fall building estimates for the second supplemental. Several key assumptions and factors drove the scope, and amount, of the request. First among those was the artificial imposition of an assumed end of hostilities by the end of FY51 (June 30, 1951). Since no one knew for certain how the war would progress, and to avoid the problems of developing plans and programs across fiscal years, the Administration decided on the imposed cutoff date for budgetary planning. Financially, pricing adjustments resulting from war-induced inflation were made to baseline budget programs and first supplemental spending plans. As with the first supplemental, another factor was the multiple agendas served by this request. In testimony to Congress, Defense Secretary George Marshall stated that the second FY51 supplemental was not solely focused on Korea, but the larger, worldwide security situation, and it was " . . . against that perspective or background that this second supplementary recommendation to Congress [was] being made."[40] In the same hearing, JCS Chairman, General Omar Bradley, amplified this point, highlighting three main thrusts behind the second supplemental. First, were the fighting needs in Korea at the time (not counting increased requirements due to the open entry of Chinese Communists—the supplemental estimates were essentially finished before the late November Red China crossing of the Yalu River); second, the need to support the buildup of forces at home as a deterrent to further conflict (essentially the start of the NSC-68 Build-up); and finally, certain steps with industry and defense preparedness in case of full-scale war.[41] Deputy Secretary of Defense Robert Lovett expounded even further. Regarding the general force buildup, he indicated this supplemental was an "... initial step in a planned 4-year effort to restore our military posture...." He said it was not a war-footing budget request, but rather aimed at creating a defense establishment that could "... be maintained over a substantial period of time without excessive strain while providing the essential quality of quick build-up from a sound base." He also emphasized the tenuous nature of the requested amounts given recent increased tensions and uncertainties. If further reversals were suffered, the military, and in particular the Army, would likely require much greater appropriations.[42]

In additional testimony, the DoD Comptroller, Assistant Secretary Wilfred McNeil, informed Congress the second supplemental was not formulated under any artificial budget caps, but rather, "... when various elements of the agreed forces [for both Korea and general build-up] should be completely equipped and ready ... and will materially affect the budgets for succeeding fiscal years [mainly concern impacting the preparation of the FY52 budget]."[43] In fact, he stated it was the first supplemental budget prepared since World War II on a nondollar-ceiling basis.[44] Of the fiscal issues he highlighted in testimony, he stressed that the second supplemental estimates were making significant adjustments for rapid inflationary pressures since the baseline budget and first supplemental were finalized in the August-September time frame. This loss of purchasing power was particularly acute in the electronics industry as well as end-use products requiring lumber and steel.[45]

When challenged by Congressman George Mahon, Democrat from Texas and Chairman of the House Appropriations Defense Subcommittee, on the need to request further funds to prepare for the possibility of an expanded conflict in Korea or elsewhere, Secretary Marshall's answer was absorptive capacity. Marshall stated the funds requested were DoD's estimates of what could actually be put to use in the economy. Further preparations would be limited without full-scale economic and manpower mobilization for total war. His estimate for $500 million under the heading of "Expediting Production" was to assist industrial preparedness.[46]

The first two supplementals of FY51, in today's dollars, individually were the two largest ever provided to DoD during the Cold War and after. They provide intriguing contrasts and the following figures offer side-by-side comparisons (pie charts on the left side are from the first supplemental Figures 3.2–3.5 respectively). With over $9 billion appropriated, the still heavily engaged Army assumed the majority share of the defense appropriation at the relative decline of the Navy

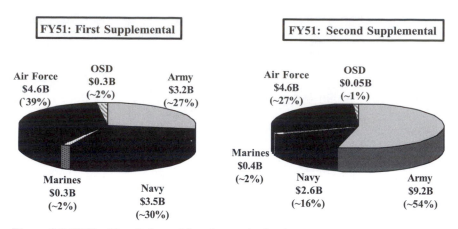

Figure 3.6 FY51—First & Second Supplementals: Service Shares Comparison

and Air Force shares. Figure 3.6 reveals the changes in Service shares, yet all three Services continued to pursue prosecution of the war as well as general force buildup. However, the pace of funding differed between the ground-centric Army and Marine Corps versus the more technology-oriented Navy and Air Force. In both supplementals, Army and Marine appropriations were always over 50 percent dedicated to war support while less than half of Navy and Air Force funds were consistently dedicated to Korea.

Some in Congress believed that the bulk of the second supplemental request was geared toward the general buildup rather than immediate fighting in Korea. Democratic Congressman Robert Sikes of Florida, challenged DoD witnesses in one hearing, stating he thought somewhere between 80 and 90 percent would go toward the general buildup rather than immediate and specific Korea needs.[47] During later congressional debate about the second supplemental, this concern was further emphasized on December 15, when the President announced an accelerated goal for the general force buildup (to reach 3.5 million under arms by June 1952) and declared the existence of a national emergency the following day. While significant sums supported the buildup, the claim of 80–90 percent appears excessive. As shown in Figure 3.7, costs associated only with the buildup actually dropped significantly, from 25 percent in the first supplemental to approximately 6 percent in the second (although buildup costs are also embedded in the "mixed" category which only increased from 41 to 52).[48] Even allowing for a significant share of the mixed category to count toward the general buildup, this figure would still fall well short of the 80–90 percent claimed by Representative Sikes at the time.

Again using the categorization approach to examine appropriations, Figure 3.8 shows the two major changes were in investments and foreign aid. Investments

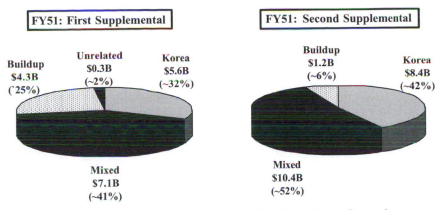

Figure 3.7 FY51—First & Second Supplementals: Functional Shares Comparison

saw a 21percent rise, largely through increased weapons procurements. Taken in concert with the increased Korea appropriations in Figure 3.7, it appears the bulk of investment increases in the second supplemental were geared for combat support overseas. The drop in foreign aid was one area where Congress denied the President's request, for example, cutting funds for Civilian Relief in Korea. Several congressmen expressed concern over the use of these funds and Congress only provided $50 million of the $100 million requested.

A smaller overall request in these types of funds, together with the congressional reduction, decreased the flexible funds available to the President—only 4 percent of the second supplemental appropriation had flexibility that 25 percent in the first supplemental contained.[49] Likewise, as a percentage, the funds requested

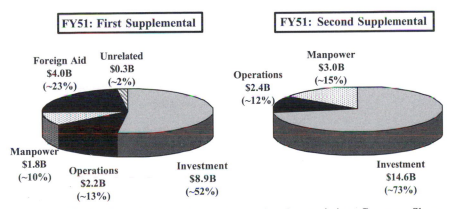

Figure 3.8 FY51—First & Second Supplementals: Appropriation Category Shares Comparison

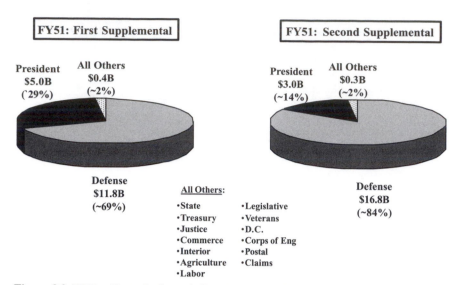

| FY51: First Supplemental | | FY51: Second Supplemental |

President $5.0B (~29%)   All Others $0.4B (~2%)

President $3.0B (~14%)   All Others $0.3B (~2%)

Defense $11.8B (~69%)

Defense $16.8B (~84%)

All Others:
•State   •Legislative
•Treasury   •Veterans
•Justice   •D.C.
•Commerce   •Corps of Eng
•Interior   •Postal
•Agriculture •Claims
•Labor

Figure 3.9 FY51—First & Second Supplementals: Department and Agency Shares Comparison

and appropriated directly to the President declined by half, although the President's and DoD's funds combined still equaled 98 percent of the total appropriation as in the first supplemental. Figure 3.9 provides the comparison of departmental/agency shares.

Regarding the sufficiency of the supplemental request to meet the needs through the rest of FY51, Representative Sikes challenged the Defense Secretary. Sikes stated that when the first supplemental was finished back in September, there was hope that requirements for the remainder of the fiscal year were covered. Yet, now Congress was presented with a second supplemental request that was larger than either the initial FY51 baseline budget request or the first supplemental. He asked directly if the new estimate would complete the needs for the year. Secretary Marshall replied he thought it would unless the situation became more critical.[50] In fact, even though the situation in the spring grew more stabilized and approached geographic stalemate on the peninsula, two more supplementals would be required to complete FY51.

Accelerating Defense Production: The Third FY51 Supplemental

In early September 1950, Congress passed the Defense Production Act (DPA). The DPA contained sweeping delegations of legal authority to the Executive to carry out defense production tasks. The President received numerous and broad authorities, including 44 specific grants of power, including:

- Purchase and allocation of materials and facilities.
- Requisition and disposal of property.
- Expand industrial capacity as well as grant/guarantee loans to do so.
- Create new government agencies to carry out DPA functions, including appointment power without Senate confirmation over most senior posts and significant hiring/firing authority.
- Make rules and regulations to carry out various provisions.
- Consult with business and labor to carry out DPA functions.
- Establish price and wage controls.
- Help arbitrate labor disputes.
- Work with the Federal Reserve System to control consumer and real estate credit.

Many of these authorities encompassed even broader powers when granted, "without regard to the limitations of existing law."[51]

The DPA contained flexible authority to borrow up to $600 million from the Treasury to help industry expand to meet growing demand and the Act authorized an additional $1.4 billion in additional appropriations to carry out the same functions. Congress stressed the President should exercise these authorities " . . . so far as practicable, on the maintenance and furtherance of the American system of competitive enterprise. . . . "[52] A judicial review process was established to hear and settle disputes under this law, but only two courts were empowered, an Emergency Appeals Court and the Supreme Court. For oversight and control, Congress created a specific joint oversight committee for Defense Production, and all the various titles contained in the Act were given specific expiration dates 1 to 2 years beyond enactment. The main emphasis of the third FY51 supplemental was significantly increased borrowing authority for industry under the DPA-granted provisions.

The third supplemental added $1 billion in borrowing authority to expand production, supporting both the intensity of Korean operations and the general buildup of forces. It also added more funds to cover operating expenses of the agencies established to carry out the DPA, such as the Defense Production Administration, Office of Defense Mobilization, Economic Stabilization Agency, National Production Board, and other similar organizations. Congress recognized the $1 billion request was based upon many uncertainties, not the least of which was how much funding industry could effectively absorb in the remainder of the fiscal year. Congress further expressed concern over the size of flexible funds, stating

> . . . The amount of money involved is so large as to have a tremendous effect on our domestic economy. If the program is well and carefully administered it will serve the

intended purpose. If it is not administered carefully it may very well result in serious disruptions in our industrial pattern and dislocations in the general economy of the nation.[53]

The supplemental also provided $47 million in increased funding for the maritime administration to support sealift for Korean War/Far Eastern operations and $66 million supporting other activities associated with military functions, and $240 million in unrelated spending. The official history of the Office of the Secretary of Defense only "credits" three of the FY51 supplementals (the first, second, and fourth) as contributing toward the Defense Department, but the third supplemental was clearly in support of the war effort and general rearmament by making significantly more funds available to implement the Defense Production Act.[54] Defense Secretary Marshall recognized the integral aspect of this funding when he told Congress, "Our request for a third supplemental appropriation for fiscal year 1951 constitutes an essential part of the general [defense] program."[55]

Closing Out the Year: The Fourth FY51 Supplemental

The final FY51 supplemental comprised funding mainly dedicated to supporting Korea. The funds either (1) corrected an antideficiency problem where Korea spending had exceeded authorized and appropriated funds in a particular account, (2) provided money for shortfalls projected in the final two and a half months of the fiscal year remaining, (3) bought back other defense programs where funds had been transferred or reprogrammed to support Korean operations, or (4) covered shortfalls in existing purchase orders and prior appropriations due to significantly increased inflation.[56] Hearings were held only for a few days in April as DoD stressed the urgency since some appropriations had gone into deficiency conditions as of 1 April.[57] While this request was considered, debate over the DoD FY52 baseline appropriation was ongoing, and hence there was concern by Congress that funds in the supplemental should only cover to the end of FY51 and not extend activities into FY52. The appropriations committees expressed frustration at the meager time to review the supplemental items; however, they recognized further corrective actions could be taken on the same or similar items in the larger FY52 baseline budget. As a result, the appropriators, "insisted funds requested in the present bill [the supplemental] shall not involve commitments to new programs which would affect decisions on the fiscal year 1952 budget."[58] Thus, approximately $42 million was cut from the DoD request where Congress felt the funds could not be spent by the end of the year.

The fourth supplemental had to account for the rapid inflation throughout FY51 that eroded the purchasing power of previous supplemental appropriations. In the Army portion of the bill, $679 million was required to cover price differentials, $577 million (85 percent) of which was solely due to inflation.[59] The

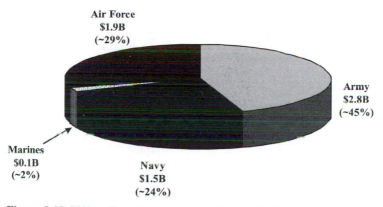

Figure 3.10 FY51—Fourth Supplemental: Service Shares

Navy included $80 million for price increases, most of which was in the aircraft procurement account. A specific amount for Air Force inflation costs was not provided, but since approximately 70 percent of the Navy's inflation was related to aircraft procurement and facilities with the remainder in the personnel accounts, it should be safe to assume with similar appropriations and procurements, the overall percentage of inflation experienced by the Air Force was the same as the Navy. Based on that assumption, the Air Force would have had $94 million committed to counter price hikes. Taken in total, inflation alone accounted for 12 percent of this entire supplemental appropriation. This inflation stemmed from overall price increases sparked by general consumer reactions to the outbreak of the war, implementation of selected materials controls, and increased government contracts for selected goods. Thus, the Korean War helped trigger the increased inflation costs added to this supplemental request.

The final FY51 supplemental enacted on May 31, had appropriations as shown in Figure 3.10–3.12. As with the second supplemental, ground combat maintained the dominant position of the Army for funding shares and the Air Force expansion efforts drove its continued edge over the Navy in percentages appropriated. Continuing the trend viewed earlier in Figure 3.7 within the supplemental request justifications and corresponding appropriations, it became harder to distinguish between funds dedicated for Korean operations and those supporting both Korea and the general buildup. Figure 3.11 depicts the split between those categories in the fourth supplemental.

Finally, Figure 3.12 reveals the continuing trend in the character of the spending. Once again, as with the first and second supplementals, the emphasis was on investment, particularly long-term procurement, in this supplemental. As a percentage, operations funding remained fairly steady from the previous supplementals and manpower funds grew slightly. In all, FY51 supplemental funding

Figure 3.11 FY51—Fourth Supplemental: Functional Shares

aimed at expanding the armed forces for Korea, and for a general buildup primarily through investments in new equipment.

Fiscal Year 52–53 Costs

Incremental costs of Korean War operations were not included in the FY52 nor FY53 DoD baseline budgets. Nevertheless, the war was largely funded throughout those years from baseline appropriations until DoD ran short on cash, then toward the end of each fiscal year, the administration would request a supplemental or antideficiency appropriation to fund the shortfall. DoD could operate this way for several key reasons. First, the rapid increase in troop strength was assumed to be part of the normal baseline of force structure and therefore the normal "peacetime" rates of pay, benefits, and consumption were assumed included in the base budget (more on extra manpower costs attributable to the Korean War in the subsequent section below). Secondly, much of the ammunition and supplies consumed came from post-World War II stock levels, and the large FY51 supplemental appropriations in procurement accounts would only start to deliver significant replacement goods in late FY52 and into FY53. The Truman administration's shortfall funding approach and congressional frustration was illuminated well in the following exchange

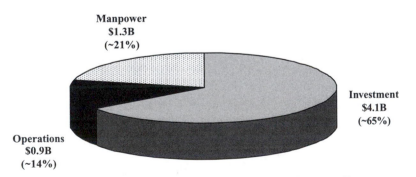

Figure 3.12 FY51—Fourth Supplemental: Appropriation Category Shares

between Secretary of Defense Robert Lovett and Senator Homer Ferguson, Ranking Member of the Sub-committee on Defense Appropriations:

Senator Ferguson: Is there anything in this budget of $51 billion plus for the battles in Korea, for the actual Korean War?

Secretary Lovett: Yes, sir.

Senator Ferguson: How much of it?

Secretary Lovett: The forces stationed in Korea are provided here on a so-called peacetime consumption rate.

Senator Ferguson: Is this peace in Korea? Is this peacetime in Korea?

Secretary Lovett: No sir; but we have no means of estimating accurately now in advance, how many shells will be expended, and so forth. It depends on the rate of activity.

Senator Ferguson: Mr. Lovett, if we do not have a way of estimating what we are going to need in Korea while the war is actually going on in Korea, how can we ever anticipate what we are going to need in a war that has not started?

Secretary Lovett: We have not anticipated needs for a war that has not started. We are estimating on the requirement of a minimum defense force. The wartime expenditures would be incalculable.

Senator Ferguson: Can we not determine, then, while this war is actually going on, what we need? Is it that we really believe that there is going to be a truce right now, and, therefore, we will not need more? Do you think that the Defense Department really feels that they are going to get a truce in Korea?

Secretary Lovett: Senator Ferguson, we come up for deficiency appropriations to provide for deficiencies caused by Korea beyond the average consumption rates.

Senator Ferguson: Why can we not get those Korean items in the regular budget? Why do we have to wait on a war that actually is taking place? Why do we not get them in here?

Secretary Lovett: You get them in supplementals because we bring one up only when we have actual provable deficiencies.[60]

Finally, DoD did not necessarily draw a fine distinction regarding what funding and force structure increases were dedicated to the NSC-68 general buildup and what was driven by Korean War requirements; hence, the overall increasing budget and force levels helped resource war needs. Due to these reasons, the clear and often detailed, line-item visibility of war costs evident throughout various FY51 supplemental appropriations no longer existed in FY52 and FY53. Beyond the much smaller supplemental appropriations in those years, determining incremental costs of the war was largely dependent upon a few cost estimates that DoD provided.

Incremental Cost Estimates

In early FY52 (August 1951), DoD estimated the Korean War incremental costs for the year by providing a minimum and maximum figure depending upon level of combat intensity and operations.

- Department of the Army: $3.9 billion minimum to $4.3 billion maximum.
- Department of the Navy: $536 million minimum to $1.1 billion maximum.
- Department of the Air Force: $325 million minimum to $450 million maximum.

Later in the year, DoD revised these figures based upon actual expenditure experience, and the best estimates it provided for FY52 were as follows:

- Department of the Army: $4.4 billion.
- Department of the Navy: $375 million.
- Department of the Air Force: $305 million.[61]

Within this $5.1 billion total, the Army slightly exceeded estimates while the Navy and Air Force came in slightly under expectation. Also worth noting in these cost figures, a large portion of the Marine Corps' support costs in Korea were borne by the Army and that is why the Department of the Navy figure appears to be lower than might otherwise be expected if full Marine costs were reflected.[62] For FY53, a complete set of incremental cost figures was not provided; however, the Army, which carried the brunt of the burden in Korea, did estimate its incremental costs that year at approximately $5 billion, roughly 9 percent more than the previous year's figure. Assuming Navy and Air Force operations tempo increased in comparable amounts to support the Army, the implied incremental costs for them equaled $408 million for the Navy and $332 million for the Air Force in FY53.

Supplemental Appropriations

Throughout FY52–53, several supplemental appropriation bills contributed to the Korean War. The first FY52 supplemental carried no DoD funding directly for Korean operations, but, it did fund other departments and agencies for functions supporting the war, other associated costs with the general military buildup, and funding that supported both efforts. Enacted on November 1, 1951, the final bill included $1.2 billion in funds either directly or partially in support of Korea. Additionally, another $372 million was provided in indirectly related functions for the general buildup of U.S force posture. As with past supplementals, the $1.2 billion was heavily biased toward investments, with 70 percent going toward procurement of shipping and strategic materials to support defense production. Also included within those funds were $162 million for various agencies to accomplish their functions related to the Defense Production Act.

The second FY52 supplemental was an amalgam of other planned supplemental funding and the military construction (MILCON)/public works bill submitted for that fiscal year. As such, the final measure contained $248 million of other defense-related activities and nearly $4 billion for military construction. This large MILCON appropriation was a cornerstone of the U.S. defense buildup and created infrastructure in 48 states and U.S. territories, as well as a dozen locations overseas. As an order of magnitude, this supplemental MILCON was five to seven times greater than average MILCON expenditures before Korea, and in today's dollars was still two to three times greater than today's annual MILCON commitments. Interestingly, there was a correlation between how much of these MILCON funds went to particular states and congressional districts, and whether or not the corresponding congressional member sat on one of the committees that exercised military oversight. This correlation was particularly apparent by tracking the House, where MILCON projects could be linked to individual congressional members by district. Of all House representatives, 50 percent had MILCON funding appropriated directly for projects in their districts while another 25 percent, particularly in dense urban areas, had MILCON projects put into bordering districts where cross-district economic and employment impacts could still be beneficial. Therefore, in addition to almost all Senators receiving MILCON benefits in his or her state, 75 percent of the House members also saw funds benefit their districts. The sum of funds in districts with MILCON projects and a representative on either the House Armed Services Committee, House Public Works Committee, or House Appropriations Committee held a 3:1 greater margin over the sum of all other members whose districts received MILCON projects as well. This correlation was not simply because these committee members added money in their districts and states—the bill tracked very closely with the President's request. Truman apparently knew how to "buy" support via appropriations in a war that was increasingly growing unpopular as well as a congressional funding irritant.

Like the first, the third supplemental bill in FY52 contained no direct Korea funds for DoD, but did provide $320 million in Korea support to other departments and agencies. Examples of these other agencies were organizations such as the Veterans Administration, the Selective Service System, and the many defense production agencies handling various aspects of industrial and economic policies. The final supplemental measure of FY52 was the June 1952, Urgent Deficiencies appropriation. Enacted on the final day of the fiscal year, it provided DoD $1.5 billion to support shortfalls resulting from Korean War operations and consumption. Unlike past supplemental appropriations, only 3 percent of these funds went toward investment, with 71 percent for operations and maintenance, and 26 percent for manpower costs.

Three supplemental appropriations provided support to the Korean War in FY53. Like the second FY52 supplemental, the first FY53 supplemental contained the DoD military construction funds for the year ($2.3 billion) and made up the bulk of the total $2.8 billion appropriation providing direct or indirect support for Korea. The other $500 million supported defense production activities and assorted operating expenses. The second FY53 supplemental primarily covered DoD manpower costs and comprised 98 percent of the $1.4 billion in total war support approved. The third and final supplemental of the year was just slightly more than $1 million in war support to provide for year-end shortfalls in the Veterans Administration and DPA activities.

Congressional Frustration

Budgeting for the war via supplementals in FY51 was understandable given the timing of events. However, congressional frustration mounted in FY52 and FY53 due to the Administration's budgetary planning assumptions and lack of war cost estimates in the baseline budgets. Continued use of artificial cutoff dates for hostilities corresponding to the end of each fiscal year irritated congressional members, particularly as DoD witnesses themselves admitted these were arbitrary assumptions for use in budget building rather than realistic expectations of what they thought might happen. Administration witnesses repeatedly expressed frustration over what they felt were inherent contradictions in trying to predict requirements for wartime operations, so far in advance, when baseline budget requests were being prepared. Karl Bendetsen, Under Secretary of the Army, made this tension clear:

> I wish to make the record clear I am not saying that [hostilities would cease at the end of the fiscal year]. I do not believe they will cease June 30, and that is not what we are saying. . . . We were given over 18 months ago a budget-planning assumption. There must be an assumption when you have a role that runs that far ahead. . . . If the Korean War continues in 1953, then, insofar as our budget assumptions and the military strength in the fiscal 1953 budget which is now before you are concerned, we will have no alternative . . . but to come before you to request your consideration of an increase in strength [funds]. This is because our 1953 budget, as stated, is based on the assumption across the board that by June 30, 1952, the hostilities will cease.[63]

Some in Congress viewed the continued use of supplementals, and essentially providing two spending bills for DoD during this time—a baseline budget and at least one extra appropriation each year to cover additional war costs—as an attempt to force tough choices onto the backs of congressional members. Regarding both financing and budgeting for Korean costs, fellow Democrat and Chairman of the

Defense Appropriations Subcommittee, Senator Joseph O'Mahoney, criticized President Truman's approach this way:

> The difference between the decision of the President and ours is this: The President said, "We will send down this budget for military expenditures but we will balance the budget by increased taxes." The Ways and Means Committee said, "No, we will not have any taxes and there is no possibility of getting any taxes," so we have to decide whether we are going to have this preparedness program and the deficit or whether we are going to avoid the deficit by cutting back. Therefore, the decisions will be made by the Congress where to cut.[64]

For all the bluff and bluster regarding vacillating war costs and accurate estimating, Congress aided and abetted the early spend-to-deficiency practice with provisions like Section 626 in both the FY52 and FY53 DoD Appropriation Acts. That provision allowed the President to spend appropriations into deficiency conditions "whenever he deems such action to be necessary in the interest of national defense."[65] Although during testimony and in committee reports, congressional appropriators said this practice should be strictly limited, and likely only necessary in funds like Army operations and maintenance accounts, Congress never put binding limits on the President in this regard. The first Eisenhower-amended FY54 DoD budget attempted to add partial Korean War incremental costs in the baseline to limit the use of supplementals, deficiency appropriations, and provide what was hoped to be a more accurate accounting of war costs in one spending bill. It is ironic that FY54 was the first year an attempt was made—the fighting stopped only 27 days into that fiscal year.[66]

Additional Manpower Costs

The full cost of DoD's manpower added specifically to fight the Korean War, and not required before or after the conflict, historically becomes evident as a significant incremental cost of war not accounted for in estimates prepared during the conflict. By FY52, senior defense officials simply considered the higher manning levels part of the baseline of the new force structure being created.[67] In hindsight, it is clear that from FY51 through FY55, a manpower mobilization and demobilization supported the Korean conflict. Those extra troop levels, with corresponding full pay and benefit expenditures, become incremental costs for the Korean War.

Fighting stopped in the first few days of FY54. A couple of years were necessary to facilitate demobilization from wartime requirements (especially since standard enlistment periods were 2 years), and for the sake of calculation, it is assumed FY54–55 still carried some of the excess troops drafted for Korea. Examining the total DoD end strength numbers throughout the 1950s also suggests

Table 3.2 Korean War Incremental Excess End Strength (E/S)

	FY51	FY52	FY53	FY54	FY55	Total (FY51–53)	Total (FY51–55)
Total Excess E/S	613,467	1,000,008	919,163	666,200	299,203	2,532,638	3,498,041
Percentage of Total E/S	19%	28%	26%	20%	10%		
TY($M) Cost	$1,670	$3,155	$3,241	$2,335	$1,168	$8,066	$11,569
CY2006($M) Cost	$22,563	$44,107	$42,345	$31,135	$15,978	$109,015	$156,128

this assumption is correct. A 5-year average of end strength, beginning in FY56, is better representative of the Cold War steady state, "peacetime" requirement for troops during this period.[68] The difference between this reflective Cold War end strength "norm," and the total end strength in each of the years FY51–55, represents a good estimate of manpower acquired solely to prosecute the Korean War. Using a per capita manpower cost rate, that excess end strength yielded a $3.2 billion cost in FY52, $3.2 billion in FY53, and $11.6 billion over the entire 5 years in added Korean War costs. Table 3.2 highlights the annual breakdown during those years.

A similar calculation will be done in the following chapter on Vietnam to show the costs of end strength specifically supporting escalation in that conflict and not required before or after the years of peak American involvement. These calculations also keep the manpower comparisons consistent and more equitable with the GWOT since excess, or what today is called "over strength" levels, in GWOT are fully funded via supplemental appropriations that pay for the war. While not added here, it would also be safe to assume some percentage of total operations and maintenance (O&M) and procurement funds were required to support these increased number of troops, and therefore the extra procurement and O&M costs should be added as well. Since it is impossible to determine what fair share percentage of these appropriations to attribute, no attempt is made to assign costs, only a recognition that the dollars required to support Korea, while specifically undeterminable, were higher than shown.

KOREAN WAR—SUMMARY

Korea precipitated, and then partially sustained itself from, a general buildup in U.S. defense forces around the globe postulated by the guiding document outlining national strategy, NSC-68. This dual buildup, coupled with the practice beginning substantially in FY52 of funding war operations out of baseline appropriations and then trying to repay those costs with supplemental appropriations, made clear determination of Korean War costs very difficult. The preceding analysis briefly summarized the salient context and major costs of federal funding applied to the Korean War from FY51–53. In particular, the analysis reviewed, to the extent possible, federal appropriations beyond those for the Defense Department that directly or indirectly contributed to the war effort. There was no attempt to review costs at the state or local level, no inclusion of any private costs incurred, nor were any second-order economic effects costs included. Likewise, U.S. aid to the Republic of Korea before 1950, and the tremendous costs of U.S. commitments to Korean security and development after FY53, continuing still today, were not considered. Even with these items excluded from the calculation, examining the full range of federal funds dedicated to the war effort exceeds the cost commonly associated with the Korean War.

Using the categories of direct Korea, mixed, and indirect costs, a rough approximation of the incremental costs can be made. From FY51–53, the incremental costs in today's dollars were:

- Directly linked to Korea: $390 billion
- Mixed costs (Korea & the general defense buildup): $216 billion
- Indirect/Related costs: $72 billion

The $390 billion indirectly attributable costs are straightforward. What becomes open for interpretation and debate is how much of the other costs should be counted. The "mixed" cost category reflected funds that were known to support both Korea and the general buildup, but uncertainty existed as to percentage composition of each category. Splitting them evenly at 50/50 percent would add $108 billion dollars to the cost of the war. Even attributing only 25 percent would still increase the cost of war by $54 billion. If one subscribes to the reasoning that all of the increased defense spending generated around the time of Korea would not have occurred without the war, then all three costs shown can be considered war costs, and the total then is $678 billion.

Three known "tails" of funding exist that are directly attributable to the war during FY51–53. They are the excess end strength drafted for the Korean War that extended slightly beyond FY53 before demobilization, debt servicing estimates for war costs not covered by increased tax revenues, and long-term Veterans Administration (VA) compensation and pension payments directly attributable to Korean War veterans and their dependents.[69] In FY 2006 dollars, expanded cost estimates to include these funding tails add:

- Excess Manpower: $156 billion
- Debt Servicing: $19 billion
- Veterans Compensation & Pensions: $148 billion (through 2000)

These three attributable costs increase the incremental cost of war by $323 billion for a combined total incremental cost of $1,001 billion through the year

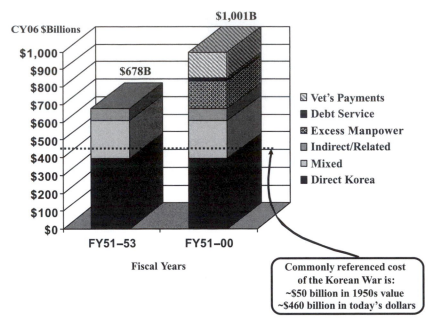

Figure 3.13 Federal Government Incremental Cost of the Korean War

2000—and the United States is still making VA payments and will continue to do so for several more decades.

Valuable insights appear from the years of "hot conflict" that were examined. First, reviewing the funding itself, several key considerations were evident:

- As a percentage, the level of investment funding—procurement, research and development and construction—was very high (approximately 50 percent) for the Korean War.[70]
- The imperatives of war provided significant increases in benefits to active-duty military and veterans, raising long-term personnel costs.
- The supplemental appropriation budgeting mechanism was used consistently in the first year of war (FY51), but haphazardly throughout the remainder of the conflict. As a result, FY51 provides the greatest transparency of costs for both Korea and the general buildup. Once costs were absorbed by regular budget funding, visibility of incremental war costs was virtually eliminated.
- Money was pushed so fast to war and buildup efforts, the American economy could not absorb it all and large unobligated balances carried over from year to year.

Secondly, from the view of the policies regarding how the war was financed and budgeted:

- Tensions between the Executive and Legislative branches over funding mechanisms increased as the conflict progressed.
- Executive funding flexibility granted by Congress declined over time; especially when no clear distinction of progress emerged, however, President Truman and, later, President Eisenhower, were both given and had broad funding authorities available throughout the war.
- Intergovernmental tension forced the famous settlement between the Federal Reserve System and the Treasury Department over maintaining control over the price of government bonds.

In the larger funding sense, particularly for DoD, Korea truly was an inflection point. "The outbreak of fighting on the Korean peninsula and the fear that it would be followed shortly by the onset of a third world war, shattered previously existing constraints and permitted defense budgets to soar . . . and did not, once the fighting had ended, shrink to anything resembling their earlier dimensions."[71] While the macro-economic impacts of this higher sustained spending were not analyzed herein, it is generally accepted that the Korean War set in motion the Cold War economy that played such a dominant role in U.S. affairs for the next half-century. Realignment of new defense industries created demographic shifts in capital and labor in the United States, moving away from old industrial centers in the Northeast and toward the new "gunbelt" in the South and West. The military and industrial infrastructure created during Korea persisted throughout the Cold War and parts of it still exist today. The financial relationships begun during this war, and fostered throughout the Cold War, between the military, industry, and parochially interested members of Congress was what led the President who ended the Korean War to warn against as he left office, "In the councils of government, we must guard against the acquisition of unwarranted influence, whether sought or unsought, by the military-industrial complex. The potential for the disastrous rise of misplaced power exists and will persist."[72]

Vietnam and Southeast Asia: 1965–1975

Get those 104 bills [Great Society legislation package] and you just watch them like a hawk. . . . Have we got a farm bill? Have we got Appalachia? Have we got a school, bill? Have we got health bill? Is medical care out? . . . We've got to pass it. Now, that's number one. That's your wife. Then you can get down to your aunts and your cousins later.

—President Lyndon B. Johnson, emphasizing priorities to
Vice President Hubert Humphrey, March 6, 1965

. . . With additional U.S. combat troops in there—and there's still a little disagreement as to how many there should be ultimately, but no disagreement as to how many there should be in the next ninety or a hundred and twenty days—they [General Westmoreland and Ambassador Taylor] feel that they can sufficiently stiffen the South Vietnamese and strengthen their forces to show Hanoi that Hanoi cannot win in the South. *It won't be that the South Vietnamese can win. But it will be clear to Hanoi that Hanoi can't win. And this is one of the objectives we're driving for.*

—Robert McNamara, Defense Secretary to Lyndon B. Johnson,
April 20, 1965

Vietnam is getting worse every day. I have the choice to go in with great casualty lists or to get out with disgrace. It's like being in an airplane and I have to choose between crashing the plane or jumping out. I do not have a parachute.

—Lyndon B. Johnson, July 8, 1965

[Of] the hundred thousand [troops requested by General Westmoreland], I may put in forty at one time, and forty at another, and twenty at another so that it doesn't scare the British and scare hell out of everybody else that we're going into a world war. . . . I'm going to talk to all of them [Congress] before we do anything. That they're going to know every bit of it. . . . I don't want to keep any secrets. I want all of them in on it with me.

—Lyndon B. Johnson, 23 July 1965

Lots of folks confuse bad management with destiny.

—Kin Hubbard, Cartoonist, Humorist, Journalist

INTRODUCTION

Direct U.S. involvement in Vietnam at some level from 1954 to 1975 ranks it as the longest period of "hot conflict" the United States has ever undertaken. The peak efforts of U.S. military involvement are generally considered to fall between President Johnson's decision to begin the sustained bombing of North Vietnam in March 1965, through the signing of the Paris Accords in January 1973. Ambiguous aims, deception at all levels of government and with the American people, failed metrics, misunderstanding the character of war being waged, and competing domestic priorities driving war strategy are but a few of the many issues raised by the U.S. experience in the Vietnam War. The operational history, errors in judgment, and resulting tragedies of how the United States conducted this war have been well documented in other accounts. This chapter will focus on the funding measures developed for Vietnam, and how some of the same problems highlighted in other aspects of the war's conduct appear in this one as well.

The earliest U.S. funding for the conflict in Vietnam was the surrogate funding provided to the French beginning in late 1949 and continuing through the fall of Dien Bien Phu in 1954. From that point through the fateful decisions of July 1965 to significantly increase U.S. troop presence, the levels of U.S. monetary aid and military advisors were incrementally increased. Several assessments of the pre-1965 costs related to these efforts put the American price of this phase between $4–5 billion total in then-year costs, not including the aid to France prior to 1953.[1] Yearly funding for military advisors was relatively small and absorbed within the annual U.S. defense budget. Other forms of aid were provided via regular foreign assistance appropriations. The remainder of this chapter examines the U.S. costs beginning in 1965 until the final U.S. retreat from Saigon in 1975.

COST AND BUDGETING OVERVIEW

May 1965: The $700 Million Confidence Vote

President Johnson believed he had all the authority he needed via the August 1964, Gulf of Tonkin Resolution to pursue operations in Vietnam. Nevertheless, as U.S. operations and air bombing campaigns expanded, he put forward a $700 million dollar supplemental request to support ongoing Vietnam operations at the beginning of May 1965. At that time, both Congress and the nation were otherwise preoccupied with the landing of nearly 20,000 U.S. troops in the Dominican Republic to respond to unrest and leftist movements in that country. President Johnson saw the congressional vote on the $700 million lump sum, maximum discretionary fund as a vote of confidence in his administration and the handling of the Vietnam escalation. It is doubtful that Johnson actually believed his own claim, but he even went so far to assert to Mississippi Senator John Stennis (D), on the day the package was submitted to the Hill, that support for the $700 million would show North Vietnam the United States was united and " . . . if we can just let them [North Vietnam] know in forty-eight hours that we're in this thing to stay, I think they'll fold."[2] Since President Dwight Eisenhower began support in 1954, this occasion marked the first time any administration asked for a specific defense appropriation for Vietnam.

Congress cleared the measure on May 6, 1965, with supplemental appropriations of $700 million specifically for support of Vietnam operations. The bill took approximately 53 hours to pass from when the President appealed to Congress to demonstrate "prompt support of our basic course: resistance to aggression, moderation in the use of power, and a constant search for peace," but the North Vietnamese certainly did not fold. Any "folding" came from Congress, which passed the measure 408 to 7 in the House and 88 to 3 in the Senate. With very little debate or questioning of war policy, Congress played a hand in fiscally facilitating the administration's gradual escalation.

Structured essentially as a transfer fund, the $700 million gave the Executive Branch maximum flexibility over how it would be spent. President Johnson also used this appropriation measure as an opportunity to demonstrate an appearance of cooperation with the Legislative Branch on the war. Lobbying Texas representative and Chairman of the House Appropriations Committee George Mahon (D) the day before passage, Johnson surmised,

> If I hadn't been there thirty years on the Hill, I would have just signed the document that came to me transferring funds. . . . So I laid my cards on the table. If they [Congress] want those helicopters to fly, if they want that fuel in them, if they want ammunition in their guns, they can pass that bill. And unless we want to pull out, why, we've got to have the funds to do it with. . . . If you don't want us to do it, we can just quit. . . . We'll see whether they [Congress] believe in the Executive being frank and candid and open with them.[3]

The frank, candid, and open dialogue—if it ever truly existed then—was about to end with the request for the Southeast Asia Emergency Fund $1.7 billion request.

Administration Deception and the Southeast Asia Emergency Fund—FY66

Leading to the fateful day of July 28, 1965, when the President announced that troop strength and operational commitments to South Vietnam would significantly increase, lay a web of deceptive statements and actions by administration officials, particularly with regards to the cost estimates that followed in August. Understated by at least five to seven times below known costs, the administration clung to the claim that only an additional $1.7 billion was needed through the end of the calendar year. Various memoirs and historical records all point to President Johnson trying to protect his Great Society legislation, and not threatening the cost of these "butter" programs with the cost of "guns" for Vietnam.[4] Johnson also ruled out a tax hike to pay for Vietnam expenses since he did not think he could get the votes, nor did he want the public debate to raise the guns versus butter question. He felt he had to hide the immediate costs of increased involvement at least until after the new year, when the bulk of the Great Society programs would already become law.[5]

The President initially did not want to request any additional funds until January 1966. The approach planned for DoD was to use existing transfer authority, unobligated balances from prior year appropriations that had carried over, and the $700 million provided in May to "cash flow" operations out of existing accounts rather than request a new appropriation. However, under growing pressure, particularly from a vocal Republican minority in Congress and a Senate Armed Services Committee's yearlong investigation into the readiness and preparedness of the military, Johnson and Secretary of Defense Robert McNamara felt the need to request additional funds. Submitted to Congress on August 4, 1965, the request for $1.7 billion in a central transfer fund entitled the Southeast Asia Emergency Fund (SEAEF) was an acknowledgment of the need for more money, yet the request avoided revealing the growing bill for FY66 now included an estimated $10–13 billion for Vietnam operations.[6] The SEAEF was considered as an amendment to the regular FY66 budget legislation that had already passed the House, and therefore it received substantial review only via hearings and questioning in the Senate.

Secretary McNamara admitted in congressional testimony that the $1.7 billion was a down payment pending additional supplemental funds that might be required in FY66, and the administration would likely submit a more detailed supplemental request in January 1966 when Congress reconvened.[7] The deception was not in stating that there might be more funding required later (everyone involved seemed to expect this requirement), but rather in the fact that McNamara already had DoD expenditures totaling more than the amount requested, and the known costs were even higher. As stated in the Bureau of the Budget documents President Johnson submitted to Congress, "This amendment [for $1.7 billion additional funds was] to meet the immediate need for additional funds to increase our military strength in Vietnam as . . . announced to the nation on July 28."[8] However, a brief analysis of this statement and the administration troop commitments, prior to and on July 28, indicate a purposefully low estimate of required costs. From McNamara's congressional testimony in February 1965, on the baseline FY66 DoD budget, he stated approximately 23,500 U.S. military personnel were in South Vietnam, and 6 months later when he testified in defense of the SEAEF, troop levels had already been increased to 75,000 without much public attention or debate.[9] This rough 50,000 troop increase carried an annual cost estimated at $1.3 billion even before the July 28, announcement to add yet an additional 50,000 troop increment immediately (theoretically adding at least another $1.3 billion in annual costs), with more troops to follow soon afterward.[10] Even before the $1.7 billion request, the overall increase of approximately 100,000 troops alone generated an annual bill of $2.6 billion merely to support the current level of operations and did not account for increased combat operations the administration envisioned. Additional aircraft strike sorties, artillery, and sea-based bombardment was planned in support of expanded U.S. combat operations.[11] Likewise, the increased operations tempo would only generate inevitable demands for more resources. On the troop-level issue alone, it is clear in hindsight why selected members of Congress challenged the administration's early funding requests and accused the President of trying to hide the costs (to protect his cherished Great Society programs). McNamara stated, "We have no desire to widen to war," but that was exactly what the administration had done without requesting sufficient resources to cover the costs.

Congress provided the $1.7 billion exactly as the administration requested it. However, DoD used the bulk of the funds, a little over $1.5 billion, for procurement items such as equipment, aircraft, and ammunition for Vietnam. Congressional documents show the immediate manpower bills resulting from increased troop strengths were initially funded with $470 million transferred from various other DoD accounts and by moving FY66 manpower funds dedicated for later in the year forward. Also, by not including in the final bill any reporting requirements or stipulations to notify Congress about transfers from the fund, Congress once again passed up an opportunity to have any influence over wartime expenditures. Executive funding flexibility in wartime is not necessarily bad, and for prompt response to changing battlefield conditions it can be a vital asset. However, in early Vietnam expenditures, there was an apparent lack of legislative probing on details of war policy and conduct. Coupled with purposeful deception by the Executive, these factors combined to help set conditions for later significant funding battles over Vietnam.

FY66 Supplemental—The Shoe Finally Drops

The follow-on supplemental that Secretary McNamara had alluded to when he testified in support of the Southeast Asia Emergency Fund in August 1965, came in the form of a $13.1 billion request in early 1966 and passed overwhelmingly through Congress in a mere 10 days in March 1966. The President got 100 percent of what he asked for, with no deviation in the composition of the appropriations requested. As a percentage increase over the baseline FY66 funding, this supplemental increased overall defense spending by nearly 30 percent, with the largest increases in both operations and investment accounts for the ground forces, as well as for aircraft procurement and military construction funds. Interestingly, the congressional defense authorization committees attended hearings on the supplemental

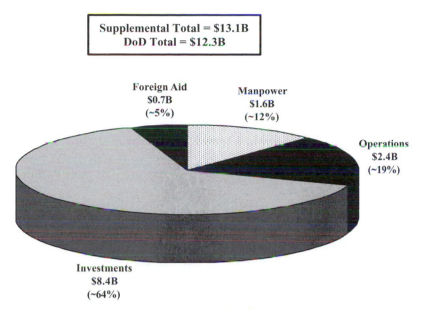

Supplemental Total = $13.1B
DoD Total = $12.3B

Foreign Aid
$0.7B
(~5%)

Manpower
$1.6B
(~12%)

Operations
$2.4B
(~19%)

Investments
$8.4B
(~64%)

Figure 4.1 FY66 Supplemental: Appropriation Category Shares

and passed measures authorizing those funds where no existing authorizations were in place like the construction, procurement, and research and development dollars. Normally, supplemental appropriations were—and are—handled only by the appropriations committees.

Figure 4.1 shows the breakout of funding according to function, while Figure 4.2 depicts the division across the military Services within DoD and aid funds appropriated to the President. The military personnel funds supported increases in end-strength for all the Services, which finally paid the bills avoided in 1965 and not funded via the SEAEF. Additionally, there were significant funds added for "operations," which included the construction, operation, and maintenance of new and expanded bases. The major percentage of the funds in the "investment" category went toward procurement of new aircraft, ordnance, and missile systems; and research and development efforts directed to support Vietnam operations. Compared with financial support to the fighting forces, the small portion of funding dedicated to aid was indicative of the financial support assistance programs received throughout the war into the early 1970s. The preference for firepower funding over aid funding was another proof the United States misjudged the type of counterinsurgency fight it was in—violating Clausewitz's admonition, " . . . that the statesman and commander have to . . . establish . . . the kind of war on which they are embarking; neither mistaking it for, nor trying to turn it into, something that is alien to its nature."[12]

Despite early and frequent questioning by some in Congress over the appropriateness of the administration's funding requests for Vietnam, there was little

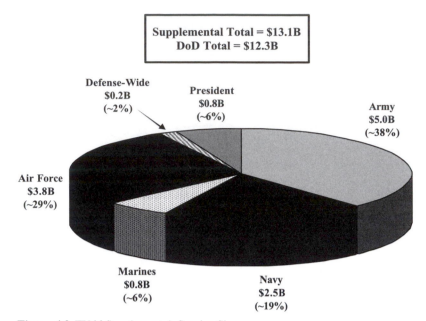

Supplemental Total = $13.1B
DoD Total = $12.3B

Defense-Wide
$0.2B
(~2%)

President
$0.8B
(~6%)

Army
$5.0B
(~38%)

Air Force
$3.8B
(~29%)

Marines
$0.8B
(~6%)

Navy
$2.5B
(~19%)

Figure 4.2 FY66 Supplemental: Service Shares

guidance, reporting requirements, or restrictions placed on the Executive through this spending measure. In fact, the only reporting requirement was a quarterly report on support provided other countries from these funds. Flexibility, however, was significantly reduced in this supplemental. The previous funds passed in 1965 and dedicated for Vietnam were granted in special transfer accounts with essentially unlimited flexibility for transfer. Given the size of this request (more than five times the size of the previous two supplementals combined), the administration likely concluded it could not get that amount from Congress in a similar unconstrained transfer fund. The request asked for the bulk of the new funds in dedicated appropriations, subject to normal appropriation rules and restrictions, thereby limiting unfettered transfer flexibility. Only 6 percent of the appropriation came in flexible funds, with an additional minor amount of flexible authority granted for emergency expenses within the operations and maintenance accounts. However, operations and maintenance funds have inherently greater flexibility for use than most other appropriations and comprised 64 percent of this supplemental.

Other Associated 1965–1966 Spending

Several other spending measures in this time frame were also germane to the cost of war in Vietnam. The first, and historically most important, relates to a passing mention between Secretary of the Navy, Paul Nitze, and Marine

Commandant, General Wallace Greene, regarding a $1 billion set-aside for Vietnam within the FY66 baseline DoD appropriations. The comment was made by Nitze on July 23, 1965, just before the President announced the major troop increase for Vietnam. Nitze told Greene DoD was under orders from the President to " . . . hold down the 'political noise level' of escalation."[13] The Joint Chiefs would not get the $12–13 billion that they estimated new deployments would cost, but as discussed above, the administration would rely on transfer authorities, unobligated carry-over balances in other appropriations, the recently provided (May '65) $700 million supplemental, and now apparently also " . . . the $1 billion already included in the 1966 Defense Appropriations."[14] At this point, the $1.7 billion SEAEF and follow-on FY66 supplemental were not yet in existence. This comment suggests the administration had already increased defense spending for Vietnam in the baseline budget without advertising the fact in the President's budget message to Congress or subsequent Executive Branch officials' congressional testimony. Funds of this amount could have easily been added into manpower or operations and maintenance accounts under the guise of increased readiness, a theme being continuously pushed by the McNamara Pentagon, without raising significant suspicion over higher funding levels, or that the money was actually planned for Vietnam expenditures. If indeed the case, the later use of the $1.7 billion SEAEF primarily for procurement investments, and using only a smaller $470 million transfer of funds for manpower in early FY66, also makes more sense—the immediate operations, maintenance, and manpower bills were apparently significantly covered by the additional $1 billion set-aside in the baseline budget. During the time the FY66 budget was developed in the Summer-Fall of 1964, supporting the number of U.S. troops then present in South Vietnam would have required roughly $500 million per year. Why would the ever cost-conscious McNamara have nearly doubled the funds required for a function in a budget submission, and not called attention to the purpose of the funds, unless he hoped to provide for an unnoticed escalation? Given budget development timelines, to have $1 billion for Vietnam in the budget submission for FY66 indicated that at least the DoD leadership, if not the White House as well, had fiscally planned for significant escalation back in 1964, and absolutely no later than January 1965 when the budget was submitted—clearly months earlier than most histories suggest and likely even before Johnson's 1964 reelection.

Other increased costs associated with the war included the expansion of military and veterans' benefits and supporting foreign aid spending. As with past and future conflicts, wartime pay and benefits increases for the troops were dramatic and began in earnest in 1965. This upward ratchet effect on military personnel entitlements created enduring cost growth that persisted long after the conflict ended. Across the board, military pay, medical benefits, and Veterans Administration benefits were all enhanced significantly during FY65–66. Also, U.S. economic aid to Vietnam over FY65–66 increased sharply, totaling nearly $2.7 billion. All of these added costs can be considered attributable to the conflict in Vietnam.

FY67—First Year Attempt at Requirements On-Budget

In FY67, the Johnson administration attempted its first year of identifying and requesting Vietnam War operations in the baseline DoD budget. The President's budget message to Congress identified $10.3 billion of DoD's overall $58.9 billion as dedicated for Vietnam, or 17.5 percent of the planned overall defense budget. In addition to support for U.S. forces, the requested funds also included support and sustainment of South Vietnamese and allied troops participating in Vietnam operations that were previously funded via the Military Assistance Programs. Secretary McNamara commented that " . . . maintenance of separate financial and logistic systems for the U.S. and Military Assistance forces is proving to be entirely too cumbersome, time consuming and inefficient."[15]

Of the $10.3 billion requested on budget, no detailed breakout by appropriations or line-item requirements was provided. Several statements do provide insights, and contradictions, on what the assumptions were in creating the estimate. First, much like the Korean War, the Johnson administration would not make predictions about when the conflict might terminate. As a result, the end of the fiscal year was assumed as an arbitrary cutoff for requested funding. During congressional testimony, administration witnesses highlighted this fact and stated if fighting increased significantly, or extended beyond the end of the fiscal year, additional appropriations would be required. Documentation of a second feature regarding funds requested revealed an inconsistency between the Office of the Secretary of Defense and the Services. At issue was whether combat attrition and consumption was included in the on-budget request, particularly for major weapon systems. Secretary McNamara stated in testimony,

> . . . We do not normally provide in advance for combat attrition of such major weapon systems as aircraft and ships because of the great costs involved. I understand that a war reserve of aircraft was once considered in connection with the military build-up undertaken during the Korean War, but rejected for the same reason. Accordingly, additional aircraft must be procured as soon as the forces are committed to combat and this was one of the largest items in our FY 1966 Supplemental request.[16]

Examination of the full set of congressional testimony surrounding the FY66 and FY67 DoD appropriations requests revealed the McNamara assertion was at least partially in conflict with previous Army testimony that indicated some aircraft attrition in Vietnam had been accounted for in development of the FY66 baseline budget a year earlier, although no one in Congress appears to have challenged the discontinuity at the time of McNamara's testimony.[17] Further testimony by other Service officials suggests aircraft attrition may have been handled similarly for both the Navy and Air Force.

Throughout testimony in the spring of 1967, congressional members continuously challenged witnesses about the adequacy of the budget to support Vietnam. OSD witnesses routinely stated the request was sufficient for the fiscal year barring any major changes. Service officials were guarded in their responses and stressed more reasons why additional funds might be required than did their civilian OSD counterparts. As a foreboding of likely supplementals, Secretary McNamara's comments about reducing other core defense programs to help keep spending down while paying for Vietnam should have served as one warning post—despite reassurances that planned Southeast Asia combat activities were covered by the funds in the budget request. McNamara stated because of the large funding demands of combat operations, "we have stretched out and deferred some programs which are not directly related to our near-term combat readiness." He concluded his opening comments in this testimony session by claiming that in elimination of "unneeded and marginal activities and deferring whatever can be safely deferred," he reduced the combined FY66 supplemental and FY67 base budget requests by roughly $15.5 billion.[18] This figure translated to an OSD managed 18 percent cut in defense funds from the combined amount apparently requested in those two spending measures by the Services. It is hard to imagine a cut of that magnitude during escalation in what became the peak years of combat involvement. These inherently prophetic comments were further indication that significant portions of Vietnam funding were being underestimated and future readiness was being sacrificed for near-term combat exigencies—actions that came home to roost as part of the hollow military readiness challenges in the early-to-mid 1970s.

The request for supplemental funds, many expected, was required to fully fund Vietnam operations in FY67 came not once, but twice. The first supplemental request was submitted in January 1967, with the FY68 budget submission. Enacted on March 16, 1967, with a little more than a quarter of the fiscal year remaining, this appropriation, and the accompanying authorization bill for the new procurement and other investment spending included, was the first opportunity the new 90th Congress had to vote on a measure directly related to the war. Despite previous and ongoing congressional concerns over funding the war, the Democratic-controlled Congress passed their President's appropriation bill with only minor modifications and broad bipartisan support; 385-11 in the House and 77-3 in the Senate. Included in the accompanying authorization bill was a Statement of Congressional Policy known as the Vietnam Declaration. In that language, Congress stated intentions to support the troops fighting in Vietnam, support for efforts to prevent expansion of conflict, and support for a peaceful settlement of the war. No binding measures or provisions over the Executive were enacted with this text; discretion in the conduct of Vietnam policy, and to a large extent the course of funding, was still ceded to the Executive.[19] Restrictive legislation on funding for Southeast Asian (SEA) operations would eventually come, but not until more negative opinions, accumulated over the growing costs in money and blood, developed the impetus for congressional funding cutoff.

As for composition and size of the FY67 first supplemental request, it was not significantly different than the large FY66 supplemental the year before. All of this appropriation went to DoD and incremental Vietnam costs. Figures 4.3 and 4.4 below show the breakout of funds.

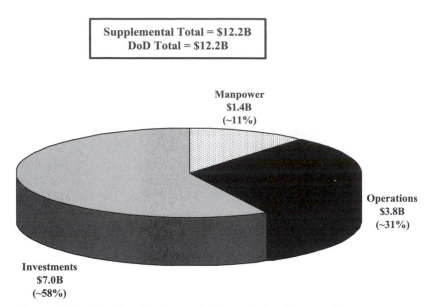

Supplemental Total = $12.2B
DoD Total = $12.2B

Manpower
$1.4B
(~11%)

Operations
$3.8B
(~31%)

Investments
$7.0B
(~58%)

Figure 4.3 FY67—First Supplemental: Appropriation Category Shares

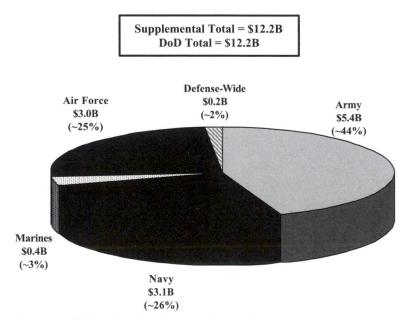

Supplemental Total = $12.2B
DoD Total = $12.2B

Air Force
$3.0B
(~25%)

Defense-Wide
$0.2B
(~2%)

Army
$5.4B
(~44%)

Marines
$0.4B
(~3%)

Navy
$3.1B
(~26%)

Figure 4.4 FY67—First Supplemental: Service Shares

Supplemental Vietnam Support Total = $743M
DoD Total = $592M

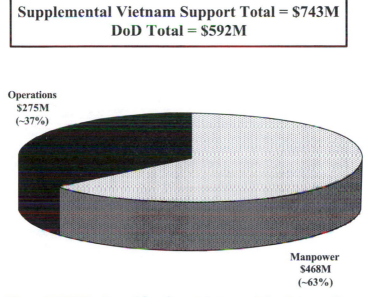

Operations
$275M
(~37%)

Manpower
$468M
(~63%)

Figure 4.5 FY67—Second Supplemental: Appropriation Category Shares

Although Vietnam funds increased by nearly 120 percent, the first supplemental's funds were not enough. Less than 2 months later, the administration requested an additional $743 million for direct or related activities supporting Vietnam: $275 million in the operations and maintenance accounts and $468 million in manpower dollars to ensure sufficient funding through the remaining month and a half of FY67. A total of $592 million (80 percent) of these funds went to DoD, with the remainder to other departments and agencies like the Veterans Administration for disabled veterans care, the Selective Service System to administer the draft, and other related functions. Figures 4.5 and Figure 4.6 below depict the breakout of funds from the second FY67 supplemental.

When finally enacted, both supplementals combined added $12.9 billion to spending for Vietnam and increased the war's share of the new total defense budget from the 17.5 percent projected when the original FY67 budget was submitted to 32 percent by the end of that year. Investment funds were the majority share of this addition at 54 percent, operations and maintenance accounts claimed 32 percent, and manpower consumed the balance of 14 percent. In summary, the FY67 planning for on-budget Vietnam spending missed the actual requirements by a wide margin. The first FY67 supplemental appropriation alone increased Vietnam spending beyond the on-budget amount by 120 percent and the second supplemental added an additional 7 percent of the original Vietnam request.

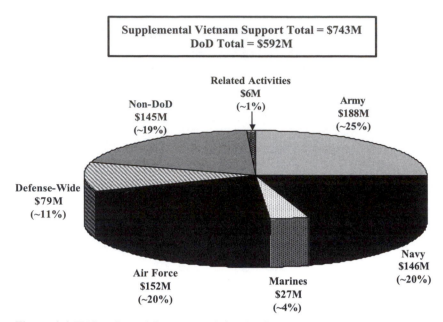

Figure 4.6 FY67—Second Supplemental: Service Shares

FY68—The Pattern Continues

By FY68, the incremental costs of Vietnam placed in the baseline budget request consumed nearly 30 percent of the DoD budget. The President identified $21.9 billion of the total $74.7 billion defense budget as Vietnam related. During testimony on the budget request, Secretary McNamara stated these incremental costs for Vietnam were estimated between $17–22 billion. McNamara testified this cost range was the best estimate that could be provided and the higher end of $22 billion was the generally accepted figure. He repeatedly stated the Defense Department could not refine this value, nor could it with any accuracy break down these costs on a monthly basis.[20] As such, little detail existed as to the composition of these funds, exact appropriations, and under what assumptions the incremental costs were determined. Given the previous record of significantly understated costs from 1964 through McNamara's testimony in early calendar year 1967 regarding the FY68 budget, a safe assumption would be to consider the $22 billion figure was the minimum of funds included in the baseline budget and consumed in support of Vietnam.

For both the FY68 baseline request for Vietnam costs and the FY67 supplemental discussed above, two major assumptions, or rules, used to create the estimates changed from previous years. First, as the Service supporting the bulk of the troops in Vietnam, the Army based the main portion of its operations and support funds on a factor of tons per man-year required. Essentially, the Army used projected troop strengths and then multiplied by this factor to build its funding estimates. For the FY67 supplemental and FY68 baseline requests, the factor was increased from the previous 5.5 tons per man-year to a figure of 7.8—the final level constrained by the Office of the Secretary of Defense to control costs. The Army Service estimates independently had suggested the figure should have been as high as 9.0 tons per man-year.[21]

The second major change from previous Vietnam budget planning was DoD now extended funding projections beyond the current year. McNamara said,

> Since we can now project our requirements for the conflict in Southeast Asia with far greater confidence than last year, we have changed our basic approach in preparing the FY 1967 supplemental as well as the FY 1968 Budget. Sufficient funds are being requested in both the FY 1967 Supplemental and the FY 1968 Budget to protect the production lead-time on all combat essential items until FY 1969 funds would become available.[22]

For ammunition, perhaps the procurement item most sensitive to changes in combat intensity, funding was projected as sufficient to continue orders through the first 6 months of FY69 using the combined FY67 Supplemental and FY68 baseline Vietnam funds. For aircraft, with longer lead times, sufficient funds were supposedly included to account for both attrition rates and production deliveries all the way through the first half of FY71.[23] McNamara further stated assumed attrition rates, operations tempo considered, and number of weapon systems employed were all factored in at higher rates than past estimates (arguably this assertion was based on the discussion of Army planning factors above; what McNamara did not state at the time was that his office artificially constrained the planning factors for fiscal reasons).[24] While appropriation-level detail of the FY68 on-budget funds were not available at the time, based upon McNamara's statements, the funding must have been heavily skewed in favor of investment accounts like previous years. Later DoD publication of incremental cost data revealed that the FY68 on-budget portion contained almost half investment funds as shown in Figure 4.7.

Secretary McNamara stated in the same testimony that funds for Vietnam, " . . . should be sufficient to cover our requirements until FY 1969 funds become available, even if the conflict continues beyond June 30, 1968 [the end of FY 68]."[25] Hence, McNamara was again, and more firmly this time, stating no requirement for supplemental funds was foreseen. However, as with FY67, events and realities of combat proved baseline funding inadequate and nearly $7 billion in supplemental funds was required. Figures 4.8 and 4.9 highlight the composition of funds in the appropriated FY68 supplemental. The supplemental was primarily money in the operations and maintenance and manpower accounts to cover shortfalls due to increased combat operations. The Southeast Asia Emergency Fund was used again as a central transfer account for the bulk of the funds and is reflected in the figures above as either in the Defense-wide share in the Service breakout, or as the SEAEF

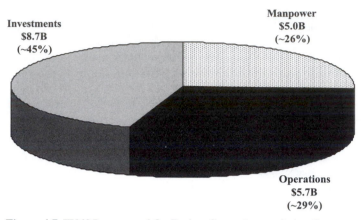

Figure 4.7 FY68 Incremental On-Budget Costs: Appropriation Category Shares

in the appropriation categories. The baseline funds had already provided enough for investments in equipment procurement, construction to support infrastructure requirements, and a small amount for research and development work on problems directly related to operations in Southeast Asia.

FY69–70: The Johnson Administration Departs

In his last two budget messages to Congress before leaving office, President Johnson apparently tried to downplay the budget and economic impacts of Vietnam

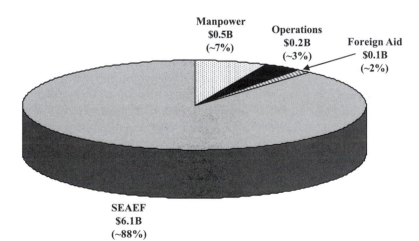

Figure 4.8 FY68 Supplemental: Appropriation Category Shares

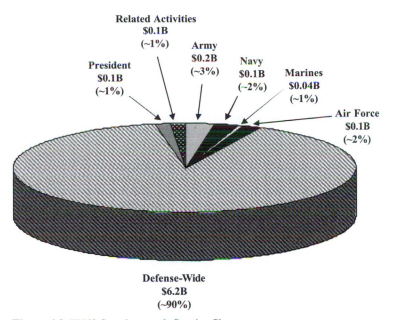

Figure 4.9 FY68 Supplemental: Service Shares

operations. The FY67 and FY68 budget messages featured Vietnam as a central element; with over 20–30 direct references in each document, linked to discussion in 9–10 different subsections, it was one of the main themes introducing the FY67 budget and was highlighted in the FY68 budget as a "top three" priority along with the Great Society programs and promoting economic growth.[26] The FY69 message was notable for its lack of emphasis in all these respects. It only contained nine references to the war, and five of those were in the national defense and international affairs sections as would be expected. Recounting progress since he came into office, this budget document appeared to be an attempt to begin writing the Johnson legacy regarding social progress, and Vietnam was certainly one legacy he did not want associated.[27] The departing FY70 turnover budget to the incoming Nixon administration followed the trend of distancing from Vietnam as the year before.[28]

Various assessments placed Vietnam costs in the on-budget estimate for FY69 at between $19.8 and $25.8 billion. The Air Force estimated the on-budget portion of Vietnam funding in FY69 was $7 billion.[29] The Army estimated its FY69 Vietnam costs in the budget request at $11.5 billion.[30] With only two Services alone almost equaling the lower overall estimate, it appears the higher end figure of approximately $25.8 billion was probably more accurate when assuming Navy, Marine Corps, Defense-Wide programs, and military assistance costs had to be included (although these additional Service and functional breakouts were not specified). The higher estimate continued the upward trend as a percentage of

DoD's overall budget with planned, on-budget costs rising from 17.5 percent in FY67, to 30 percent in FY68, and to 33 percent in FY69.

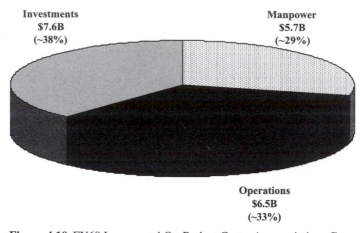

Figure 4.10 FY69 Incremental On-Budget Costs: Appropriations Category Shares

Investment funds still remained the majority of the incremental on-budget funds, but as the war reached its peak of U.S. presence and involvement, the composition of the on-budget funds between investments, manpower, and operations began to achieve more balance among these functions.

This increasing, on-budget allowance was still not enough, and further, albeit smaller, supplemental appropriations were required. The FY69 supplemental appropriations carried $2.5 billion more for DoD in Vietnam. Additionally, $0.5 billion was provided to other departments and agencies in support of the war efforts.

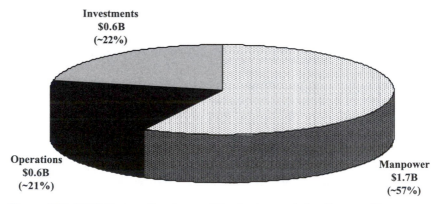

Figure 4.11 FY69 Vietnam Supplemental Funds: Appropriation Category Shares

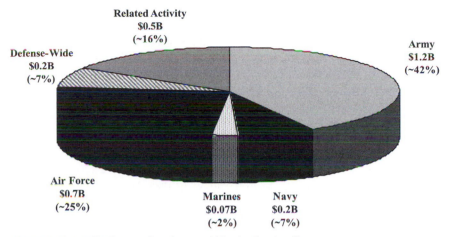

Figure 4.12 FY69 Vietnam Supplemental Funds: Service Shares

By the end of the fiscal year, war costs had risen $3 billion over estimates due to a higher operations tempo stemming from events like the Tet Offensive that occurred after the FY69 estimates were prepared and hence increased costs.

Congressional Concerns: 1965–1969

Throughout the 1965–1969 period of escalation and rising costs, congressional frustrations with Johnson administration financing and budgeting continued to mount. Beyond a relatively few initial war opponents like Senator Wayne Morse, many members felt it was not a matter of the war costing too much; rather, they felt the estimates placed before them were obviously too low and comprehensive military operations needed more funding. This concern extended to such issues as long-term readiness and preparedness for other challenges and it conflicted with the assumptions Secretary McNamara used to build the estimates. Further, there was a collective frustration at the continued assurances of sufficient funding that failed to stem the need for supplemental appropriations when DoD ran dangerously short on funds. Lastly, congressional frustration may have been most acute in not having full war costs visible when the annual appropriations process was underway. There was a bipartisan and bicameral expressed desire to balance war costs with domestic spending and appropriate revenue levels, but such needs could not be met as war costs were only presented piecemeal. Even as Richard Nixon became President, congressional concerns remained over Vietnam funding. Part of the angst was not just over Vietnam funds, but perceptions of bloated budgets and poorly performing weapon systems. All combined, these concerns generated wider public criticisms and greater congressional scrutiny as the FY70 budget made its way through the appropriation process.

The accuracy of cost estimates for Vietnam, and the forthrightness of Executive information concerning those costs, plagued Congress after McNamara and Johnson left office. Democratic Senator Richard Russell, Chairman of the Appropriations Defense Subcommittee, remarked to the new Secretary of Defense, Melvin Laird, "I think you will recall that I could not agree with the cost estimates of this war given by former Secretary McNamara."[31] Early in his tenure, Laird wrestled with problems that had surfaced in both House and Senate hearings during the previous years, especially the hidden costs in the defense program resulting from Vietnam. Those costs associated with reconstituting stock and inventory, repair and replacement of equipment not already provided for, and meeting backlogs remained obscured. Laird, like McNamara before him and even former Defense Secretaries Louis Johnson, George Marshall, and Robert Lovett, all suffered from the same problem—there was no established standard procedures or accounting records for estimating and capturing war costs. Yet, by and large, Congress provided most of what the administration requested and with few restrictions during Johnson's last months and Nixon's first year in office.

FY70: The American Ebb Flow Begins

Coupled with the congressional concerns over DoD costs in general, and Vietnam costs in particular, was a consensus developing on the Hill to reduce growing deficits by cutting federal spending. President Johnson had pushed for tax increases to cool an overheated economy and help curb the growing inflation trends. After a long and cantankerous debate, Congress passed the Revenue and Expenditure Control Act of 1968. It gave the President his desired tax hike, but at a cost of legislating spending reductions and rescissions. This budget cutting began in FY69 and gathered further momentum with the incoming Nixon administration. The lame duck Johnson budget submission for FY70 contained $25.4 billion for Vietnam War operations. The revised Nixon budget, prepared in the spring of 1969, reduced the Vietnam on-budget portion of the DoD budget request to $24.9 billion.[32] Spending reductions and fiscal constraints even began to dictate military operations. Joint Chiefs Chairman, General Earle Wheeler, testified that planned B-52 sorties supporting Vietnam were being reduced from 1,800 per month in FY69 to 1,400 per month based on " ... an action taken in response to the budget reduction requirement. Although the military factors standing alone would not have called for a reduction, we shall, nevertheless, be able to support the conflict. ... "[33] Another example was nearly $1.1 billion removed by reducing the projected ammunition consumption in Vietnam for FY70.[34] Clearly, the tide had turned on swelling budget projections to prosecute the Vietnam War.

However, budget estimates were just that—estimates. FY70 was generally regarded as the first year Vietnam was fully absorbed on-budget. While largely true, DoD still required an additional $2.3 billion to cover higher pay costs in response to war-generated inflation and substantial cost-of-living increases. Supplemental appropriations also were required to finance $800 million of war support in other areas.[35] These combined costs exploded the myth that the Vietnam War was fully on budget by FY70.

FY71–74: De-escalation, Vietnamization, and Funding Reductions

The main challenge in examining Vietnam War costs from FY71 through the end of American involvement was that all the on-budget numbers were classified at the time and line-item detail was sorely lacking. The classification was due to the drawdown of forces by Nixon and the desire not to reveal planned or anticipated troop strength, or levels of effort, by inference from budget numbers. After the fact, DoD provided macrolevel numbers of incremental costs and the breakout of each year; FY71–74 is shown in Figure 4.13. The Vietnamization Plan is evident in an examination of the changing composition of these three categories of spending. Investment funds, which were noted earlier to have started declining from a majority share prior to FY69–70, fluctuate slightly but remain well below the 60–80 percent range they commanded in the first years of the stepped up war efforts. This sustained lower percentage of equipment and infrastructure required made sense as the U.S. force levels continued to drop. Manpower costs obviously dropped as well as troops were brought home and demobilized. The operations account share increased as aid and assistance to the South Vietnamese increased significantly.

The augmentation of higher DoD pay costs continued with supplemental appropriations, and these extra appropriations also helped cover rising costs in the Veterans Administration and other readjustment benefits for the troops returning home. Table 4.1 summarizes the combined amounts of supplemental appropriations devoted to incremental Vietnam costs as the American war began to wind down. The spike in FY74 supplemental funding was mainly comprised of: more than $1 billion in added operations and maintenance funds and $800 million in various types of procurement to begin addressing DoD shortfalls from Vietnam War operations, and $50 million in reconstruction and refugee aid to Southeast Asia.

Another issue during these years was the chimera of a "peace dividend." When DoD budgets reached their peak in the late 1960s, Vietnam cost between $20–30 billion annually. Many felt that removing $20 billion from the defense budget for other priorities would, therefore, be a relatively easy task once the war ended. However, the task proved more difficult than expected. Several factors complicated the issue. First, without a precise estimate on what was really spent on Vietnam from inside the budgets, it was naturally difficult to determine how much correspondingly could be taken out. Second, similar to Secretary Laird's earlier lament, the hidden costs of items deferred, program reductions, and

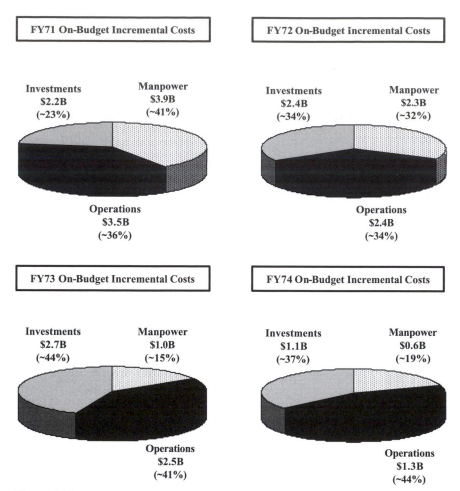

Figure 4.13 FY71–74 Incremental On-Budget Costs: Appropriation Category Shares

schedule slippage required additional funds when conflict ended. The problem here was a traditional one; war funding generally runs out before the war bills are fully paid. Using the Navy as example, General Wheeler emphasized this challenge:

> Over the past several years maintenance of the fleet and the building of new vessels have been shoved ahead of us in the interest of economy and because of the cost of the Vietnamese war in order to hold the budget down to some reasonable level.... While the Navy, in my judgment, has been put in a worse position than either the Air Force or the Army during the Vietnamese war, it is quite true that all three services are going to need improvements and modernization [after the war ends].[36]

Table 4.1 FY71–75 Supplemental Appropriations Incremental Costs in Support of Vietnam

$Billions	FY71	FY72	FY73	FY74	FY75	Total (FY71–75)
TY($B) Cost	3.6	2.9	1.6	5.8	3.9	17.8
CY2006($B) Cost	21.2	16.0	7.5	24.9	16.4	86.0

The Army also experienced the cutbacks and dropped production on several types of helicopters and combat vehicles below anticipated attrition rates, buying only enough to sustain the production lines.[37] Finally, unique to Vietnam was the effort to shift to an All-Volunteer Force (AVF) around the same time the conflict ended. Resourcing an AVF, even at smaller levels than peak-Vietnam manpower levels, would require more funds, not less, than a conscription-based force.

Congressional Concerns: 1970–1975

The cleavages in American society caused by the Vietnam War are well documented in other works and need no recounting here. What does bear merit for discussion are the effects on financing and budgeting the war, and by extension fundamental war policy itself, from these various pressures. Needless to say, by the early 1970s public opinion was widely against continued U.S. involvement in Southeast Asia. Congress began to reflect this sentiment in actions using the power-of-the-purse. Beginning with the FY70 DoD Appropriations Act, the Hill enacted a series of restrictive appropriations to limit slowly, then cut off, funding for the war. From FY70 through FY74, Congress included various provisions and rider amendments in regular DoD and foreign aid appropriations, supplemental appropriations, and even continuing resolutions used to extend funding into a new fiscal year. The first rider mentioned above prevented the President from introducing ground troops into either Laos or Cambodia. The decisive restrictive appropriation came in the FY74 Continuing Appropriation, Section 108, which stated:

> Notwithstanding any other provision of law, on or after August 15, 1973, no funds herein or heretofore appropriated may be obligated or expended to finance directly or indirectly combat activities by United States military forces in or over or from off the shores of North Vietnam, South Vietnam, Laos or Cambodia.[38]

The President always maintained he had the constitutional authority to direct force as Commander in Chief and consistently fought these restrictive appropriations.

Additionally, the Executive had the Gulf of Tonkin Resolution (until its repeal in 1971) and a series of specific war supporting appropriations since the $700 million was approved in May 1965 to point to for legitimization. Ultimately, the dispute produced the War Powers Resolution in 1973 that attempted to force the Executive into certain behaviors regarding the use of U.S. military forces.

Another funding mechanism Congress used to force behavior was reducing the funding flexibility provided to DoD in its annual appropriations bill, as well as increased reporting and oversight requirements. The annual amounts for General Transfer Authority and highly discretionary emergency and contingency funds were gradually reduced or eliminated. Secretary Laird challenged this restriction during the FY71 debate, arguing for greater transfer authority (at least 2 percent of the overall DoD appropriation) to handle unforeseen requirements. As part of the overall negative climate surrounding the war, Congress sustained the reduction in flexible contingency and emergency funds normally provided to the Department. Not only did Congress decrease the amount of flexible funds normally provided, but also the sharp increase in inflation made the actual power of those fewer dollars even less.

Other Costs

Other direct federal spending occurred for the war, but is not usually included in the common Vietnam cost assessments that focus on DoD funding. Managing the draft, aiding and assisting Veterans, and providing for foreign aid programs are just a few examples of other types of war costs. Such spending has been included in the calculations for this chapter where the costs could clearly be identified as supporting Vietnam efforts. Another often overlooked cost was one discussed regarding Korea—the increased manpower that in hindsight was clearly only brought onboard to support the war. Previous analysis of the baseline budgets and supplementals from the Vietnam years captured certain incremental costs of manpower; that is, the combat pay, hazardous duty pay, and other similar items that stemmed from the war. The basic pay, allowances, and other peacetime benefits were considered part of the base DoD program and not attributed to the war effort. Knowing now that was a large manpower increase solely to support the war, the baseline costs of that increase can be considered an incremental cost of war.

Examining the 4 years of increasing troop levels in Vietnam from 1965 through 1968, and comparing those to the preceding 4-year average DoD end strength, reveals that an estimated 2.1 million man-years worth of troops were "extra" for the war at an estimated cost of $12.6 billion. Likewise, the "extra" troops for the war from 1969–1972 when the bulk of the drawdown was completed, compared to the following 4-year average shows 2.9 million man-years in additional troops

Table 4.2 Vietnam War Incremental Excess End Strength (E/S)

	FY65	FY66	FT67	FY68	Total (FY65–68)	
Total Excess E/S	24,195	462,444	745,754	916,340	2,148,733	
Percentage of Total E/S	1%	15%	22%	26%		
TY($M) Cost	$132	$2,506	$4,366	$5,616	$12,620	
CY2006($M) Cost	$1,296	$22,383	$36,973	$45,210	$105,862	

	FY69	FY70	FY71	FY72	Total (FY69–72)	Total (FY65–72)
Total Excess E/S	1,302,079	908,767	557,051	165,966	2,933,863	5,082,596
Percentage of Total E/S	38%	30%	21%	7%	—	—
TY($M) Cost	$8,839	$7,566	$5,245	$1,910	$23,560	$36,180
CY2006($M) Cost	$66,877	$51,163	$33,118	$10,592	$161,750	$267,612

with a cost of $23.6 billion. These costs reflected in Table 4.2 below should be added to the incremental cost of war in Vietnam.

Other federal costs included are items like military construction legislation supporting the war effort and foreign aid funds, whether military or economic in character, directed toward the countries in Southeast Asia during this time period. All of these costs are reflected in the Summary section that follows.

VIETNAM SUMMARY

What did the war cost? The Statistical Abstract of the United States lists $107 billion in FY67 dollars in incremental costs from 1965–1977. In today's 2006 dollars, that equates to roughly $677 billion. The source quoted for this cost estimate is the DoD. In terms of incremental, overall federal expenditures, between 1965 and 1975, the estimate tabulated herein is approximately $160 billion in then-year costs ($895 billion in today's 2006 constant dollars). Just using DoD figures understates the federal government costs by $218 billion in CY06 adjusted dollars. Adding excess end strength, debt servicing, and long-term veteran's compensation and pensions through 2000 adds an additional $386 billion in today's dollars.

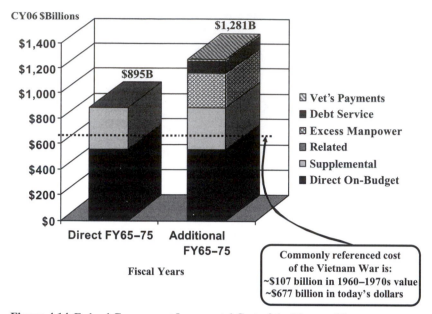

Figure 4.14 Federal Government Incremental Cost of the Vietnam War

These figures do not include the costs of American efforts in support of the French before 1954, and direct American advisory efforts in the decade that followed 1954–1964. Including these costs would certainly add billions more in today's values. It is interesting to note that veterans and their eligible beneficiaries from the Vietnam War will not stop collecting payments until after the middle of the twenty-first century—roughly 100 years after the conflict took place. Only then can a final tally be attempted to describe the true fiscal magnitude of the Vietnam War.

Of course, other costs could be attributed to the war. Indirect or second order effects costs can be calculated, estimates of the macroeconomic effects of heightened wartime spending, earnings loss of casualties, local- and state-level expenditures, opportunity costs, and a host of other issues can all be estimated and attributed depending on what assumptions are made. Due to the inherent uncertain nature for some of these required assumptions, and for the sake of brevity, these types of costs are not included in this analysis.

Increasing defense outlays for Vietnam and baseline defense needs helped fuel the inflationary trend throughout the late 1960s. Defense spending was estimated to have generated at least 7 percent of the gross national product (GNP) during the period of peak involvement in the mid-to-late 1960s; however, the pressures of higher spending with minimal increases in taxes fueled inflation as the consumer price index rose from 111 percent at the beginning of 1966 to 117.5 percent by the fall of 1967. The inflation toll on the economy, coupled with mounting casualties, and general public disenchantment with the war all led to increased criticism of military spending—even spending beyond direct Vietnam support. Coupled with news stories over spiraling program costs and missed performance goals in systems like the C-5A transport plane, the F-111 (TFX) fighter-bomber, the Anti-Ballistic Missile (ABM) System, nuclear-powered surface ships for the Navy, and others, all contributed to public pressures to cut defense funds as the war ended for the United States.

Beyond mere defense budget cuts, the Vietnam War impacted the American psyche in numerous ways creating a variety of legacies in our government, military, and society. Perhaps the enduring fiscal challenge created by Vietnam, that may influence future conflicts, is the tension between the Executive and Legislative over power-of-the-purse and flexibility in wartime. This Constitutional struggle always becomes more acute when lives are in the balance, and many of the issues that stem from it, such as congressional restrictions on the commander in chief authorities, funding cutoffs, and the War Powers Resolution itself, all remain unresolved. The courts have shown a reluctance to rule on these issues and thus decisions are left to the realm of politics—that Clausewitzian pull-and-tug between the government, the military, and the American people. The Global War on Terrorism (GWOT) has already seen the effects of the post-Vietnam legacy, and it is unlikely to be the last war to do so.

Global War on Terror: 2001–?

.

A social movement can rouse people when it can do three things: simplify ideas, establish a claim to truth, and in the union of the two, demand a commitment to action. Thus, not only does ideology transform ideas, it transforms people as well.

—Daniel Bell, Sociologist

Being killed for God's cause is a great honor achieved by only those who are the elite of the nation. We love this kind of death . . . as much as you like to live . . . it is a duty on all our umma to do so.

—Usama bin Laden

Great harm has been done to us. We have suffered great loss. And in our grief and anger we have found our mission and our moment. Freedom and fear are at war. The advance of human freedom—the great achievement of our time, and the great hope of every time—now depends on us.

There is only one force of history that can break the reign of hatred and resentment, and expose the pretensions of tyrants, and reward the hopes of the decent and tolerant, and that is the force of human freedom. Advancing these ideals is the mission that created our Nation. It is the honorable achievement of our fathers. Now it is the urgent requirement of our nation's security, and the calling of our time.

Whatever it costs to defend our country, we will pay.

—George W. Bush, U.S. President

Peace does not follow conflict with the same directness [as conflict follows peace]. The ending of conflict is a specific enterprise. It belongs neither to war nor to peace, just as a bridge is different from either bank it connects.

—Georg Simmel, Sociologist

INTRODUCTION

> Americans have known wars—but for the past 136 years, they have been wars on
> foreign soil, except for one Sunday in 1941. Americans have known the casualties
> of war—but not at the center of a great city on a peaceful morning. Americans have
> known surprise attacks—but never before on thousands of civilians. All of this was
> brought upon us in a single day—and night fell on a different world, a world where
> freedom itself is under attack.[1]

8:46:40 AM, September 11, 2001: 101 minutes later, 2973 lives and hundreds
of billions, maybe even trillions of dollars—those are the magnitudes of U.S. losses
on that fateful day. Averaged over that hundred-minute time span between the first
New York airplane strike and the collapse of the second World Trade Center tower,
measuring 9/11's rate of loss per minute makes it perhaps the greatest combined
loss rate in U.S. history—greater than even the battle of Gettysburg, the attack on
Pearl Harbor, and D-Day on the Normandy beaches in 1944. If numbers are to be
believed, only the final assault in the Civil War battle of Cold Harbor experienced
an average of more men killed per minute (losing Americans on both sides), and
no U.S. battle has exceeded the billions per minute lost in monetary cost. The
damage wrought by 19 men in four airplanes was truly stunning in its impact—
both on the American psyche (perhaps the greatest unquantifiable cost), and in the
American response. The attack launched what has become known as the Global
War on Terror (GWOT).

The GWOT has been characterized as the greatest security challenge in the
new millennium. Many have called it a generational, or decades-long conflict. In
this sense, the United States finds itself in a similar position to the late 1940s.
Emerging from World War II as the preeminent victor, the United States entered
an ideological conflict with world communism and the USSR. It took several
years and the onset of the Korean War to forge consensus behind the decades-
long strategy of containment that emerged victorious from the Cold War some
40–50 years later. If the GWOT prognoses are correct, this war is the long-term
conflict that the United States must decide how to prosecute, and concomitantly,
how to resource. The 1990s were the bridge Simmel describes between the two
conflicts—unfortunately, it was already crossed before determining what to do on
the other side.

As the unrivaled victor from the Cold War, the United States is now trying
to craft the long-term strategy and goals for fighting the GWOT. If the GWOT is
analogous to the Cold War in this sense, then the various campaigns underway
in Afghanistan and Iraq are the modern forms of extended "hot" conflicts. The
following sections outline the cost of these significant GWOT operations using
methods similar to those for examining Korea and Vietnam. Additionally, because
the GWOT data is more abundant, richer in detail, and readily available, the GWOT
analysis will also include how spending plans and appropriations have actually
been implemented where appropriate.

This analysis will not examine the GWOT's financing issues and assumes that all of the GWOT costs are included as deficit spending. Given the administration budget priorities, commitment to significant baseline budget increases in defense spending, and commitment to tax cuts, there is no reason to believe any of the incremental GWOT spending would have occurred without the events of 9/11. Nor is there any evidence of an attempt to raise revenues to cover the increased expenditures since 9/11. The emphasis in this chapter will be on budgeting, composition of spending, and legal authority issues, even though there are hundreds of other issues regarding the fiscal aspects of resourcing the GWOT. This discussion will focus only on a handful of concerns with the greatest implications for policymakers. As with the analysis on Korea and Vietnam, only incremental costs will be categorized as attributable to the cost of the conflict. Fortunately for accounting purposes, most of the GWOT funding to date has been done via supplemental appropriations that make visibility of the appropriations easier in comparison to much of the funding for Korea and Vietnam. This approach is particularly the case with DoD operations in Afghanistan and Iraq that have essentially all been carried or reimbursed using supplementals. Homeland security spending, however, both in the Department of Homeland Security and other departments and agencies, has over time largely shifted into the annual baseline budgets making that tracking more difficult, the details of which will be discussed in further detail later.

Unlike previous conflicts, DoD GWOT cost estimating benefited from the post-Cold War work of the 1990s to provide more accurate cost estimates in support of contingency operations. Previously, cost estimating for conflicts was done in a more ad hoc manner, with much left to the discretion of the services without any standardization for their estimates. While cost-estimating techniques served reasonably well for Desert Shield/Desert Storm and smaller operations like Somalia, Haiti, and Panama, Operation Joint Endeavor in Bosnia generated estimates that were in error by a significant amount. Resulting from these experiences, DoD developed a tool to standardize a cost breakdown structure, better understand incremental costs, and provide standard cost data drawn upon experience gained from past contingency operations.[2]

The Contingency Operations Support Tool (COST) provided the improved technique for estimating the cost of contingency operations. In the early stages of planning, when little is known about an operation, COST can create an immediate rough estimate followed by more detailed estimates as more information becomes available. The COST created the basic skeleton of the DoD supplemental requests for GWOT with modifications and add-on expenses not included in the computer model added when necessary.[3] The COST model and methodology are worth mentioning here as GWOT experience has shown two distinct advantages for its use. First, the tool is widely accepted by both the Executive and Legislative branches. This acceptance has helped in developing trust and understanding of the funding estimates throughout the military, civilian leadership in the Executive Branch and Congress. COST has also helped produce supplemental estimates over the past 5 years that were much closer to monthly implementation rates when compared to the experience of supplemental budgeting in both the Korean and Vietnam wars.

FUNDING HISTORY—THE SUPPLEMENTALS

9/11 Initial Response—The FY 2001 Supplementals

At one and a half pages, the "2001 Emergency Supplemental Appropriations Act for Recovery from and Response to Terrorist Attacks on the United States," signed into law one week after the attacks, was perhaps the shortest and simplest war supplemental appropriation in U.S. history. It provided $40 billion as an emergency response fund to the President with broad discretion. It did include provisions for congressional oversight, but not nearly as stringent as the typical post-Vietnam controls for a conflict. The Act required that half the funds be dedicated "... for disaster recovery activities and assistance related to the terrorist acts in New York, Virginia, and Pennsylvania. ..."[4] It further required that $20 billion be enacted in future legislation once more detailed spending plans could be developed, and that another $10 billion not be made available for transfer to departments and/or agencies until 15 days after the Director of the Office of Management and Budget (OMB) submitted to the House and Senate Appropriations Committees plans for proposed allocation and use of the funds. Finally, it required that OMB make quarterly reports to Congress on the use of the funds. The President received considerable more flexibility on immediate use of the remaining $10 billion. The fast congressional response, significant sum, and reasonably broad latitude provided for implementation of these funds reflected the public's "rally-around-the-flag" mood regarding the seriousness of the attack.

The President distributed most of the initial $10 billion rather quickly, most before the end of September 2001, with the remainder following later in the fall and in the spring of 2002. The $10 billion requiring an OMB spending plan was developed and reviewed by the Executive Branch through September and October and the plan was submitted for the full amount to Congress by the end of November 2001. The final $20 billion, requiring enactment in a subsequent emergency appropriations bill, followed shortly after. OMB submitted the distribution estimate for the $20 billion on October 16, 2001. Congress passed the measure as separate titles within the regular FY02 DoD Appropriations Act as the "Department of Defense and Emergency Supplemental Appropriations for Recovery from and Response to Terrorist Attacks on the United States Act" (PL 107-117), which the President signed on January 10, 2002. The White House made minor adjustments to these overall amounts up through the summer of 2002 as circumstances and events dictated changing resourcing priorities.

Despite broad bipartisan support for the supplemental resources in response to 9/11, differences emerged over policy priorities regarding both the total amount and allocations within the $40 billion. The White House remained concerned over

Table 5.1 The $40 Billion Emergency Response to 9/11

Purpose	Executed Transfers (1st $10B)	15 Day Wait Transfers (2nd $10B)	Admin Request ($20B)	House Version HR 3338	Senate Version HR 3338	PL (107-117)	Total $40B
Bioterrorism	$0	$175	$1,587	$2,160	$3,046	$2,834	$3,018
Defense	$5,900	$7,915	$7,349	$7,348	$2,000	$3,500	$17,315
Humanitarian and other Foreign Aid	$824	$412	$0	$0	$0	$50	$1,286
Investigation and Law Enforcement	$188	$119	$1,179	$1,158	$2,367	$2,270	$2,577
Preparedness	$4	$11	$655	$539	$450	$438	$452
Public Diplomacy	$12	$44	$0	$19	$0	$19	$75
Recovery from Attacks	$960	$60	$5,166	$4,578	$6,503	$5,023	$6,043
Security Infrastructure	$592	$131	$1,390	$1,422	$2,676	$2,843	$3,566
Aviation Security	$1,211	$409	$415	$490	$508	$540	$2,160
Victim Relief	$312	$725	$2,260	$2,285	$2,473	$2,479	$3,516
TOTAL	**$10,000**	**$10,000**	**$20,000**	**$20,000**	**$20,000**	**$20,000**	**$40,000**

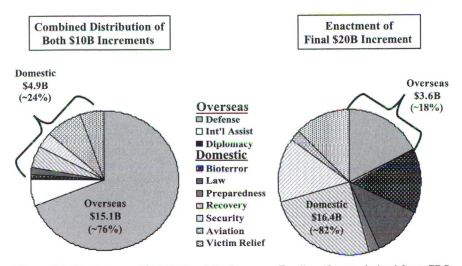

Figure 5.1 Breakdown of $40 Billion 9/11 Response Funding (figures derived from CRS data and analysis)

rising deficits, arguing that the $40 billion total emergency fund was sufficient at the time and the administration would request more if future needs arose. However, many on the Hill were looking for immediate resource increases above the $40 billion, particularly with an eye toward New York City relief and recovery. The President indicated he would veto any FY01 legislation attempting to exceed the $40 billion mark.[5]

Of concern to some in Congress was whether sufficient resources were devoted to comprehensive recovery efforts in New York, Pennsylvania, and Virginia. Some initial analytic work by the Congressional Research Service (CRS) is helpful in understanding these concerns. CRS grouped the spending measures associated with the initial $40 billion response package into ten general categories. Three of those categories, *Defense, Humanitarian & International Assistance*, and *Public Diplomacy*, broadly represented funding dedicated to pursuit of the GWOT overseas (although a small portion of DoD funding was also used at home for homeland defense activities, repair of the Pentagon, etc.). The remaining seven categories used by CRS represent various response, preparedness, and security spending for the U.S. homeland. Table 5.1 and Figures 5.1–5.2 (adapted from Congressional Research Service analysis) show the administration's distribution of the first two $10 billion increments and the requested verses congressionally enacted final $20 billion across those ten general categories.[6]

By modifying the President's request for the remaining $20 billion, Congress shifted emphasis away from defense appropriations and slightly away from recovery activities toward items like funding for combating bioterrorism, aviation infrastructure and security, law enforcement investigations, and direct aid to victims of 9/11. Figure 5.1 and Table 5.1 clearly shows these categories enjoyed some of the largest percentages gains over requested amounts. Defense fell from over

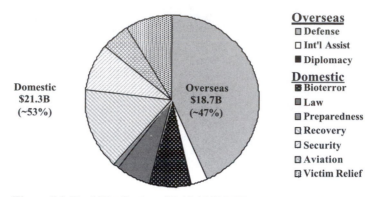

Figure 5.2 Total Distribution of Initial $40 Billion Emergency Response (derived from CRS data)

half of the overall planned funding to $17.3 billion, or 43.4 percent of the total activities. Recovery activities that the administration would have allocated $6.2 billion (15.5 percent) were now appropriated $6 billion (15 percent) of the total. These decreases made room for the increases highlighted above[7]:

	Pres Req	Congress APPN**
Combating Bioterrorism	$1.8B	$3.0B (7.6%)
Aviation Security	$2.0B	$2.2B (14.3%)
Direct Aid to Victims	$3.3B	$3.5B (8.8%)
Investigations/Law Enforcement	$1.5B	$2.6B (6.5%)
Security Infrastructure	$2.1B	$3.6B (8.9%)

**Percentages shown are of the total $40B.

Despite the congressional reduction to DoD appropriations, the administration's general priorities for defense remained roughly intact and many lawmakers anticipated further requests for defense later in the year that could fix any "shortfalls" that might result.

An alternative to the CRS categorization is to examine the appropriation line items grouped by three simple categories: contributions to homeland operations, operations in Afghanistan, and other worldwide or unspecified GWOT activities (not to include Afghanistan). This accounting of the appropriations as approved is reflected in Figure 5.3.

The major shift between this breakdown and the CRS categories is a shift of approximately $2.2 billion dollars out of the CRS "Defense" category over to the Homeland in this analysis. This change reflects the contribution to domestic security and recovery efforts provided by the Defense Department under the $40 billion response package—5.5 percent of the total provided. Another important fact in this view is that Afghanistan is "underreported." Later analysis that examines the final expended cost reports developed by DoD will show that Afghanistan spending is higher than reflected in the initial look at the appropriations for it. The

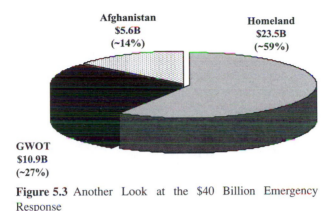

Figure 5.3 Another Look at the $40 Billion Emergency Response

main reason for this difference is the significant flexibility granted to DoD through use of the Defense Emergency Response Fund (DERF).

The DERF was established as a sort of central holding account within DoD where the Secretary of Defense could transfer funds to various existing appropriations as changing conditions created requirements for expenditures. Unlike regular budget proposals and appropriations dedicated to specific functions, the DERF gave DoD greater flexibility on how, where, and when to apply resources without having to return to Congress for reprogramming authority.[8] Included within that authority was authority to use DERF for National Foreign Intelligence Program activities funded by DoD, and authority to use a portion for payments to key allies participating in the GWOT, like Pakistan and Jordan. The allied reimbursement provision was a significant departure from past experience when military assistance funds were only managed by the State Department. This authority greatly enhanced DoD's position, particularly that of its Combatant Commanders, as key negotiators with these countries. Further flexibility was created by allowing the use of the funds until expended, instead of establishing a specified cutoff date, which was usually the end of the current or designated fiscal year. Transferring funds to existing appropriations for obligation and execution also caused them to be tracked separately rather than simply having them added all at once, up-front, to large lump-sum appropriation accounts.

FY 2002 Emergency Supplemental (PL 107-206)—Transitioning from 9/11 Response and Recovery to the Offensive

Debate over the broad shape of policy priorities and the extent of executive branch funding authority continued in development of the FY02 supplemental (PL 107-206). Submitted by the President in March of 2002, it was not enacted until early August. Several key tensions that contributed to the prolonged debate on Capitol Hill included: the Legislative-Executive and partisan divisions over

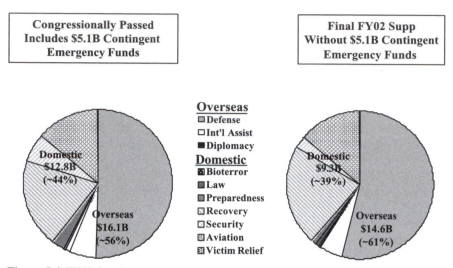

Figure 5.4 FY02 Supplemental Composition (derived from CRS data in Any Belasco and Larry Nowles, Supplemental Appropriations for FY2002: Combating terrorism and other Issues, CRS RL 31406 (Washington, DC: GPO, 2002) 10)

priorities; the attempted expansion of DoD's role in administering military aid; the growing concern over the continued use of, and large sums in, the DoD DERF account; the congressional role in war policymaking through appropriations; and the politics of adding controversial amendments to supplemental legislation that supported the troops in harm's way.

The Legislative-Executive tension centered on the inclusion of an additional $5.1 billion in "contingent emergency spending" by Congress (above the $25 billion in emergency spending). Budget rules required both the President and Congress to designate appropriations as emergency funds to avoid 2002 spending caps. By Congress declaring those funds contingent upon a presidential determination, and adding an "all or none" provision to invoke the $5.1 billion, the President had to submit a budget amendment designating either all or none as emergency funding. Many items were included in this designated spending package, but of greatest benefit to administration priorities were $1 billion for DoD, $400 million for veterans' medical care, and $450 million in various foreign aid funds. Despite these inclusions, the President announced on August 13 that he would not use the contingent emergency funds; however, the administration would request approximately $1 billion worth of those items in an amended FY03 request, as well as funds for the Transportation Security Administration, foreign aid to Israel, the Palestinians, and international HIV/AIDS work. By choosing to not use those funds, the President changed policy priorities that Congress had initiated. Homeland security was the area most impacted. As a result, the majority of enacted funds for preparedness activities and infrastructure protection were not used. Again using the CRS categorization of funding, Figure 5.4 depicts the changing priorities from the congressionally passed version of the legislation (with the $5.1 billion contingent funds included), to the enacted version when the President chose not to use those funds. Although DoD and foreign aid funding declined slightly, the overall percentage of funds geared for overseas operations grew from 56 percent to 61 percent, thereby increasing the trend reversal from previous GWOT supplementals where emphasis on domestic GWOT priorities had grown. Part of this decline was natural as initial relief and recovery efforts from 9/11 were underway, but what suffered declines in the final FY02 spending were domestic items such as law enforcement, preparedness, and infrastructure security.

The administration's economic and military aid request again revealed the Legislative-Executive tension. Unlike the priority differences discussed above, this issue revolved around the request to insert language stating, "notwithstanding any other provision of law," into the aid portions of the bill. Essentially, this designation would have waived all legislative constraints on delivering aid to countries with antidemocratic practices, weapons proliferation concerns, or late with debt payments to the United States (all conditions that would otherwise deny aid). The issue was one of separation of powers, where Congress was unwilling to provide a blanket surrender of their oversight rights and responsibilities. Ultimately, a temporary waiver was provided for those countries late on debt payments, which enabled most of the aid transfers that the administration sought to occur. However, Congress held in place many specific restrictions (on Columbian aid for example), and denied authority to use funds to support indigenous forces engaged in combating terrorism activities.

On the partisan front, the proposed bill developed by the Republican controlled House made minor changes to the President's request (only about $350 million different in total), but the Democratic controlled Senate's differences were much greater. The Senate added nearly $3 billion more than the administration's request, much of it in funding for homeland security functions. The Senate also included several provisions, including one restricting the President's ability to designate spending as emergency—key to allowing spending to exceed established budget caps.[9] The President strongly opposed the Senate version of the bill, threatening veto for it being both more restrictive on executive flexibility and for exceeding his proposed spending limit. The OMB Director, Mitch Daniels, even hinted in mid-July, 2002, the supplemental could be reduced due to limited time remaining in the fiscal year and the ability, or lack thereof, to allocate and spend $25 billion or more in funds before the end of the fiscal year.[10]

Party control also produced a bicameral fracture when the administration requested authority for DoD to administer $580 million in funds for foreign governments to assist in the GWOT. The proposal would also grant DoD the authority to choose the recipient governments of this aid. While neither chamber adopted the administration's proposed language, the two chambers agreed that DoD could reimburse key allies for logistical support up to $420 million. Differences arose over controlling funds beyond direct reimbursement, as was the case with payments to Jordan and Pakistan. The Republican-controlled House sided with the administration and the Democratic-controlled Senate argued for control in the

State Department, where such authority had traditionally resided. The ultimate solution was to require concurrence and joint reporting by both the State and Defense Departments, rather than DoD alone.[11]

Regarding the DERF, the administration requested that the bulk of DoD funding go into the DERF again to preserve flexibility to respond to operational changes, wartime imperatives, and uncertainties. Of the $14 billion requested for DoD, $11.3 billion was placed in the DERF. With only $78 million congressionally earmarked for North American Air Defense (NORAD) enhancements, the Secretary of Defense received the unlimited ability to transfer funds from the DERF to any other defense appropriation as he determined with only a 15-day prior notification to Congress. Additionally, Congress granted SECDEF the ability to move $275 million of these funds to other activities outside the scope of that envisioned for the DERF. In fact, the DERF became the *preferred* choice for flexible funding, so much so that DoD requested a hedge of $20 billion ($10 billion for continued wartime operations and $10 billion for various departmental functions in support of the GWOT efforts overall) in the regular FY03 budget request. Ultimately, Congress rejected this request.

Despite the large DERF appropriation in FY02 supplemental, there was growing concern among some members of Congress regarding continued use of the DERF. Some congressmen feared that the DERF gave DoD a "blank check" and abrogated Congress' "power of the purse" prerogative. Others expressed anxiety over losing transparency of DERF monies once they were transferred and merged with regular appropriation accounts. Because of these concerns, Congress rescinded $224 million in unobligated balances residing in the DERF account from the FY01 emergency supplementals. While DoD acknowledged the visibility problems, the DERF at least provided a clear audit point when the funds were moved to the various appropriations with corresponding statements of intended purpose—something sorely lacking from the wars in Korea and Vietnam.

As was the case in the President's FY01 supplemental request, the cost of war in Afghanistan was not specifically highlighted in his request for FY02. DoD estimated the total FY02 deployment cost for Operation Enduring Freedom (OEF) to be approximately $10.4 billion. Of this total requirement, $3.7 billion was covered by DERF funding from the previous supplementals. Behind that estimate were assumptions that operations and force levels in and supporting Afghanistan would remain steady throughout the remainder of the year. Instead, the end of the fiscal year DERF cost reports revealed that mobilization, combat operations, and transportation for all of OEF had consumed $12.6 billion, resulting in a monthly "burn rate" of funds of just over $1 billion.[12]

Congressional activism through appropriations bills also surfaced more in the FY02 supplemental. Increasing oversight and activism could be expected in appropriations measures as attempts to ensure good stewardship of the people's purse strings. The language included regarding assistance to the government of Colombia in the battle against narco-trafficking was one case of clarifying funding and associated authorities. However, Congress often used these spending bills as a means to push into the strategy and policy arenas. An example of appropriations language to help dictate policy could be seen in the requirement for the President to give congressional committees updates on Afghanistan. He was to provide:

> . . . two reports setting forth a strategy for meeting the security needs of Afghanistan in order to promote safe and effective delivery of humanitarian and other assistance throughout Afghanistan, further the rule of law and civil order, and support the formation of a functioning, representative Afghan national government. The first report, which should be transmitted no later than 30 days after enactment of this Act, should report on the strategy for meeting the immediate security needs of Afghanistan. The second report, which should be transmitted no later than 90 days after enactment of this Act, should report on a long term strategy for meeting the security needs of Afghanistan and should include a reassessment of the strategy to meet the immediate security needs if they have changed substantially.[13]

The comprehensive nature of the reporting requirements went far beyond ensuring the effective use of appropriated funds. Afghanistan was not the only subject in this supplemental either. Title II of the bill was called the "American Servicemembers' Protection Act of 2002," and contained numerous legislative prohibitions on members of the U.S. armed forces being subjected to jurisdiction of the International Criminal Court—clearly a policy issue not directly related to appropriating funds. One of the attractions of the war supplemental spending bills was that members of Congress could often get amendments and language added they otherwise could not have done through other, more focused, legislation.

Since war supplemental bills have usually moved fast through the congressional process and been viewed by many as "must pass" items to show support for the troops, they have often attracted legislation otherwise hard to enact. An impasse existed over the overall budget resolution for FY 2003, and the supplemental spending bill was unsuccessfully tried as the means to resolve the budget deadlock. Several Senate amendments were proposed to extend budget enforcement mechanisms, including the PAY-GO rules. These measures were originally put in place and then extended under the auspices of the Budget Enforcement Act from the early 1990s and were due to expire at the end of FY02. Likewise, there was an attempt to prevent the administration from canceling the Army's Crusader artillery program as well. These unrelated measures to the central purpose of the war appropriations resulted in extending debate and slowing passage. Ultimately, the various budget-related amendments were rejected by close votes. The supplemental as passed nevertheless did incorporate some budget resolution business, including an increase to the U.S. debt ceiling.[14] Even with the DERF from prior supplementals, because OMB's incremental release of funds to DoD made the Department's financial situation grim by July. The services had been "cash flowing" operations since the start of OEF and would reimburse accounts as DERF dollars were made available. With existing DERF appropriations running out, DoD spent out of 4th Quarter regular appropriations to the point where the civilian payroll for the last month of the year was already gone. The DoD Comptroller, Dov Zakheim, was concerned enough about the Department's cash position and need for additional funds that he drafted an article published on July 17, warning of dire circumstances if the congressional conference did not resolve these extraneous issues and complete work on the supplemental before the August recess.[15] The public spotlight and private pressure from the administration on congressional leadership provided enough force to move these issues through and avert the funding crisis.

The FY2003 Supplemental—Fight over Flexibility

Submitted to Congress by the President on March 25, 2003, six days after the opening salvos of Operation Iraqi Freedom (OIF), and enacted a short three weeks later, the FY03 Supplemental was the first payment on the war in Iraq as well as a continuation of other GWOT operations. Timing was critical. Iraq operations leading up to the war had been conducted by cash flowing from other existing appropriations. As a result, DoD's fiscal year 2003 financial condition was tight by the time OIF hostilities began. Congress planned a spring recess beginning on April 12, so swift passage was essential. The opening stages of the Iraq campaign reinforced the shift of GWOT funding away from defensive priorities and, with virtually 90 percent of the $78.5 billion appropriated to DoD and international aid for overseas operations, firmly put the resourcing priority back on the offensive. Despite this significant shift in policy and the critical timing issues for this supplemental, the prominent story line in this funding measure was the fight over flexibility in control of funds.

One of the largest disparities between the structure of an administration funding request and congressional approval came about on passage of the largest supplemental dollar amount hitherto approved—the FY03 Supplemental.[16] The disconnect was not in total dollar amount; in fact, Congress added additional funds above the President's request. The troubles centered on the appropriation's deference granted (or denied) the Executive Branch in use of the funds. Of $62.4 billion requested for DoD, the administration wanted 96 percent, or $59.9 billion, placed in the DERF, allowing extreme flexibility with little-to-no congressional direction in actual use of the money. Likewise, the President requested similar flexible accounts (albeit in much smaller amounts) for homeland security operations and counterterrorism. The administration sought maximum flexibility to respond to changing requirements in both Iraq and the wider GWOT. If granted, this request would have dramatically reversed the declining trend since 9/11 of the percentage of funds granted with broad discretionary flexibility. Congress reacted in a similar fashion to its denial of the large DERF requested in the baseline FY03 DoD budget, and viewed the request as a threat to Congress' jealously guarded power of the purse.

In its report on the bill, the [House Appropriations] committee said the need for flexibility "does not obviate the need for Congress to be fully involved ... in establishing the terms and conditions under which the appropriated funds are to be used." "We did not create huge slush funds to be used at the discretion of the agencies," [HAC Chairman] Young said. Ranking Democrat David R. Obey of Wisconsin said the bill "honors our responsibility . . . to keep the power of the purse in the legislative branch of the government."[17]

On the Senate side of the Hill, Christopher J. Dodd (D) of Connecticut added, "To allow the kind of flexibility the White House is looking for with the money involved here is dangerous. It's bad precedent."[18] Clearly, congressional opposition to the requested flexibility was bicameral and bipartisan. When finally enacted, the supplemental provided most funds to dedicated appropriations and functions, although it still left a portion to the administration's discretion.

Flexibility of Funds in GWOT Supplemental Appropriations			
% of Funds with:	**FY2001**	**FY2002**	**FY2003**
Broad Flexibility	~50%	~41%	~15%
Limited Flexibility	0	~5%	~8%

Essentially, Congress took the bulk of the funds DoD requested in the DERF and directly appropriated them to the accounts where DoD had anticipated they would be spent. Figure 5.5 shows congressional distribution of the bulk of the funds compared to the original DERF request. Of the $59.9 billion DoD requested in DERF, Congress provided $46.5 billion in the spending categories DoD had estimated. The remaining funds were directly appropriated into various accounts for functions like coalition support, working capital funds, military construction, and a new creation, the Iraq Freedom Fund.

The resulting flexibilities in the bill came in several forms. The most significant was creation of the Iraq Freedom Fund (IFF) account. The FY03 supplemental

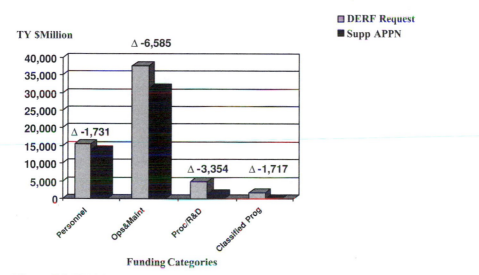

Figure 5.5 FY03 Supplemental: DERF Request vs. Appropriations Provided

eliminated the DERF account (any remaining DERF balances were merged with the new IFF).[19] As a flexible fund, the IFF initially was given $15.7 billion. Within that amount, Congress earmarked a portion for several functions, with both minimum and maximum limits on transfers. In the original supplemental request, DoD identified several classified programs with funding needs. Congress directed a minimum of $1.77 billion in the IFF to these requirements. Additionally, as the price of oil had risen from when the DoD estimates were prepared, Congress also directed a minimum of $1.1 billion for fuel costs. This combined $2.9 billion was a sort of constrained flexibility mandated by Congress. Additionally, another $2.4 billion of the fund was capped with various maximum transfer limits to support requested functions such as: coalition support, research, and development, U.S. Coast Guard operations, counterterrorism training, and extinguishing anticipated oil well fires and initially repairing Iraqi oil infrastructure.[20] These measures provided a degree of flexible spending up to the authorized amounts, assuming the full amounts were transferred. The remaining $10.4 billion was the true "unfettered flexibility," as it was referred to by the DoD Comptroller, equivalent to approximately 17 percent of the total DoD appropriated funds in the supplemental.[21]

Table 5.2 Iraq Freedom Fund (IFF) Structure in FY03 Supplemental

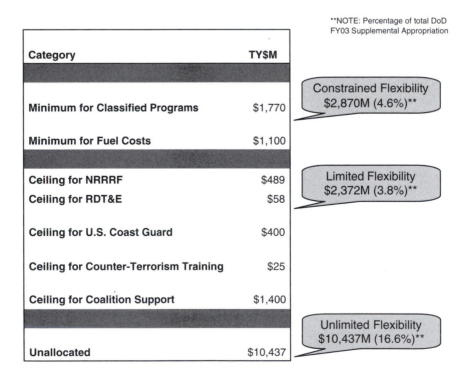

**NOTE: Percentage of total DoD FY03 Supplemental Appropriation

Category	TY$M	
Minimum for Classified Programs	$1,770	Constrained Flexibility $2,870M (4.6%)**
Minimum for Fuel Costs	$1,100	
Ceiling for NRRRF	$489	Limited Flexibility $2,372M (3.8%)**
Ceiling for RDT&E	$58	
Ceiling for U.S. Coast Guard	$400	
Ceiling for Counter-Terrorism Training	$25	
Ceiling for Coalition Support	$1,400	
Unallocated	$10,437	Unlimited Flexibility $10,437M (16.6%)**

Other, smaller, flexibilities were also granted. Congress added $500 million to the limit of general transfer authority granted in the annual FY03 DoD appropriation. The supplemental bill itself carried a special $2 billion transfer authority on the directly appropriated (non-IFF) DoD titled funds in the supplemental. Also, $150 million in flexible transfer authority was built in for contingency construction accounts (with prior congressional notification).[22] Similar to previously initiated authority after 9/11, Congress continued to grant the administration authority to reimburse key cooperating nations, up to a $1.4 billion limit from this fund. However, the administration, finding no support in either chamber of Congress, was denied the authority to transfer up to $150 million to support irregular or indigenous forces in foreign countries. Allowing the executive to become involved in paramilitary operations, in unspecified countries, despite the support it might provide to GWOT efforts, was a Pandora's box Congress was unwilling to open. Congress also agreed to expand two other smaller, existing flexible authorities by matching the DoD request to increase the Commanders-in-Chief (CINC) Initiative Fund (CIF) from $25 million to $50 million, and provide slightly less than the requested increase in the Secretary of Defense's Emergencies and Extraordinary Expenses (EEE) Authority from $34.5 million to $50 million. These smaller accounts and authorities also provide means for the DoD to respond to urgent needs in the field. In addition to the flexibility afforded by new IFF dollars highlighted above, DoD also had total transfer authorities over funds increased by $2.5 billion with broad flexibility and $1.6 billion with more limited flexibility. In sum, all of the flexible funds and transfer authorities together gave DoD ability to shift approximately 25 percent of the supplemental funds as required for changing circumstances—significantly less than the more than 40 percent flexibility that was granted in the 2002 supplemental.

Aside from the battles over flexible funding, the specific costs of named combat operations were not identified in the administration's funding requests. The ongoing operations in Afghanistan and other locations comprising Operation Enduring Freedom, and the DoD costs for homeland defense (mainly air patrols and increased base security) comprising Operation Noble Eagle (ONE), combined in a monthly total slightly more than $1 billion.[23] Based on this rate of expenditure, it was estimated these operations required $6–8 billion of the supplemental funds to complete the remaining 6 months of the fiscal year. The overall breakout of funds and the DoD breakout are provided in Figures 5.6 and 5.7.

The COST model, along with the tracking of expenditures by named operations, led to the development of a metric which gained significant attention during 2003 and has become a staple of funding discussion regarding the war—the "burn rate." Burn rates referred to the amount of funds obligated to each operation and usually tracked on a monthly basis. Monitoring them has become a concern beyond merely the comptrollers writing checks and trying to "balance the books"; burn rates have now attracted considerable attention from Capitol Hill and the media as well. This prominence led to different ways of calculating the burn rate. The obvious method was to count everything spent in a given month on a particular operation. However, if recalculated by excluding nonrecurring

- **DoD:**   **$62.60B**
  - MILCON/Corps of Eng: $0.24B

- **Dept State (DoS):**   **$0.61B**

- **Dept Justice (DoJ):**   **$0.50B**

- **Bi-Lateral Economic Asst:**   **$2.70B**
  - USAID/Economic Support Fund

- **Other Bi-Lat Econ Asst:**   **$2.50B**
  - Iraq Relief and Reconstruction Fund

- **Homeland Security:**   **$3.90B**

- **Military Assistance:**   **$2.20B**

- **Aviation Industry Relief:**   **$2.40B**

- **Other Dept's/Functions:**   **$1.20B**

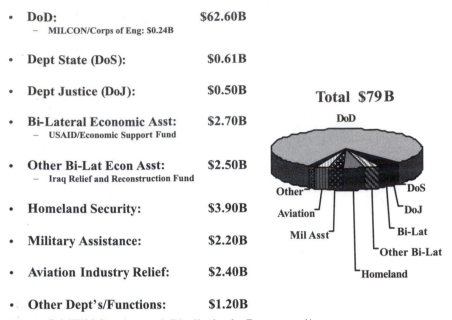

Figure 5.6 FY03 Supplemental: Distribution by Department/Agency

- **Personnel:**   **$13.90B**

- **Ops & Maintenance:**   **$31.20B**

- **Procurement/R&D:**   **$1.50B**

- **Classified Programs:**   **$1.70B**

- **Military Construction (MILCON):**   **$0.20B**

- **Work Capital Fund (WCF):**   **$1.10B**

- **Coalition Support:**   **$1.90B**

- **Counter-Narcotics:**   **$.034B**

- **Iraq Free Fund (IFF)**
  Undistributed: **$10.40B**

- **USCG Reimburse:**   **$0.40B**

- **Other Undistributed:**   **$0.17B**

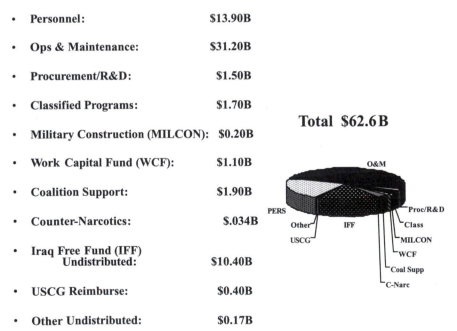

Figure 5.7 FY03 Supplemental: DoD Distribution by Function

procurement programs and one-time contracts, DoD assumed this method provided a more accurate assessment of operational tempo spending (and a decreased burn rate figure). If the cost of procurement programs and other one-time contracts were included, it increased average monthly obligations to produce a higher burn rate. As stated before, the recurring cost burn rate for all of OEF and ONE was averaging $1.1 billion per month. The average monthly burn rate for OIF in FY2003 was $4.2 billion.

Security and assistance to the civilian aviation industry was the one area where Congress added significant funds, nearly $2.4 billion, more than the President's request. Included in this industry aid package were funds for compensation of costs associated with the strengthening of flight deck doors and locks on aircraft required by the new Aviation and Transportation Security Act, and remittances to U.S. flag air carriers for air carrier security fees to the Transportation Security Administration. Additionally, above the direct costs appropriated, the supplemental granted authorities to continue suspension of collecting airline security service fees, extending war risk insurance, and extending unemployment benefits to members of the industry. These combined measures created additional federal revenue losses and expenditure increases outside the supplemental appropriations. The Congressional Budget Office (CBO) estimated costs of these factors at between $675 million and $1 billion, placing the total cost of airline assistance provided in the bill between $3–3.5 billion.

Another phenomenon impacting resources—and seen in previous conflicts—appeared for the GWOT in the FY03 supplemental—the military benefits ratchet. Whether developed through a general sympathy toward the troops, politicians' need to be seen taking care of the fighting military, public demand, a combination of these or other reasons, various pay and allowances, medical benefits, veterans benefits, and other such "entitlement" spending tended to make significant and permanent increases—the ratchet effect of war. In the FY03 Supplemental, Congress increased Imminent Danger Pay (combat pay) and Family Separation Allowances for U.S. military personnel at an estimated cost of $650–825 million, depending on sustained troop levels overseas. This benefit increase was adopted as a floor amendment on a voice vote with little-to-no deliberation of long-term cost implications, but was certainly a move to show Congress "cared" about the troops. While the supplemental bill only made the increase effective for that fiscal year, Congress later made the increases permanent. This has been the trend with virtually any temporary increase in benefits—once awarded, never withdrawn. Later GWOT-related legislation will likely amplify this effect, with significant expansion to other benefits as well.

Another distinctive aspect of this spending bill was, given its size, the minimum amount of unrelated pork spending attached to it. The airline provisions, which the President felt were much too large in dollar terms, were at least related to response/recovery from 9/11 within the industry. The House bill remained fairly free of add-ons; however, SAC Chairman Stevens allowed add-ons of approximately $675 million in unrelated spending. Various amendments and negotiations cut a considerable portion of these before passage, enough for HAC Chairman Young to state it was the "cleanest" supplemental ever to get through Congress.[24]

Once enacted, DoD assessed its portion of the supplemental would be sufficient to cover the GWOT requirements, to include the wars in Afghanistan and Iraq, for the remainder of the fiscal year. In fact, funds proved to be slightly in excess, as evidenced by completing the end of FY03 and having $3.5 billion of the remaining IFF account later rescinded in the FY04 DoD Appropriation Act.[25]

FY 2004 Emergency Supplemental—Continue Operations, Address Reconstruction

Summary of Request and Appropriation

The purpose of the FY04 supplemental was to sustain the level of support necessary to continue military operations in Iraq and Afghanistan. The DoD, which would spend the majority of the funds, developed the request in late August-early September of 2003. The following major assumptions for what was included guided the request: incremental costs to continue current operations; reserve component mobilization; approved orders for units to deploy to Afghanistan and Iraq, with logistical support to include air/sealift and intelligence support; Guantanamo Bay detainee operations; critical depot maintenance activities (that could be accomplished in FY04); critical procurement purchases; and critical military construction. The estimates were built on assumptions that force levels and operations tempo at the end of FY03 would continue through the beginning of FY04 and that there would be a modest drawdown of U.S. presence in theater supporting Iraq by the end of FY04 (from the 140–150,000 U.S. troop level to approximately 99,000 by the following October) while sustaining two multinational divisions totaling approximately 20,000 troops. The level of effort in Afghanistan was assumed to remain in steady state throughout the year. Additional funds were requested in the IFF, with appropriate lift and sustain (L&S) authorities, to serve as a hedge either to support coalition troops, or replace them by mobilizing up to four U.S. Reserve enhanced separate brigades.[26] Operation Noble Eagle, the continued DoD efforts at enhanced homeland defense, were also included in the FY04 supplemental. The FY04 supplemental was also the first GWOT spending request that clearly broke out the proposed spending by major operations/components:

- Operation Iraqi Freedom $51.5 billion
- Operation Enduring Freedom $10.5 billion
- Operation Noble Eagle $ 2.2 billion
- Coalition Support $ 1.4 billion
- Iraq Reconstruction $20.4 billion
- Afghan Reconstruction $ 0.8 billion[27]

Compared to the request, the enacted supplemental provided a reduction in funds specifically for reconstruction of Iraq: $18.649 billion in the Iraq Relief and Reconstruction Fund (IRRF) and $983 million for administrative support costs for the Coalition Provisional Authority (CPA) (included $75 million for the CPA Inspector General and $50 million for reports). It also provided an increase in funds for Afghanistan: $1.164 billion in total aid to Afghanistan. Funds available to DoD were provided in the following major appropriation accounts:

Military Personnel	$17.8 billion
Operation and Maintenance (O&M)	$37.3 billion
Procurement, Research & Development	$ 5.9 billion
Other accounts (included storm damage and USCG funds)	$ 4.2 billion
Total funding appropriated in the supplemental	$65.2 billion
Funds available to DoD (excluding classified programs)	$60.0 billion[28]

Election Year/Timing Concerns

The timing of the FY04 supplemental request submission brought into question the impact of the 2004 presidential election campaign cycle and timing of public debate over these funds. Considering past GWOT supplemental spending bills, and looking ahead to both the FY05 and FY06 supplemental requests, the administration likely wanted to avoid the funding issue during the height of an election campaign. The FY01 emergency response spending for 9/11 had been clearly event-driven in its timing. The FY02 supplemental request, submitted in March of 2002, seemed to make sense in that DoD was approximately 6 months into OEF, and was approaching the mid-point of the fiscal year when a review was normally conducted. The FY03 supplemental immediately followed the start of OIF and was also roughly concurrent with the mid-fiscal year review point. Likewise, the FY05 and FY06 supplementals would later be submitted shortly after the annual budget submissions in February of their respective years, and also would approach the mid-fiscal year point of ongoing operations, when burn rates and levels of effort were better understood.

Several factors contributed to the timing of the supplemental request. If the FY04 supplemental, the largest on record at the time, had been requested in the spring of 2004, it would have been during the heart of the presidential primaries and likely have supplied much fodder for the Democrats to use against the incumbent. Also, had congressional debate and passage of the supplemental been extended into the summer—like the FY02 supplemental—it would have again been timely campaign material for the nominating conventions and detracted from other messages that the President wanted to portray. Requesting the funding in the fall of 2003 would ensure the prominent debate over a bill under active consideration would be completed roughly 1 year prior to the election, and, if the request was appropriately sized, it would carry through the remainder of FY04. Allowing the first 2–3 months of FY05 to be funded by drawing from regular FY05 appropriations would further submerge the issue during the presidential campaign schedule.

An alternative explanation, or contributing factor, for the early fall 2003 request for 2004 supplemental funds was the impact of funding the newly established Coalition Provisional Authority (CPA) under Ambassador Paul Bremer in Iraq. CPA took over governing and reconstruction functions in Iraq in May 2003 from the prewar organization devoted to this function, the Office of Reconstruction and Humanitarian Assistance (ORHA) under retired Lieutenant General Jay Garner. While the FY03 supplemental provided $2.5 billion in the Iraq Relief and Reconstruction Fund (IRRF) for the President to use, the CPA essentially ran the entire country through the summer of 2003 on appropriated IRRF funds and Iraqi seized and vested assets that were available.[29] Based on the rate of consumption, by August 2003, it became clear to the CPA that its funding sources would run out around November–December of 2003. While in Washington in August, Ambassador Bremer made it clear to senior officials, including the President, that the CPA would soon be in dire straits unless additional funds were provided to run operations in Iraq. In support of an early 2004 supplemental, the CPA had prepared a $20.3 billion estimate that provided a foundation for the ultimate request.

When compared to the remainder of the dedicated GWOT supplemental spending bills, the election year influence and CPA funding situation together point to the rationale for the apparent timing anomaly of the FY04 supplemental.

Financing Concerns

The issue of war financing finally came into the public debate led mainly by the Democrats in Congress. The administration viewed additional borrowing as a satisfactory method of continuing to finance the war supplementals since the economy was still recovering from recession and the tax cuts were spurring growth. Additionally, OMB estimated that actual outlays of the $87 billion would lag over at least 2 or more years and therefore the entire $87 billion would not appear in the final FY04 deficit figure. Critics on the Hill argued that domestic programs absorbed the brunt of funding cuts and continuation of large deficit spending was economically dangerous. Dozens of congressional speeches were made critical of previously passed tax cuts being in conflict with the need to fund the supplemental request. Several amendments were offered that would have reversed various tax cuts to offset the mounting war costs. Other options would have limited reductions in planned marginal tax rates for 5 years for those in the top tax bracket—a measure designed to increase revenue by $87 billion to offset the supplemental costs. Ultimately, these tax change measures were defeated; however, they did raise some of the public awareness regarding war costs.

Authorities and Flexibility

The legislative-executive tug-of-war regarding flexible funds continued throughout the FY04 supplemental debate. Congress continued the reimbursement authority for DoD to key cooperating nations, but reduced the administration's request by $250 million to a maximum $1.15 billion total and required Secretary of State consultation.[30] Again, DoD requested increased general transfer authority within the supplemental funds between accounts, and again Congress provided it, but in a reduced amount (granted $3 billion vice $5 billion requested).[31] Likewise, Congress again allowed transfer of funds for contingency construction, but approved $150 million vice $500 million requested.[32] The most controversial flexible authority developed in this bill was that to train and equip (T&E) Iraqi and Afghani forces. The administration wanted $200 million in T&E for the new Iraqi Army (NIA) and the Afghan National Army (ANA), plus authority to use the funds in other nearby nations. Congress agreed to $150 million (a compromise between Senate-recommended $200 million and House-recommended $100 million), but specified for use only in Iraq and Afghanistan—not other countries at the administration's discretion.[33] Just as with previous congressional denial of funds to assist indigenous forces, or previous attempts at aid authorities for unspecified locations, this portion of the request was an anathema to Congress.

Perhaps the most outspoken Senate critic over the power of the purse authorities and flexibility granted the Bush administration was Senator Robert Byrd (D) of West Virginia. He proposed an amendment (Senate Amendment #1888) in the reconstruction funding to eliminate Executive flexibility to reallocate reconstruction funds without prior congressional approval. The amendment was tabled by a close vote (49-46), but reflected the growing anxiety some members of Congress had regarding the constitutional tension on control of funds.

Reconstruction

Perhaps the most divisive issue of the FY04 Supplemental debate was how to structure the reconstruction request for the roughly $20 billion that the President requested. Several bipartisan arguments were advanced for making a portion, if not all, of the Iraq reconstruction request a loan. These arguments included:

- Desire for greater international contributions/matching fund commitments.
- Concern over U.S. deficits and not receiving any eventual return revenue from investments made in Iraq's future.
- Outcry that the U.S. was funding programs in Iraq when corresponding domestic programs were not fully funded.
- Feedback from previous official statements that Iraqi oil revenue would be able to finance Iraqi reconstruction.[34]

These arguments led to a series of House and Senate amendments offered to structure the funding in a variety of ways, shift priorities, delay implementation, and slash the requested total amount. Most amendments were defeated within their respective chambers, but when both versions of the bill were passed and sent to conference, the Senate bill carried a provision structuring $10 billion as a grant and $10 billion as a loan with various provisions. The House then overwhelming (277-139) passed a motion to instruct their conferees to accept that Senate amendment. Only significant political pressure applied by the administration resulted in overturning the loan proposals in conference, and that reversal was only passed by a two-vote margin. The administration's four central arguments put forth against loans were:

- The legal question of who could assume sovereign responsibility for binding Iraq to repayment commitments. The U.S.-led Coalition Provisional Authority under Ambassador Paul Bremer was in effect the acting sovereign authority and significant concern surrounded perceptions of U.S. officials making guarantees of future payments back to the United States.
- The negative impact of increasing Iraq's existing debt burden already estimated at $200 billion.
- The hypocrisy charge against a United States actively seeking donations from the international community, yet itself unwilling to contribute full aid in the form of a grant. During congressional consideration of the bill, a donor's conference took place in Madrid and there was concern other donors would back away if the United States did not express confidence in delivering grant assistance.
- That it would further overall perceptions in the Middle East that the United States was only interested in gaining control of Iraq's oil riches.

Another administration concern, ultimately dropped in conference, was the House provision requiring officials who controlled reconstruction funds to be subject to congressional confirmation. This provision was in direct response to a White House announcement that Condolezza Rice, Special Assistant to the President for National Security, would assume an active role in coordinating stability and reconstruction activities. Some congressional members expressed concern since Rice was not subject to Senate confirmation and could not be compelled to readily provide account to Congress. Compounding congressional angst was the President's request to put the Iraq reconstruction aid fully within the Iraq Relief and Reconstruction Fund (IRRF), a fund established in the FY03 supplemental initially with $2.5 billion dollars. By placing reconstruction inside the IRRF account, the CPA (operating under DoD) would be directly responsible for those funds, rather than the State Department, which directed traditional aid programs that were subject to an entire construct of foreign aid legislation. Ultimately, Congress passed $18.6 billion for the IRRF (also designated transfer of $210 million to other aid activities, resulting in $18.4 billion dedicated to Iraq), and required joint State and Defense Departments' concurrence.

From the financial perspective, the major issue with reconstruction funding at this point was the question of absorptive capacity. The World Bank and UN Development Program published an Iraqi needs assessment in conjunction with the Madrid donors conference and suggested $36 billion in requirements over 4 years for areas not covered by the $20 billion CPA proposal the President requested in the supplemental. The challenge noted by the World Bank/UN report was that it was likely Iraq could only effectively absorb approximately $5 billion in aid during the first year. This assessment was based upon previous postconflict experience, and the estimated condition of the Iraqi society and economy. Increased aid funding above realistic absorptive capacity generally had presented problems of corruption and funds abuse. The other enduring challenge with international aid commitments is the follow-through on delivery. Every country's donation pledge is first subject to domestic political concerns within the donor country. Additionally, some countries have limited means available to actually deliver the intended aid if it is a donation-in-kind vice a cash pledge.

Benefits Ratchet

The military benefit increases begun in the FY03 supplemental continued to ratchet upward in the FY04 supplemental. The temporary increases to Imminent Danger Pay and Family Separation Allowances initiated in April were extended by this supplemental despite administration objections.[35] Senate Amendment #1816 further increased benefits by offering the DoD TRICARE health insurance coverage to reservists (and their families) who were either unemployed or otherwise not eligible for employer-sponsored health insurance programs. This increase was a significant expansion of benefits without attendant cost considerations or appropriations provided. Furthermore, the administration worried that civilian companies would take advantage of this change by hiring military reservists for potentially higher salaries but with no medical coverage because a reservist could get full coverage under TRICARE. Such actions would further cost growth within the military healthcare system—a condition that has occurred over the past several years as the TRICARE benefit has increased in both scope and eligibility. Other Senate Amendments, albeit at smaller costs, added family assistance programs for the National Guard, and pay differential replacement for federal employees who experienced a pay reduction as a result of reserve military service; removed food and subsistence payments for military members while hospitalized; increased transitional health care to troops mobilizing, demobilizing, or separating from military service; and increased funding ($1.3 billion) for the Department of Veterans Affairs.

Also attempted by the Senate in the supplemental, but later withdrawn and incorporated into the regular FY04 defense authorization bill, was the repeal of a Civil War era ban on acceptance of concurrent receipt for military retirees. Essentially, this law required an offset in retired pay equal to an amount of VA disability pay being received by the same retiree. Previous attempts at repealing this legislation had been unsuccessful, but the imperative of appearing to "take care of the military" during a time of war enabled a compromise deal to phase in concurrent receipt payments over a 10-year time span. Estimates placed initial costs at $1.4–1.7 billion per year to DoD in accrual payments and another $1.0–2.5 billion per year in further Treasury payments. This entitlement increase was projected to further grow resulting in initial 10-year costs between $26–32 billion—all for an entitlement increase that has no benefit to the young troops serving in the GWOT today. It will only accrue to those few who stay for a career into retirement and are eligible for some disability payments—all events that are years into the future.

The House also passed amendments similar to the Senate for IDP and FSA increases and subsistence payments while hospitalized. The House also added other family advocacy programs, and travel benefits for troops returning on two-week rest and recuperative leave program during deployment. The House turned down an amendment by only one vote that would have given $1,500 pay rate bonuses to everyone serving in Iraq and Afghanistan.

The final conference-passed bill included many of these proposed benefit increases. The expanded medical coverage for reservists was legislated as a 1-year trial, but has since become a standard part of the benefit. The added funds for the VA were dropped, but only to be included later as part of the regular VA annual funding bill. In total, the FY04 supplemental only further enhanced the trend to increase military "entitlement" spending.

Congressional Activism

The issues of congressional oversight and policy involvement seen with Afghanistan in the FY02 supplemental were magnified with regard to Iraq in the FY04 supplemental. The first policy issue was one of military end strength. Several attempts were made to insert amendments increasing the end strength of active duty personnel, particularly in the Army. Many congressional members had heard complaints from constituents about extended and repeated National Guard and Reserve mobilizations, and the attempt to add more troops was a natural reaction. The administration's main response was from Secretary of Defense Donald Rumsfeld, who repeatedly asserted DoD had sufficient total end strength but the wrong capabilities mix. Rather than adding troops, Rumsfeld preferred to transform existing troops into more deployable units and in greater numbers with skill sets in demand. While the FY04 supplemental amendments to add troops were all defeated, the issue remained a significant point of contention between the administration and Congress.

Congress also dictated significantly increased reporting requirements for DoD with regard to the conduct and costs of the war. Multiple amendments were passed

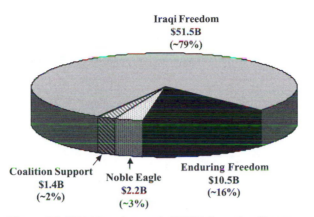

Figure 5.8 FY04 Supplemental: GWOT Operation Shares

and a consolidated set of requirements were adopted in conference. Additionally, more reporting requirements were developed for reconstruction efforts in both Iraq and Afghanistan. The CPA was required to make a detailed submission of projects and progress. Senator Byrd further tried, but failed, to make the head of the CPA subject to congressional confirmation.

FY04 Supplemental Composition and Execution

Figure 5.8 shows how the supplemental funding was split across the various major operations.

Of the total $87 billion appropriated, $18.6B was for Iraqi reconstruction, and a minor percentage for other departments and agencies, leaving DoD with approximately $66B. Figure 5.9 indicates that the bulk of DoD funds were dedicated to supporting the Army in Iraq and Afghanistan.

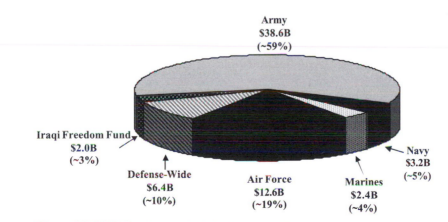

Figure 5.9 FY04 Supplemental: DoD Component Shares

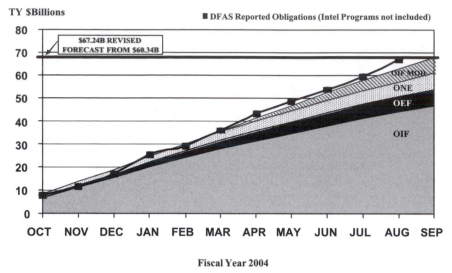

TY $Billions

■ DFAS Reported Obligations (Intel Programs not included)

Figure 5.10 FY04 Supplemental: Projected and Actual Obligation Rates

The Defense Financial Accounting Service (DFAS) tracked actual expenditures by named operation each month. The various shaded wedges on Figure 5.10 were the projected costs for each of the operations and the sloped dark line shows actual total by month costs reported by DFAS. In the aggregate, actual costs tracked closely with projections throughout the year. However, there were variations due to changing circumstances on the ground. Increased violence in Iraq in the Spring of 2004, and the associated decision to increase force levels, resulted in the spending increase shown by the "OIF Mod" wedge.

By the time the FY05 baseline DoD budget was submitted in February 2004, total costs from the FY2004 Supplemental were running as follows (excluding classified programs execution):

Operation Iraqi Freedom (OIF)	($22.1)
Operation Enduring Freedom (OEF)	($ 3.1)
Operation Noble Eagle (ONE)	($ 1.8)
Total	$27.0

The average monthly burn rate for OIF by that date was approximately $4.0 billion, when nonrecurring procurement programs were excluded. The $4.0 billion represented a more accurate assessment of operational tempo in Iraq. If the cost of procurement programs were included, the average monthly obligations increased to $4.4 billion.

Monthly obligations in Iraq increased by $100–130 million a month between April–May and the end of the fiscal year because 20,000 additional troops were retained in Iraq for an additional 90 days (1st Armored Division ($390 million)

and because of the early deployment of two Marine Expeditionary Units (MEUs) and a brigade of the 10th Mountain Division ($311 million)). It is worth noting, at this point, the FY04 monthly costs in Iraq were nearly the same as for FY03, despite having fought the major combat phase in 2003 during roughly the same time frame. Counterintuitive at first glance, these expenses were consistent with general contingency operations experience where the sustained care and feeding of personnel costs more than usually short duration combat operations. While FY03 included a short and intensive combat phase, the average number of personnel deployed in Iraq for subsequent operations in FY04 was actually greater than FY03.

At the same time, in Afghanistan, costs equaled $3.1 billion and the average burn rate was estimated at $612 million per month (including spending for procurement). If the spending for investment projects was removed, the monthly incremental costs were $600 million. While slightly lower than FY 2003, excluding some one-time depot maintenance and procurement for the replacement of equipment and munitions used during August and September of 2003, the contingency operations costs were overall relatively stable at a monthly rate running between $700–$900 million. DoD anticipated monthly costs would generally stay within this span over the fiscal year. At home in Operation Noble Eagle, total costs equaled $2.3 billion with a monthly burn rate of approximately $467 million.

By the April/May 2004 time frame, DoD was concerned about having sufficient 2004 supplemental appropriations remaining to sustain operations in Iraq through the rest of the fiscal year. The funding challenge looked very difficult, but was still manageable. Just beyond the fiscal mid-year, the Department believed it had sufficient resources to cover requirements in Iraq through the end of September. On the eve of the mid-year, FY04 budget review in April–June, DoD asserted that it would have a better idea about the likely sufficiency of FY04 resources for Iraq after the review was completed. Despite early Spring congressional questioning regarding the sufficiency of FY04 supplemental funds and the potential need for early GWOT funding in FY05, the administration aimed to transfer funds from overall appropriations to cover any FY04 shortfalls and "cash flow" operations in early FY05 from baseline FY05 budget funds while preparing a supplemental request by early calendar year 2005—a request DoD asserted would be informed by costs actually being experienced at the time. The administration did not originally intend to ask Congress for additional FY04 funding, but instead use transfer and reprogramming authority from both baseline appropriations and GWOT funds to cover shortfalls, if granted the increased authority to transfer funds as required.[36] Going into the summer, of the $2.1 billion in general transfer authority provided in the FY04 DoD Appropriations Act, only about $400 million remained. Absent new appropriations, the Department absolutely needed additional transfer authority in FY04 to implement the program.

DoD began to take a variety of measures to cover anticipated shortfalls, including: reducing other costs in normal base support, acquisition, and maintenance activities; transferring funds between appropriations; and deferring or canceling nonwar related activities in order to support the GWOT. The most flexible—and easiest—means for DoD to handle the costs was through the use of transfer authority between appropriations. However, by mid-June, the Department had used most of its annual fiscal year authority and had not nearly enough left to cover all of the estimated shortfalls perhaps in excess of $12 billion. Based on DoD's reported obligation of supplemental funds and the military services' own forecasts as of June 2004, the Government Accountability Office (GAO) estimated virtually all of the $12 billion projected shortfall was largely in the four services' operations and maintenance accounts as well as some of the manpower accounts. Not surprisingly, the largest projected shortfall was $10.2 billion in the Army's operations and maintenance appropriations.[37]

Several factors drove the accelerated spending above the FY04 supplemental planning figures. Increased operations tempo (OPTEMPO) during heightened tensions and fighting in Fallujah and other cities was a critical factor. This increased OPTEMPO negated several key assumptions upon which the FY04 supplemental was built, to include: the plan that U.S. military personnel in Iraq would decline by approximately 30–40,000 by the end of the fiscal year; the greater use of cheaper sealift vice more expensive airlift to support the operations; and replacement units would be more lightly armored and create fewer transportation costs. Events on the ground in Iraq demonstrated the flawed nature of the original assumptions. Likewise, the tougher security environment significantly increased logistics support costs and force protection requirements (i.e., more heavily armored ground vehicles).

These major unforeseen expenses of increased OPTEMPO combined to create congressional concern over funding sufficiency. Spring 2004 marked an increase in congressional skepticism over the administration's plans for shifting funds to cover costs. While an outright break in loyalty between the President and congressional Republicans did not occur, there was bipartisan support on the Hill to provide more specified funding for DoD, rather than increasing Executive Branch authority and prerogatives over spending. Such measures contrasted with the administration's desires. Increasing congressional discontent with the conduct of, and lack of progress in Iraqi operations, was expressed through the funding issues.

FY05 Defense Appropriations Act—The $25 Billion Bridge Supplemental

The FY04 shortfalls came to light as a congressional review was underway on the regular annual FY05 defense bills. The House and Senate Armed Services Committees were finishing their respective work on the FY05 defense authorization bill and chose to push for a $25 billion "down payment" authorization on anticipated FY05 supplemental needs. Pushed by Congress, supported by the military, and debated in the press, the administration finally relented and requested a $25 billion Contingency Emergency Response Fund. The initial request DoD envisioned would have placed the bulk of the $25 billion into a flexible account where DoD could transfer appropriations as required. Congress resisted the idea of that much control for the Executive.

This authorization also marked a greater congressional involvement in formulating supplementals and war spending. It had been common practice before that only the appropriations committees hammered out the details of supplementals before they went to final floor votes. The authorization committees provided their input for how funds such as the $25 billion should be used, passing their bills with separate titles authorizing various appropriation recommendations. Generally, following the authorizers' template, the appropriations committees provided the corresponding appropriations with a few modifications. One key element in the approved bill for $25 billion was contained in the General Provisions, Section 9001:

> Appropriations provided in this title are available for obligation until September 30, 2005, unless otherwise so provided in this title: Provided, that notwithstanding any other provision of law or of this Act, funds in this title are available for obligation, and authorities in this title shall apply, upon enactment of this Act.[38]

The appropriations committee's leaders pushed this language for both altruistic and selfish reasons. By enabling FY05 funds to be spent in FY04 (assuming the bill was enacted in time) to help cover projected FY04 shortfalls before DoD ran out of funding, the defense appropriators also created an imperative to complete their spending bill first (in late July/early August) to not only sustain DoD, but also get the bill approved before Congress adjourned for the extended Labor Day recess and fall election campaign travel. It worked—the President signed the bill into law on August 5, 2004 thereby enabling Section 9001 language to avert a FY04 funding crisis. Ultimately, in FY04, $2.2 billion of this FY05 advance appropriation was used to cover shortfalls and urgent needs including: $1.1 billion for urgent operational requirements and force protection as identified by the military services, $1.0 billion for increased worldwide fuel costs, and $100 million for the Commander's Emergency Response Program.

Often commonly referred to as the "Bridge Supplemental" since it provided $25 billion to DoD to "connect" funding from the shortfalls at the end of FY04 to the later request for a dedicated FY05 supplemental the following spring, the funding provided a boost across multiple appropriations. As Figures 5.11 and 5.12 show, the Bridge Supplemental focused on sustaining the engaged ground forces, with 70 percent of the total Service funding dedicated to the Army and Marines, and the Navy and Air Force each receiving approximately 2 percent for their respective supporting roles and missions. Overall, 15 percent of the funds were placed in the Iraqi Freedom Fund (IFF) account, but half of those were earmarked by Congress for transfer to specific classified programs and reimbursement for Coast Guard operating expenses, which left approximately 7 percent for Secretary of Defense discretionary use.

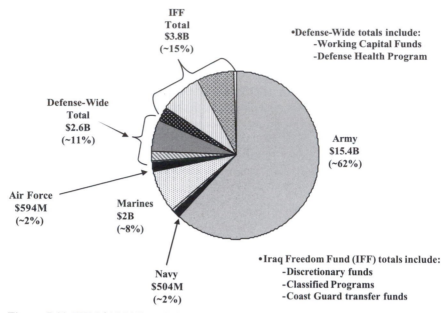

Figure 5.11 FY05 $25 Billion "Bridge Supplemental:" Component Shares

A separately titled appropriation in this act also gave the State Department $685 million toward the construction and support of the new American embassy and missions in Iraq. The $25 billion appropriated for DoD, plus the State Department embassy funding, were incremental costs in direct support of the Global War on Terror.

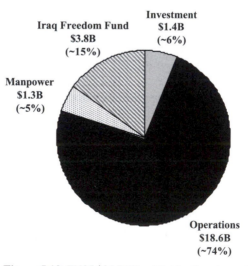

Figure 5.12 FY05 $25 Billion "Bridge Supplemental":
Appropriation Category Shares

A separate provision also gave DoD $1.5 billion in general transfer authority from within the fund, which equated to 6 percent of the $25 billion. Other specified transfer authorities included:

- $500 million for combined Secretary of Defense and Secretary of State mutually agreed upon use to train and equip Iraqi and Afghan security forces (commonly referred to as Train and Equip (T&E) authority).
- $300 million for the Commander's Emergency Response Program (CERP) in both Iraq and Afghanistan.[39]
- Unspecified amounts to transport, supply, and otherwise support coalition forces in Iraq and Afghanistan (commonly referred to as Lift and Sustain authority).

These authorities were simply that—an authority only—and did not have the accompanying appropriated funds provided.

The act also continued the trend of increasing congressional inquiry and monitoring of war finances, and therefore indirectly, an increased Congressional presence in overseeing the war. Congress levied numerous reporting requirements on the Executive Branch (mainly DoD), including a new biannual, comprehensive report that required more details on funding expenditures, assessments on force protection initiatives, operations and readiness issues, equipment status and repair, personnel statistics, various National Guard and Reserve issues, reconstruction status, and foreign aid involvement. Likewise, Congress also included language aimed at forcing the administration to provide future cost estimates for operations and reconstruction in Iraq and Afghanistan. This act was another example of the legislative use of funding mechanisms to shape war policy.

FY 2005 Emergency Supplemental—Continuing Operations, Buying Down the Backlog, and Questioning the Funding

Summary of Request and Appropriation

Submitted just a few days after the President's FY06 budget in February 2005, the FY05 supplemental request represented the second and final installment when added to the $25 billion "Bridge Supplemental" already provided. For DoD (again the largest recipient of funds), the total funding needed for the year was just under $100 billion. The new supplemental and remaining bridge supplemental funding combined were intended to cover the requirements. Figures 5.13 and 5.14 show the division of funds between the two appropriations.

The ground rules for building DoD's portion of the supplemental were very similar to FY04 with a few notable exceptions. First, there was no large request for Iraqi reconstruction; in fact, much of the roughly $18 billion appropriated the year before was still waiting to be obligated and executed for various projects.[40] The main reason for delay was the continuing security challenge in Iraq. The need

FY05 Supplemental Request

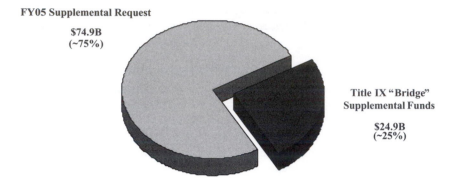

$99.8 Billion (Gross Requirement)

Figure 5.13 FY05 Total GWOT Funding Requirements

to accelerate security capacity led to a new request for $5.7 billion for training and equipping Iraqi government forces (also requested $1.3 billion to do similar initiatives in Afghanistan). Also new in this supplemental was the request for $854 million in the CERP, the first time specific funds were requested for this purpose rather than relying on flexible authorities to use other funds for it. Another major departure from past GWOT supplementals was the significant request for recapital-ization funds, the repairing and replacement of worn out and damaged equipment

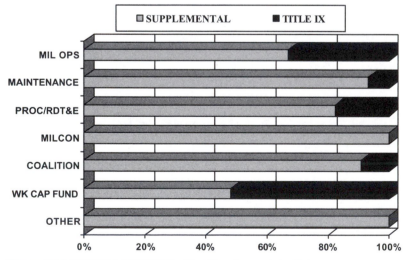

Figure 5.14 FY05 Total GWOT Funding Requirements by Category

in Iraq and Afghanistan (approximately $16 billion in procurement-related re-capitalization investment, and $5 billion in maintenance). Congress endorsed this funding, as it had been a common theme in congressional questioning in previous supplementals. Finally, one of the more controversial proposals was the request for $5.3 billion to support the Army modularity initiative, essentially a program to reorganize the Army divisional combat unit structure into more numerous and better deployable Brigade Combat Teams (BCTs). The other notable difference in FY05 was that Operation Noble Eagle had no supplemental funds requested for its homeland defense mission. The net result of these major changes resulted in this supplemental requirement being roughly $20 billion greater than the year before.

Troop rotations, and the security requirements of Iraqi elections, also drove changes in the funding profile required. The supplemental request used planned troop strength in Iraq that varied over the course of the year. Normal unit deployment rotations always created temporary spikes in troop levels during their overlapping period in theater. In addition, to provide security in the run-up to the Iraqi elections, total troop levels were increased. In the early part of FY05, there were about 138,000 troops in Iraq; by the January elections, that level had increased to approximately 160,000. With the successful completion of the elections, total troop levels began to drop by the summer. Afghanistan retained a relatively stable average troop level of 18,000 during the year. To support these commitments, the supplemental requested funding for more than 160,000 mobilized guards and reservists for FY05. It also requested funds for a temporary increase of 29,400 active duty Army soldiers and 2,675 additional active duty Marines, to alleviate stress on both the active and reserve forces and help with the fundamental restructuring of ground units as part of the Army modularity initiative.

Of the total almost $100 billion for DoD in FY05, roughly $60 billion was dedicated for military operations in Iraq and Afghanistan. In addition to the three new initiatives highlighted above, the other $40 billion went to functions like:

- Classified operations and other War on Terror costs (~$8 billion).
- Fuel and working capital funds (~$4 billion).
- Increased health care (~$1 billion).
- Military construction (~$1 billion).
- Coalition partner activities (~$2 billion).
- Other functions such as CERP; Counter-drug activities; a special project in Jordan; morale, recreation, and welfare programs, etc. (~$2.4 billion).

Also requested were funds for other agencies, totaling roughly $6 billion, and another $950 million for response to the December, 2004 South Asian tsunami needs. Altogether, funding for DoD totaled $82 billion in the FY05 emergency supplemental.

Budgeting Concerns—Cost of War on Budget

Including the cost of war in regular budget submissions, questioning what should be legitimately considered emergency spending, and future cost-of-war projections were all issues that had attracted some attention since 2002, but the bipartisan call grew louder in Congress with the FY05 supplemental. The administration continued to insist that supplementals were the appropriate mechanisms for funding immediate, urgent needs to fight the GWOT and deal with major unanticipated costs and emergencies. Executive Branch officials repeatedly emphasized the desire to not build up baseline budgets for what were assumed to be shorter-term or nonrecurring costs of the GWOT. Not only did this desire apply to DoD requests, but international activities (Department of State) as well. Long-term, ongoing costs for U.S. presence in Iraq and Afghanistan were included in the base budget for FY06, but one-time, short-term costs were included as part of this supplemental request. An example of a one-time cost in the supplemental was building the embassy in Baghdad. Examples of "ongoing needs" in the base budget were programs for building democratic institutions and economic growth. Increasing congressional interest in placing war costs on budget and eliminating use of supplementals as the main funding mechanism became more apparent as both chambers endorsed those measures in nonbinding language. Likewise, in a 2005 debate on the FY06 budget resolution, Congress began setting aside a war cost "placeholder" in the budget resolution ($50 billion) and appears likely to continue the practice as long as the administration does not provide advance estimates for war costs.

The regular, annual DoD appropriations language for both FY04 and FY05 contained a Senate recommendation that stated war costs should be a part of the baseline budget. The FY05 supplemental language became more specific, and while still just a Senate recommendation, it had both bipartisan and bicameral votes of support this time. In rather pedantic fashion, the finding outlined historical examples of making war costs part of the baseline (including the Bush administration's FY05 decision to put Noble Eagle in the base budget), highlighted continued administration noncompliance with past recommendations, and called for future estimates of war costs.[41] With a majority of Senators approving their language in all three bills, and for the first time having a House motion instructing their conferees to accept this Senate language (which passed by 417-4 votes), this language clearly reflected a tightening congressional intent to put war costs into the normal budgeting process.[42]

Authorities and Flexibility

Several authorities and inherent flexibilities afforded through the supplemental funding requested by the President raised concern and debate on the Hill. First was Congress' initial view of the $7 billion requested for training and equipping (T&E) Iraqi and Afghan security forces. Traditional military assistance funding had been under the direction of the State Department, with a long-established body of legislation to govern implementation. The administration's request would have established both policy authority, and ultimate funding control, of this T&E program solely within the DoD. Multiple defense officials conducted numerous briefings on the proposed Iraqi Security Forces Fund (ISFF) and Afghanistan Security Forces Fund (ASFF) to a variety of congressional staffers and members, in hopes of assuaging concerns and providing greater clarity of intent. Even Secretary of State Rice defended the invasion of traditionally State Department turf and assured the Hill that corresponding State Department missions were involved. Congress relented almost entirely on this issue, providing the full amounts requested, but added stipulations requiring formal Secretary of State concurrence on spending and added more congressional reporting and oversight requirements.[43]

The second issue was other foreign assistance requested, including: funds for the Palestinian Authority, a GWOT Partners' Fund and a Solidarity Fund to reward GWOT allies with economic and military assistance, funds for the Darfur region in Sudan, and even funds for Afghan reconstruction. Congress opposed such supplemental funding mechanisms that bypassed much of the oversight and regulations established on similar programs by the Senate Foreign Relations and House International Affairs Committees, and the Foreign Operations Appropriations Subcommittees. While providing aid in all of these areas, Congress reduced many of the amounts and generally invoked the same—or more stringent—requirements than done through the regular appropriations and oversight processes.[44]

A third issue related to the continued use of an emergency designation for much of the spending. Whether binding or not, established budget caps could be exceeded when an emergency was declared. The administration claimed an emergency was present, but increasingly congressional members were not so certain.

Finally, DoD continued to press for the increased authority to transfer funds. Congress obliged with a portion of what was requested, resulting in a $3 billion special transfer authority for supplemental funds and an additional $2.7 billion in general transfer authority for baseline budget appropriations. Yet the cumulative transfer authority in the FY05 baseline appropriation, bridge fund, and supplemental only totaled 2 percent of the total funds available to DoD. When added to the IFF granted in the bridge supplemental, and the limited flexibility funds in the ISFF, ASFF, and CERP accounts, all told DoD only had flexibility over roughly 4 percent of the nearly half trillion dollars available in FY05. This amount was a significant decline from the 40–50 percent range of flexibility granted during the first 2 years of the GWOT.

Timing Concerns

Expeditious passage of the supplemental became a thorny media and political issue in the spring, as it appeared that DoD was running out of money. Even with the bulk of $25 billion in bridge funds available and various transfer authorities to move money, the heightened troop levels for elections, increasing violence, and subsequent increase in operations tempo put a significant strain on the cash flow in DoD, particularly the Army. As the supplemental debate continued in Congress throughout March and April, projections showed the Army would run out of operations and maintenance funding my mid-to-late May, and manpower funds shortly thereafter. Discussion then arose on whether DoD would have to invoke the Feed and Forage Act that allowed suspension of antideficiency laws to continue critical operations and spending without appropriations. As this fact came to light in hearings and the press, the bill underwent debate instead over a significant number of immigration reform proposals. Originally proposed in late 2004 during debate and passage of the Intelligence Reform Act, mainly by Representative James Sensenbrenner, these immigration proposals were withdrawn under pressure from congressional leadership to get the reform bill passed expeditiously, with a promise to include them in an early and critical FY05 bill in the spring. The publicity surrounding DoD's funding crisis probably helped build consensus in the Senate for a unanimous cloture vote to end debate, eliminate nongermane provisions, and enabled the President to sign the bill on May 11, 2005.

Army Modularity

The goal of the Army's multiyear Modularity program is to reorganize the service into more agile, self-contained units with increased capabilities for future deployments—and in the near term, deployments to Iraq and Afghanistan. The program is scheduled to produce ten new deployable combat brigades when completed. The FY05 supplemental fight over this issue was not if the Army should be structured this way, but rather, why was it being funded via supplemental if it would take years to complete? The administration maintained supplemental funds would upgrade units rotating in and out of the theater, thereby reducing cumulative time troops were deployed and easing stress on the force. Absent the war, modularity would still occur, but at a slower pace over a longer period. According to DoD, the supplemental addressed the impact of operations tempo on the troops' rotation schedules, and by accelerating the initiative, DoD gained increased combat effectiveness in the GWOT. Modularity is designed as a multiyear program and beginning in FY07, it is to be funded in the baseline budget. In the interim, to upgrade equipment and reorganize units deploying to Iraq, the FY05 supplemental funded three additional brigades, while FY06 funds for this initiative would be sought via supplemental as well.

Benefits Ratchet

The phenomenon of benefits ratcheting upward continued in the FY05 supplemental. DoD requested an additional $176 million for the Defense Health

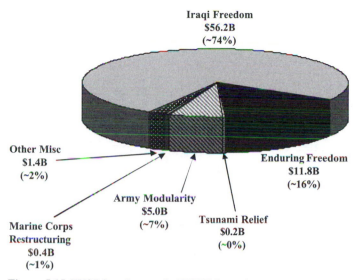

Figure 5.15 FY05 Supplemental: GWOT Operations

Program, in part to fund the expanded benefits from the previous 2 years for activated reservists and their families. The supplemental also expanded various injuries and insurance compensations for those injured or killed in the war. The Death Gratuity payment to families was increased from $12,000 to $100,000. The Serviceman's Group Life Insurance (SGLI) expanded significantly in coverage, from $250,000 maximum to $400,000 maximum, as well as adding special death gratuity up to $150,000 for death incurred in connection with OIF/OEF and partial reimbursement of SGLI premium payments. Also added were provisions for an additional $100,000 in insurance coverage for traumatic injuries, allowing dependents of deceased members to remain in military housing for longer time periods, and greater travel benefits for families of wounded service members. All of the payment benefits were made retroactive to those qualifying deaths since OEF began in October of 2001. The cost implications of these expanded benefits depends on the number of members assigned to designated areas, and operations and the number of deaths occurring in, or determined to result from, such operations or areas. However, at the time the supplemental was enacted in May 2005, the retroactive application of the new benefits to OEF and OIF veterans alone bestowed about $376 million to the survivors of qualifying deaths.

FY05 Supplemental Composition

Figure 5.15 shows how the supplemental funding as requested was split across the various major operations.

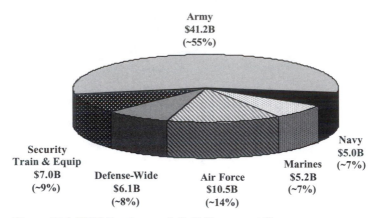

Figure 5.16 FY05 Supplemental: DoD Component Shares

Figure 5.16 indicates the bulk of DoD funds were still dedicated to keeping the Army in the field in Iraq and Afghanistan as well as accelerate the modularity initiative. Likewise, as ground operations increased, so to did the Marine Corps share of funding relative to previous years, while the Air Force share notably droppedoff as the focus of efforts shifted into counterinsurgency.

Finally, Figure 5.17 shows the breakdown by appropriation categories and depicts the commitment to begin recapitalization in this supplemental with

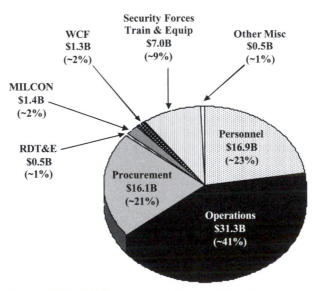

Figure 5.17 FY05 Supplemental: Appropriation Shares

21 percent of the funds going into procurement as well as a significant portion of the operations and maintenance for repair work.

COST OF WAR AT HOME—HOMELAND SECURITY SPENDING SINCE 9/11

The attacks of September 11 brought greater attention to the tracking of federal funding for homeland security spending. Even after the 2002 creation of the Department of Homeland Security, funding for homeland security functions is spread among more than 200 appropriation accounts within the federal budget and crosses virtually every department and agency in government.[45] Further complicating the funding picture is that much of these funds are carried within larger programs not considered to be homeland security related. The Office of Management and Budget (OMB) prepares an annual report to Congress on homeland security spending. The OMB report is created from data reported by the various Executive Branch departments and agencies. Unfortunately, while OMB provides some guidance for reporting these requirements, standardization is not mandated. The Government Accountability Office (GAO) found that of the seven agencies that account for approximately 90 percent of the total homeland security spending, they each developed different methodologies to provide their spending estimates to OMB.[46] With these difficulties in mind, both the GAO study and CBO analysis referenced above, categorized homeland security spending in the six mission categories defined in the President's *National Strategy for Homeland Security*:

- Intelligence and warning
- Border and transportation security
- Domestic Counterterrorism
- Protection of critical infrastructure and key assets
- Defense against catastrophic threats
- Emergency preparedness and response

All spending in these categories is domestically focused and arguably defensive in nature. Both studies also considered the separate accounting for overseas activities such as embassy security and some intelligence efforts classified as Overseas Combating Terrorism Funding (OCTF). The OCTF does not include DoD efforts in Iraq, Afghanistan, and other locales whose costs are captured under the OIF and OEF cost accounting.

Considering the OMB data as analyzed by CBO/GAO, there are clearly incremental cost increases in baseline homeland security budgets after 9/11. The FY01–02 baseline budgets, both prepared prior to 9/11, were running in the $15–17 billion range. Beginning in FY03, baseline homeland security spending expenditures jumped to over $30 billion, increasing to over $40 billion by FY05.[47] Supplemental funding, which began immediately after the 9/11 attacks through FY05, also increased the incremental costs. Based on the data, the FY03–05 on-budget incremental costs attributable or resulting from the GWOT are approximately $48–50 billion. Adding supplemental funding (~$85 billion) since FY01 for security and recovery response to 9/11 results in approximately $135 billion spent in total on homeland security as incremental costs.

GWOT SUMMARY

Through FY05, the GWOT has created approximately $489 billion in direct costs to the federal government. These costs include the initial response to the attacks of 9/11, operations in Iraq and Afghanistan, Operation Enduring Freedom activities in the Horn of Africa and Philippines, increased homeland security spending and Operation Noble Eagle in the United States, and various selected foreign aid and similar payments to countries for aid in supporting GWOT. Collectively, the United States has spent approximately 1.6 times more on offensive actions ($303 billion), than on defensive measures at home ($186 billion). This balance continues to be a discussion point as the overarching debate on strategy for fighting this long war develops.

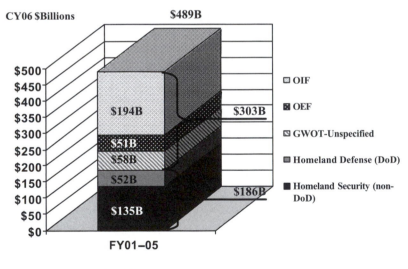

Figure 5.18 Federal Government Incremental Cost of the War on Terror

At this time, the administration had submitted its FY06 emergency supplemental request to Congress for $72.4 billion to continue the GWOT efforts. This funding was in addition to the $50 billion already provided in the FY06 budget resolution. While congressional passage is still pending, the bulk of those funds are expected to be appropriated. The themes highlighted in the previous GWOT supplemental analyses will not disappear: Congress questioning the need for flexible funds like the Iraqi Freedom Fund, a debate over further expansion of personnel benefits, concern over incorporating the cost of war into baseline budget requests, as well as a host of operational and policy issues related to U.S. progress in Iraq and Afghanistan. Larger than just a single year concern, the debate extends to what should now be considered incremental war costs and what is now the "normal" level of costs for doing business in the post-9/11 world.

It is too soon to tell what the longer-term costs like debt servicing and veteran's costs will be. Even less clear, are the impacts future GWOT operations may have on other costs to the nation. President Bush stated in his 2002 State of the Union Address:

> America is no longer protected by vast oceans. We are protected from attack only by vigorous action abroad, and increased vigilance at home. Americans are asking: How will we fight and win this war? We will direct every resource at our command—every means of diplomacy, every tool of intelligence, every instrument of law enforcement, every financial influence, and every necessary weapon of war—to the disruption and to the defeat of the global terror network.[48]

Despite the rhetoric, there still does not appear to be a broad and commonly accepted consensus in the country on how to design, implement, and fund GWOT strategy. Does the United States have the right balance between offensive and defensive capabilities in this war? What exactly defines offense, when the goal in this war is not always to attack and destroy opposing forces? Chairman of the Joint Chiefs of Staff General Peter Pace said in his February 2006 Posture Statement to Congress, "Thankfully, the daily life of the average American citizen reflects none of the hardships or shortages we associate with a nation at war."[49] The paradox then is, will this truth help or hinder the American public's understanding of the magnitude of the challenge presented by the GWOT and the sacrifices that may be required to sustain it as a multigenerational war?

Resourcing Considerations: Enduring Lessons and Issues from Extended Conflicts Past and Present

RESOURCING CONSIDERATION # 1

War cost estimates before conflicts are always wrong.
Determining war costs after a conflict is a task in the eyes of the beholder.

> In short, absolute, so-called mathematical, factors never find a firm basis in military calculations. From the very start there is an interplay of possibilities, probabilities, good luck and bad that weaves its way throughout the length and breadth of the tapestry. In the whole range of human activities, war most closely resembles a game of cards.[1]

The above quote from Clausewitz's *On War* is the simplest explanation of why estimating war costs in advance is problematical. Without recounting the many estimates provided before and during the three conflicts examined, the shortest and most equitable summary encompassing all of them was they were all wrong. The story of virtually every year of both the Korean and Vietnam Wars was a history of shortfalls and the need for more money. The GWOT estimates have been aided by the use of simulation tools to help produce war funding requests whose accuracy has improved over that of past conflicts, but even these estimates have been inexact. As a general rule, the more assumptions are examined and flexibility built into the estimates to account for potential changes in the assumptions, the greater utility the estimate/budget will provide.

Assumptions also play the lead role in determining costs after a conflict. Deciding what direct costs are appropriate to include is conceptually difficult and the actual accounting task equally challenging. Determining second order effects and associated costs, as well as macroeconomic impacts of war spending is even more problematic—fraught with numerous and challengeable assumptions. Of the cases examined, the direct cost determination for the Korean War was complicated by the overlapping general buildup of U.S. forces associated with the NSC-68 containment policy. Especially after the first year, rarely were distinctions drawn between funds dedicated for each task within the DoD budget. Other large sums were appropriated in support of infrastructure development, defense mobilization, and production throughout government and the industries that supported both tasks concurrently with little differentiation. Vietnam was inherently difficult because the Johnson Administration in particular was not forthcoming about identifying war costs and the Nixon Administration classified most of the information after 1970. In both Korea and Vietnam, major portions of the war costs were either absorbed by or moved into baseline DoD appropriations, making detailed tracking of what was actually expended for war efforts virtually impossible. By comparison, the cost information available for GWOT is much richer in detail and more accessible. The diverse nature of GWOT, however, makes determining what should be considered a more comprehensive endeavor, especially when media attention has fixated on Iraq and tends to equate all war related costs with that effort.

When studying the cost of war, one should always challenge what items are included and the assumptions behind the associated figures. A survey of the literature on the subject found no case where two conflicts were compared using reasonably equitable costs estimates grounded in similar assumptions and methodologies. As such, most cost comparisons drawn between GWOT today and past conflicts are meaningless.

RESOURCING CONSIDERATION # 2

Wars eventually transition from supplemental budgeting to baseline budgets.

The timing and manner of war funding, moving from supplemental into baseline budgets, varies circumstantially. Korea was essentially paid for with baseline DoD funds in the second and third year of conflict, despite no formal budget for it, and then supplemental or deficiency appropriations replaced the shortfalls later in the year. Not until FY54 were portions of the war requirements planned for in the annual DoD budget, but the cease-fire 27 days after the start of the fiscal year rendered the on-budget experience nil. Vietnam was attempted on-budget in significant amounts for the first time in FY67, but required 3 years' worth of huge supplemental appropriations before the on-budget portion of the funding began to approximate the annual war costs. To date, the GWOT has remained the anomaly to the war-on-budget practice, although that is true only in the active overseas conflicts associated with Operations Enduring and Iraqi Freedom. Operational Noble Eagle, a significant portion of DoD's homeland defense mission, was taken on budget beginning in FY05 and most other homeland security expenditures in

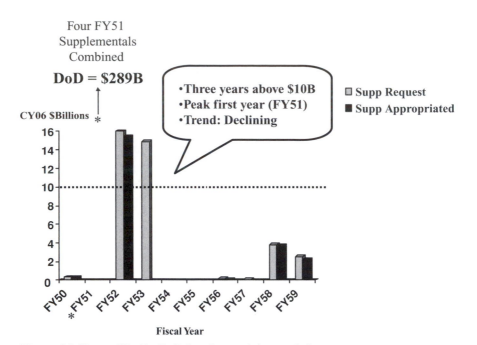

Figure 6.1 Korean War Era DoD Supplemental Appropriations
Note (1): Due to scale, FY51 amounts are not directly plotted.
Note (2): FY52 and FY53 totals do not include the annual Military Construction appropriations that were added to supplementals in those years. *Note (3)*: FY53 Supplemental request was for $14.9 billion. Funds were provided, but through transfer from other accounts and not new appropriations, hence, the appropriated amount in Figure 6.1 is zero.

various other departments and agencies associated with the war on terror have been in the annual baseline budgets since the Department of Homeland Security was created. That said, the GWOT supplementals are ahistoric in terms of magnitude, duration of consecutive appropriations, and upward trend.

Figures 6.1–6.3 show the DoD-only, supplemental appropriations requested and appropriated during each period of conflict and surrounding years. Reviewing all the DoD supplemental appropriations since 1950 adjusted into constant year 2006 dollars, $10 billion appears as a good reference when considering what constitutes a "large" supplemental, and is a quick and reasonable figure to look for to determine when extended conflicts significantly transition to baseline budgets.

The first two FY51 supplementals for Korea, in constant dollars, were the largest ever received by DoD during the Cold War. The four supplementals that year combined provided DoD almost $290 billion. After this incredible sum of funds, Korean War supplemental funding quickly declined over the next 2 years, but still exceeded the $10 billion threshold (the amount requested in the FY53

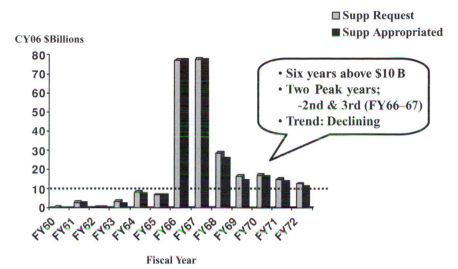

Figure 6.2 Vietnam War Era DoD Supplemental Appropriations

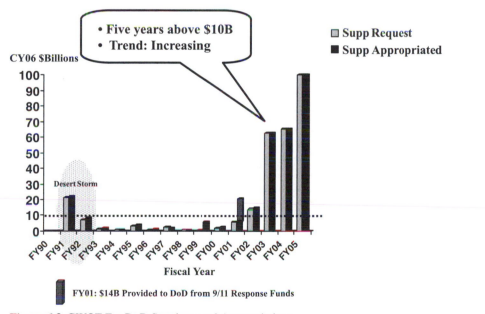

Figure 6.3 GWOT Era DoD Supplemental Appropriations

supplemental was provided by Congress, but through transfer from other existing appropriations rather than new funds and is why the appropriated amount in Figure 6.1 is zero). These amounts are consistent with a funding history that did not accommodate the conflict costs into advance budget planning until FY54. Vietnam escalation was gradual through FY65, and the first month of FY66 is when President Johnson announced the major increase in commitment. Correspondingly, FY66 and FY67 were the 2 peak years of supplemental war appropriations, and as greater attempts were made to place more accurate estimates of the war requirements in the baseline budgets, the supplemental appropriations quickly declined to around the $10 billion mark, finally going below it in FY72. The common supplemental funding profile trait for these conflicts was the supplementals were at their peak in the first couple of years of conflict and then quickly diminished to near or below the $10 billion threshold.

The GWOT's supplemental appropriation profile clearly shows the fundamental difference with previous funding experience, but as the next *Resourcing Consideration* will detail, the use of supplemental appropriations has several advantages usually unacknowledged.

RESOURCING CONSIDERATION # 3

The question of using supplemental vice regular baseline budgets to fund periods of extended conflict (greater than one year) is a perennial wartime argument.

The same arguments in the baseline budget versus supplemental budget debate for war costs resonate through all three conflicts examined. Supplemental appropriations have one overriding advantage for funding war activities; they are prepared much closer to time of need and, therefore, will be the best representation of actual amounts and pace of appropriations required to support the war. This argument has echoed in comments from multiple Defense Secretaries involved in these three conflicts.

> Louis Johnson, Korea, circa 1950: I think we will have to come back with a supplemental request involving naval aircraft procurement ... for Air Force public works and ... for public works for the Army. In the changing world conditions, about which we can tell more later, the Army and the Navy will then be able to give you a fair estimate of the amount needed for public works in those services, something that cannot be done intelligently today [testifying in defense of the 1st FY51 Supplemental and while the regular FY51 DoD Appropriations Bill was still on the Hill awaiting approval].[2]

> George Marshall, Korea, circa 1950: I feel that we are going to have to come in here again after we have gone further into the situation and have seen how it

develops and had time to figure out exactly how we are going to meet the further requirements.... There is not time to consider such matters now. It seemed to us that this was about all we could digest efficiently at this particular time [stated while testifying in defense of the 2nd FY51 Supplemental].[3]

Robert Lovett, Korea, circa 1952: ... We have no means of estimating accurately now in advance, how many shells will be expended, and so forth. It depends on the rate of activity.... We come up for deficiency appropriations to provide for deficiencies caused by Korea beyond the average [peacetime] consumption rates [the incremental cost]. You get them in supplementals because we come up only when we have actual provable deficiencies [testifying in defense of the FY53 Defense Appropriations Bill].[4]

Robert McNamara, Vietnam, circa 1966–67: I think it would be irresponsible for us to come forward, now, today, with a higher figure [in base budget for war costs], because it is extremely difficult to estimate the level of combat operations 18 months in advance, and very wasteful if we are to estimate on the high side, and quite unnecessary.... To the extent that we can finance our operations with the presently requested funds and push the timing of the submission of a supplemental into the future, I think we will be able to come forward with a more precise estimate of our total requirements.[5]

Donald Rumsfeld, GWOT, circa 2005: I've been asked why war costs are included in the supplemental rather than in the annual defense budget. Let me explain the process and the problem. The annual budget process takes up to 12 months for DoD to plan and clear through OMB a budget. I started last month to prepare the budget that will be submitted to OMB in December. Then in OMB for a month or two and the president's consideration. In February it comes up to the Congress. Then it takes eight or nine more months in the Congress for the process to pass it. And then it takes 12 months to execute it. That's a total of two and a half years in a fast-moving world where things are changing. The reality is, as Congress has recognized, is that there are appropriate uses for a supplemental. And the supplemental period, of course, is much shorter. It could be plus or minus 10 months if one thinks of the time to develop it and then the time to submit it, get it approved and then to execute it. In war, circumstances on the ground can change quickly. What was not urgent at one point may prove to be urgent later as the enemy strategies shift and new challenges arrive. So a supplemental allows for somewhat more accurate estimates of costs and, importantly, quicker access to needed funds.[6]

These statements were made by five Secretaries of Defense, both Democrat, Republican and one nonparty affiliated, retired five-star general, during three different conflicts over a 50-plus year time span. Despite that diversity, it is easy to see how one could interchange the speakers name and date on any of these quotes and still have the same fundamental argument made by any Secretary, for any conflict, during any time period. Given these facts, today's drumbeat call to place war costs on budget warrants reexamination.

The main arguments against continued use of the supplemental mechanism are:

- Need to include war costs with other annual budget and revenue discussions for the year in question. The budget resolution becomes an artificial document when enormous supplementals are routinely approved outside of the established budget caps thereby impacting the federal balance sheet.
- Supplemental appropriations are a "separate checkbook" that lacks transparency.
- Supplementals "hide" the cost of war from the Congress and public.
- Supplementals are an easy mechanism for congressional members to add "pork barrel" items they could not get through regular appropriations.
- The defense authorization committees are essentially precluded from influencing since supplemental funding bills are the sole purview of the appropriations committees.
- The time compression usually surrounding supplemental requests does not allow for effective oversight.
- It is too easy for the military to fund other than direct and immediate war costs in supplemental appropriations (argued in Korea concerning the general buildup of forces, and the current high profile example pointed to in Army transformation/modularity initiatives funded via supplemental appropriations in FY05 and requested via supplemental in FY06).

Other issues, such as partisan politics, apparent constitutional objections, and overall dislike of the costs involved have been levied against supplemental war appropriations. An often-stated advantage of placing war costs in baseline budgets is a theoretical assurance that war policy gets better exposure and debate by Congress and the public. The supposed effectiveness of war costs in baseline budgets is the implied solution to various concerns just listed. However, an examination of the experience with Korea, Vietnam, and even the GWOT reveals some of these assertions are exaggerated or flawed. The following points correspond to the previous arguments against supplementals, with examples from the analysis, and suggest a hybrid method of incorporating a "top-line" estimate of war costs in the budget resolution, while still using supplemental appropriations for line-item details developed later, and closer to the time of need, may be the best solution:

- *Need to include war costs with other annual budget and revenue discussions.* Agreed, this needs to be done for extended conflicts. There is no way to rationalize long-term federal budgets and economic impacts without incorporating these requirements. While determining war requirements far in advance is always difficult, for the first few years of a new conflict it is likely to be a fruitless task. However, once a conflict is more "established," that is, the level of effort and overall funding required becomes more predictable, it is reasonable that overarching budget requirements could be provided to the Congress and American people for debate and inclusion in the budget resolution. A partial step in this direction has occurred over the past 2 years. The congressional Budget Committees, on their own accord, have set aside $50 billion in the budget resolution for war costs and expected supplemental appropriations. It was a good first step, now what is needed is better dialogue and estimates of this top-line figure to be worked between Congress and the Executive Branch. No matter what overall budget level is established, supplemental appropriations provide the flexibility of using emergency designations on requested funds. This designation allows higher spending not subject to budget caps or enforcement rules, if and when they are in effect, if war circumstances dictate change (although vociferous opponents of supplementals would likely view this as a disadvantage).

- *Supplemental appropriations are a "separate checkbook" that lacks transparency.* Supplementals can be considered a separate checkbook, and if used exclusively (or mainly) for war costs, they actually provide for greater transparency. Analysis of all three conflicts consistently proved this point. The most accurate records and cost estimates for Korea were in the four supplementals from FY51 that covered the full war effort that year. Once Korean costs were being absorbed out of baseline funds, and more intertwined with the general build-up requirements, visibility of war costs became blurred. Similar findings occurred with Vietnam funds; the greatest transparency was in the large supplemental request in FY66 and the supplemental budget portion of war requirements in FY67 covered by two supplementals. Vietnam cost estimates from the period when costs were largely in baseline budgets are very murky. Comparably, GWOT was relatively easy to audit for war costs mainly because of the extensive use of supplemental budgets. The transfer of funds from flexible accounts provided in many GWOT supplementals to existing appropriations also provided another set of auditable documents for how funds were used.

- *Supplementals "hide" the cost of war from the Congress and public.* As just described, experience shows supplementals dedicated solely for war costs provide much greater visibility for Congress and the public. Supplementals do reveal requirements later in the budget process which could account for some of the accusations of "hidden costs," but if supplementals are used in conjunction with providing an overall advance estimate in the budget resolution, this argument no longer has any merit.

- *Supplementals are an easy mechanism for congressional members to add "pork."* This fact is true; it is always a danger with supplementals, and it occurred in all three conflicts examined. Senator McCain recently complained, "in last year's emergency request [FY05], I counted $5 million in unauthorized earmarks."[7] While unnecessary spending is always regrettable, $5 million in spending measure of roughly $75 billion is but a mere fraction of 1 percent. Overall, the extent of congressional restraint in adding pork in the recent GWOT supplementals, when compared to Korea and Vietnam experiences, is commendable.

- *The authorization committees are essentially cut out of the process.* Under current practice they are, but they have not always been. In both Korea and Vietnam, the Armed Services Committees and the Defense Sub-committees from the Appropriations Committees held some joint hearings on supplemental war appropriations. In fact, in some years, the Armed Services Committees passed separate authorizing legislation for portions of the supplemental requests, usually regarding military construction, procurement, and research and development funds. If it desires, Congress could organize oversight of war supplemental requests any way that it views as appropriate.

- *The time compression usually surrounding supplemental requests does not allow for effective oversight.* This frustration has been expressed in all three conflicts and remains a challenge. There is no easy way around the time demands of conflict, and timeliness for war appropriations needs to be improved with the Executive Branch as well. Perhaps greater congressional use of authorization and policy oversight committees when dealing with questions regarding peace, war, and war conduct would leave fewer issues to deal with when considering spending bills. That said, spending measures will always be used as a last resort by the Congress if it feels the need to do so.

- *It is too easy for the military to fund other than direct and immediate war costs in supplemental appropriations.* This issue has mixed results depending upon interpretations of what constitutes legitimate war costs. Prior, informal arrangements between the Executive and Legislative Branches regarding what are appropriate war costs for supplemental requests may preclude these types of disputes.

There are several disadvantages to placing war costs in baseline budgets. In addition to the long lead-time argument made by every Defense Secretary, when war funds are absorbed within the greater appropriation accounts of baseline budgets, visibility for tracking specific war costs is usually diminished than if retained in supplemental spending measures. When the conflict ends, it also becomes harder to make precise determinations on just how much funding can be removed from the baseline budget. This difficulty was prevalent in both previous conflicts examined, especially Vietnam. The concern is particularly acute for operations and maintenance funding which does not have discrete quantities of items or people to match against like, the procurement and manpower accounts, and could be a significant problem if GWOT operations are placed on-budget because a large percentage of the GWOT costs today are operations and maintenance related.

One advantage of having war costs in a baseline budget request loaded with other desirable items is that it makes it harder for Congressmen and Senators to vote against based on their possible objections to war policies and conduct. The mechanism to attack war-related costs in this case is through the amendment process. Conversely, war funds contained in a separate, stand-alone bill creates a more honest opportunity for members of Congress to vote funding support based on the merits of the war and associated policies. While voting "yea" on a clearly defined supplemental war appropriation does not constitute a legitimization of Executive war power, nor does it infer complete agreement with every element and aspect of war policy and conduct, it does enable Congress to take a clear, unambiguous position on overall supportability of the war effort. The ambiguity of a member of Congress voting in support of a war appropriation contained within a more expansive appropriations bill, but then verbally opposing the war overall, is removed. The American people get a clear-cut, accountable position from their Congressman, and both Senators, regarding the conflict when appropriations are structured in this manner.

In summary, the hybrid method of eventually providing top-line estimates for war costs in budget resolutions that give visibility to Congress and the American people as to the cost of war—while still retaining the advantages of flexibility, timeliness, and greater accuracy in supplemental appropriations for the line-item budget details, may be the best compromise approach to budgeting for extended conflict.

RESOURCING CONSIDERATION # 4

Flexibility in appropriated funds is often critical and usually diminishes over time.

Inherent flexibility in appropriated funds essentially means the ability for Executive Branch officials to shift funds from priority to priority, or have accounts specifically established with transferability to other funds, with little to no restrictions. This aspect of funding war is a critical tool in rapidly responding to battlefield conditions and evolving needs of those conducting operations. In all three conflicts, experience has shown that early on, flexibility is more broadly granted in both the amount of funds and scope of authority. Experience has also shown, in every case, that flexibility has decreased over time in extended conflict.

Flexibility in funds goes right to the heart of the constitutional tension between Congress' power-of-the-purse and the Executive Branch that operates with the appropriations. If the conduct or cost of war is increasingly called into question by the public, Congress can be expected to restrict this freedom of action from the Executive. In an extreme case, such as Vietnam, Congress may not only remove flexibility in the funds, but deny the funding altogether. In the aftermath of Vietnam and Iran/Contra, tougher congressional scrutiny of war monies and limited Executive latitude should be expected, especially as the conflict progresses.

To paraphrase Clausewitz: the greater the extent that war is perceived to be political in nature, the more likely that constraints will restrict the means—and funding is the one means that enables virtually all the others. Two examples from the GWOT experience illustrate both ends of this spectrum. Immediately after 9/11, responding as a nation that had been physically and dramatically attacked, Congress appropriated $40 billion in a matter of days, with tremendous presidential discretion over use of the funds. There was broad consent among the public and elected officials this measure was the necessary and appropriate course of action. In contrast, before Operation Iraqi Freedom, where greater division existed over the prospective war's ends, ways, means, and even the need to go to war, Congress completely denied the administration's request for all war funds in a flexible transfer account. By design, this built-in constitutional tension will never be "resolved."

If the problem is inevitable, what should the policy/resource planner do? For a long-term conflict, Congress is not likely to grant broad flexibility in both amount and scope of funds indefinitely. Where possible, placing needed funds in existing and structured appropriations provides a level of reassurance to Congress that they have appropriate mechanisms in place to conduct oversight. The greater challenge comes when traditional appropriations, account structures, governing laws, and regulations cannot respond to the ever-changing needs of an operation. When current methods fall short, one approach may be to request flexible funds that are limited in scope to a set of specific missions. In this manner, there would exist some balance between Congress' desire for control and oversight (funds constrained to one functional area of operations) and the Executive's need for flexibility to respond to war's dynamic conditions (enough flexibility and high discretionary authority within that particular functional area). A current example of this approach might be the Iraqi and Afghan Security Force Funds developed in the FY05 supplemental. The lump sum monies provided in each account can be transferred and merged with any existing appropriation as circumstances dictate changing requirements, but the overall purpose of the funds remains constrained to training and equipping security forces in each country. While a very useful tool provided initially in 2005, it would have been even better to develop and request this type of fund and associated authorities earlier in the conflict. Developing these funds will require greater—and earlier—coordination between operational planners and funding professionals to ensure that likely contingencies are accounted for in the estimates and corresponding authorities requested to provide necessary flexibility. As with any of these challenges, dialogue at all levels, in advance of funding needs, will likely go a long way in helping develop the trust and confidence needed by Congress to provide, and the Executive Branch to manage, such flexible accounts.

RESOURCING CONSIDERATION # 5

Authorities often matter as much, and sometimes more, than money.

Granting legal authority for certain functions, particularly with regard to funding various initiatives in wartime, is often a key to success. In the Korean War, for example, the authorities granted under the Defense Production Act were essential in providing the necessary materials and support to industry for the force buildup. President Johnson used the broad authority of the Gulf of Tonkin Resolution to undertake military escalation for several years in Vietnam. Recently, the GWOT has seen an expansion of many existing authorities and the creation of new ones to prosecute the conflict. Given the GWOT's complexity, the need for new authorities should not be surprising. Authorities such as Emergency, Extraordinary Expenses (EEE), Combatant Commander Initiative Fund (CIF), Combating Terrorism Readiness Fund (CbTRF), and Overseas Humanitarian Disaster Assistance and Civic Aid (OHDACA) existed before the GWOT began, and most provided for funding in the tens of millions of dollars. The Afghan Freedom Support Act (AFSA) drawdown authority, Acquisition Cross-Servicing Agreements (ACSAs), Support to Key Cooperating Nations, Commander's Emergency Response Program (CERP), Lift and Sustain (L&S), Train and Equip (T&E), Rapid Acquisition Authority, and others are illustrative examples of authorities used in the GWOT today. Interestingly, most of these newer authorities use funds in the hundreds of millions, or even billions, of dollars.

Several examples highlight other valuable lessons. Authorities for foreign aid are sensitive and cross-jurisdictional committee boundaries in Congress. Likewise, aid authorities requested for unspecified locations or functions are an anathema on the Hill. Vietnam provided many examples to Congress why it should not grant broad latitude in this regard, and it has been very leery to do so regarding the GWOT. While an Administration can always request whatever authorities it chooses, it is probably foolhardy to make operational plans contingent upon receipt of this type of authority. If aid or funding reimbursement requirements are anticipated for countries that otherwise violate U.S. legal restrictions, all efforts should be made to justify why temporary waivers are required. Combatant Commander justification is especially helpful in supporting the requirement.

To the maximum extent possible, policy and resource planners should anticipate the conflicts needs and request new or expanded authorities if required. Authorities are grants of trust. Early, deliberate discussions with Congress to develop mutually supportable authorities are generally more successful than trying to grant or change authorities in extreme situations. In conjunction with the authority request, recommend a specific regimen of reporting requirements and if appropriate, Executive regulations that will guide, monitor, and provide sufficient visibility to Congress for oversight. The Commander's Emergency Response Program (CERP) is a good recent example of this approach. Commanders from the Central Command area of responsibility repeatedly emphasized the importance of this program and granting the authority down to the battalion and small-sized units in the field. DoD established governing instructions, largely satisfying Congress, for appropriate regulations and obviating the need for extensive legislation to govern. Likewise, DoD has been responsive to Congress when questions have arisen regarding use of the program and continued CERP evolution and program growth has been strongly supported on the Hill.

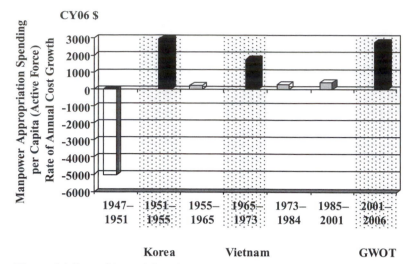

Figure 6.4 Rate of Annual Cost Growth in DoD Manpower Spending per Capita
Source: Data for graphic taken from FY06 DoD Green Book. Large aberration in the 1947–1951 time period resulted from post–World War II demobilization. The 1973–2001 time period is broken into two segments because of a significant accounting change that occurred (1984–1985) in how retirement accrual payments were scored (tracked) in the federal budget relative to the DoD manpower accounts.

RESOURCING CONSIDERATION # 6

Extended periods of conflict typically increase military personnel benefits and entitlements.

Whether initiated by the military, civilian defense leadership, Congress, pressure from the public or other interest groups, increased spending and authority for permanent "entitlement-like" benefits for the military community generally occur during extended periods of conflict. Benefit increases historically have gone toward active duty, reserve and national guard forces; however, recently in the GWOT, the military retiree community has received significantly increased benefits as well. Figure 6.4 shows the annual rate of increase in manpower spending per capita for active duty forces during several time periods since World War II.

Clearly, the three periods of conflict highlighted in the shaded time frames show abnormal rates of annual cost growth when compared to the longer periods of relative peace.

What does this chart imply for the future? Policymakers and resource planners should anticipate and consider the impact on the defense program when extended hot-conflict is undertaken. For example, in today's GWOT, with the existing force size and rate of cost growth, the funding requirements indicate an increase by as much as $3.8 billion per year. While significant supplemental funds can offset the danger to the defense program of this increasing requirement, concern should be raised about the prospect that large supplemental funding will not continue indefinitely. While some of the future costs will be mitigated when conflict ends—such as Imminent Danger Pay and Family Separation Allowances— the permanently authorized changes in entitlements, like medical benefits and other pay increases, will persist. Other impacts to consider are required future increased expenditures, such as spending in the operations accounts for the Defense Health Program, increased Veterans Administration costs, payments from Treasury trust funds for benefits, and any other personnel benefits that are not reflected in Figure 6.4.

RESOURCING CONSIDERATION # 7

Budget outlays directly related to a conflict extend longer than usually realized.

Direct federal outlays attributable to specific conflicts usually extend much further into the future than most people realize. Repairing and replacing equipment lost in combat is one obvious example of funding requirements that can extend a few years beyond the end of hostilities. Another common continuing expense is debt payments, if the war was financed at least partially with borrowing and deficits. Perhaps the longest term of payments directly resulting from conflict comes in the form of Veterans Administration (VA) compensation and pensions. These payments alone can extend for up to a century past conflict termination by the time all beneficiaries and entitled survivors have been paid. As VA benefits increase in both amount and eligibility, "retroactive" cost growth occurs on payments for past conflicts. Figure 6.5 shows the compensation and pension payments for veterans of both Korea and Vietnam, and these figures do not include the cost of medical care and other potential benefits beyond the monthly compensation/pension payments.

Data for this chart is available through the year 2002 as depicted.[8] Korean War payments reached their peak in 1980, 30 years after the start of the conflict, and are not expected to end until the middle of this century.[9] Vietnam payments as of 2002 are still increasing. Both conflicts will require budget outlays for several more decades.

Veterans' benefits have been estimated to cost two to three times more than the original direct cost of any conflict. When embarking on extended conflict, policymakers and resource planners should consider what cost growth will occur in Veterans Administration programs, budgeting for that cost-growth in the short term, and consider the impacts on longer-term revenue-outlay perspectives.

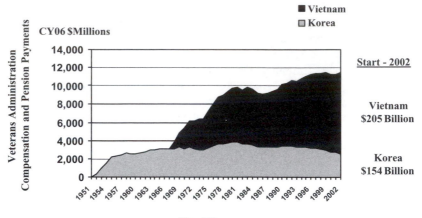

Figure 6.5 Veterans Administration Compensation and Pension Payments, Korean and Vietnam Wars: Inception Through 2002

RESOURCING CONSIDERATION # 8

Predisposed outlooks of political leadership matter heavily in financing war—effects of those decisions can have a major impact on long-term funding sustainability.

No American war has ever been fought entirely with a blank check approach to funding. Spending or economic capacity limitations have always served directly or indirectly to restrain expenditures. As the United States entered the Korean War, President Truman was colored by his experience from World War II and the heavy debt borrowing to finance that conflict. Determined to avoid large deficits that he saw as dangerous, Truman proposed greatly increased taxation to put Korea on a pay-as-you-go basis. He did not fully achieve that goal, as Congress was reluctant to enact all the tax measures requested, but taxes did rise sharply during the war. As the war grew increasingly unpopular in U.S. public opinion for a variety of reasons, so did the associated higher tax burden. Those taxes contributed to public demand to end the war.

In the early part of Vietnam escalation, President Johnson was so determined to pass legislation for his Great Society programs that not only did he forgo early tax measures to pay for the war (because they might have raised questions regarding his domestic programs), he also purposely hid the costs of war as long as possible to protect these other priorities. The resulting deficits and inflation were but two more issues that fed public demand to end American involvement. Tax cuts to spur the economy have been a pivotal priority during President George W.

Bush's tenure. It is clear there is no intention to use the tax mechanism to create revenues to finance war expenditures. While the debate over the danger of rising deficits continues, clearly there is a risk that public concern over this issue could create a political consensus to take action. Such public concern not only generated spending reductions in the closing years of Vietnam, but also after the Reagan era Cold War buildup of the early 1980s.

A long-war in particular will be more susceptible to variations in spending levels and emphasis over time, especially if it is not commonly viewed as a dire matter of national survival. The President's priorities and economic views will likely hold the most influential sway over how a conflict will be resourced, but Congress, holding the power of the purse, can have a tremendous impact, especially if the thoughts of its members differ from those of the Chief Executive. It is important for mid-level policy and resource planners to recognize the preconceived ideas and vested interests of senior leadership will potentially impact the willingness of the American democracy to fund a war, especially a long-term one.

RESOURCING CONSIDERATION # 9

Early in war planning there will likely be concern over airing cost of war estimates in public. The close-hold nature of revealing costs may preclude application of appropriate resources and a conflict may start short of the funds required.

Reasons for keeping cost of war estimates closely held are varied. For example, early in Korea, President Truman held back on estimates and supplemental requests for two main reasons: to avoid early strains on the economy, and due to potential impacts on the 1950 mid-term congressional elections. President Johnson kept Vietnam war cost estimates artificially low and under-resourced until he had the bulk of his Great Society legislation enacted. In the GWOT, early Operation Iraqi Freedom planning did not include significant resources for so-called Phase IV operations, or the postconflict stability activities. Different reasoning can be attributed for this, however, subsequently; some government officials assumed away concern over resources when Deputy Secretary of Defense Wolfowitz asserted Iraqi oil revenues would self-finance a large measure of reconstruction activities. Without a perceived need for funding, there was no imperative to advance plan and put in place early other assets that would have probably established a better postconflict environment than the one faced today in Iraq. Little can be done to change the fact that political factors will influence how a President decides to fund a war. For conflicts perceived as wars of choice, there will be a greater tendency to downplay the early cost estimates—which may unfortunately lead to increased expenses as the war progresses.

RESOURCING CONSIDERATION # 10

In election years, timing matters more than ever.

Clausewitz said, "war is politics by other means," and one should rightfully expect politics—including domestic politics—to influence war, and by extension, war financing and budgeting. If the conflict is viewed as one of choice rather than one of necessity, or if the threat is not deemed immediate, funding issues will likely receive severe scrutiny, especially in election years. Yet domestic political concerns will have some degree of impact on funding in any type of war. President Truman delayed a much needed second supplemental for Korea in FY51 until the November 1950 mid-term election was over. Hoping to be elected in his own right, President Johnson did all he could to hide planned and growing costs of Vietnam escalation until after the 1964 election and passage of his Great Society programs. He further obscured war costs in the face of growing unpopularity surrounding Vietnam and rising inflation at home in the run-up to the 1966 mid-term election. Recently, the timing of the FY2004 supplemental appropriation for the Global War on Terror was at least partially affected by the 2004 presidential election schedule, which had implications for funding shortfalls experienced later that fiscal year.

Policymakers and resource planners should probably assume an approaching election year will cause deviation from planned or ideal fiscal schedules, especially if using supplemental appropriations as the main budgeting vehicle. The rule of experience suggests politicians prefer to avoid serious debates over war financing and budgeting as an election approaches. If funding decisions will likely come too late because they follow an election, or be forced to occur much earlier in advance of an election, plans should be made and implemented early to ensure war efforts have adequate resources to carry through these timing anomalies. Reductions, and/or deferrals of other requirements, may result. Such effects will often cause cost growth in remaining portions of the program and budget, and war-spending requests should account in advance for these second-order impacts.

RESOURCING CONSIDERATION # 11

Expect significant congressional "activism" from the start.

Congress' Constitutional power to appropriate funds, declare war, and sustain and regulate the armed forces has always made it active in questions of military funding. The national security environment created in the aftermath of Vietnam and Iran/Contra has only heightened the congressional oversight of military spending, especially during conflict. Examining legislation from the three conflicts revealed a growing trend toward more reporting requirements, prior approval requests for activities and fund transfers, and other similar oversight and control mechanisms.

In Korea, much of the authority granted to the President was simply that, and little to no reporting and follow-on permissions were required by Congress. Vietnam began in much the same fashion, but as the war dragged on and support declined, more and more requirements were levied to answer to Congress. Of course, Congress ultimately used restrictive appropriations first to limit, then outright cut off, U.S. military operations in Southeast Asia. From the start, the GWOT has had significantly more reporting requirements, and money reprogramming authority requiring prior congressional approval, than either Korea or Vietnam. Policy and resource planners need to recognize early on that a free hand in spending money is not likely and significant time and energy must support congressional demands for information. Failure to provide timely, quality information will usually spark further frustration, requirements for even more reporting, and restrictions.

RESOURCING CONSIDERATION # 12

Tension and suspicion often surround war-spending requests.

It has been said, money is the root of all evil. Second probably only to the concern over the cost in lives, the tension over control and use of funding for war is perhaps one of the most visceral ways tension can be driven into the three elements of Clausewitz's trinity that must be kept in balance; the government and its rationality, the military and its creativity, and the people and their passions. The cases examined here have highlighted four different manifestations of this tension along several pathways inside the trinity. First is the difference of opinion between the military and civilian authorities in government. In the early stages of both Korea and Vietnam, military estimates of costs required to conduct the wars were overruled by civilian officials in both the Pentagon and the White House. In Vietnam, this tension persisted through much, if not all, of the conflict. Military resource requests were cut back dramatically for a variety of financial and political concerns. This is reflected by the number (1) on Figure 6.6. The next two examples come from the part of the trinity represented by the government and rationality. The first of these is manifested by tension and suspicion within the Executive Branch alone. GWOT resourcing over the past several years has seen a sharp contrast between the Pentagon's military and civilian leadership on one side and the White House Office of Management and Budget (OMB) on the other. As the watchdog for overall federal spending, OMB has routinely attempted to limit spending for the GWOT. Several wartime functions had funding significantly reduced or delayed, creating tension between line agencies trying to complete wartime missions and OMB trying to limit spending. Part of the genesis for this concern, which can also develop between Congress and the Executive Branch, is that the military will try and push through nonessential items in a war appropriation measure that it could not get through the regular appropriation

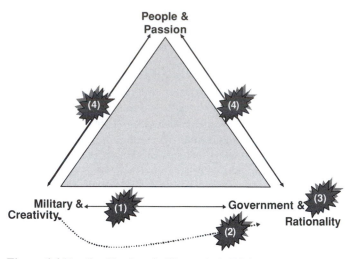

Figure 6.6 Funding Tensions in Clausewitz's Trinity

process. This division within government and rational guidance is represented by number (2). The second point of conflict within government is represented by number (3), and illustrates the more traditional tension over funding between the Executive and Legislative Branches. This tension has manifested itself in different ways in every American conflict, with the most dramatic of these disconnects being Vietnam, when Congress forced the end of American involvement by cutting off appropriations. Additional tensions, represented by number (4), arise when confidence gaps occur between the American people and the government and/or the military, which can undercut the public's passion for the war effort. This tension was also most clearly evident in the Vietnam experience, but also manifest in the latter stages of the Korean War, and has grown regarding Iraq since the President's declaration in May 2003 that major combat operations had ended.

These tensions can be overcome or mitigated by early, and frequent, engagement between the actors involved. In the government, this dialogue needs to be led by senior political appointees and elected officials. The devil is in the details and too often details are left to, and get decided by, staff level organizations rather than senior officials. There would likely be great profit (figurative and literal) if the principal officials throughout the Executive and Legislative Branches could meet and agree early on principles for funding extended conflict. Informal agreements, established early, as to what will be considered appropriate for inclusion as war costs and how funding mechanisms will be structured for them could eliminate some of the tensions described above. Having such informal agreements assumes, of course, a general consensus on two questions: that the conflict is necessary, and broad concurrence exists on its conduct and goals. Without that, Clausewitz suggests, one should return to the beginning to reevaluate "since war is not an act of senseless passion but is controlled by its political object, the value of this object must determine the sacrifices to be made for it in *magnitude* and also in *duration*."[10] Any extended conflict without this broad understanding seems doomed to failure beyond just the resourcing needs.

Conclusion

A fundamental conclusion drawn from the conflicts examined is that the direct costs of war are higher than usually attributed in documentation. That fact is true even without including the costs of second order effects—making a war's ultimate bill higher still. Chapter Six offered general insights in considering options during extended periods of "hot" conflict. The remainder of this conclusion will highlight some issues surrounding resourcing the "long-war" concept as it applies to a general, decades-long sustained effort in the GWOT, analogous in many respects to the sustained 40- to 50-year Cold War effort. The term "long-war" is widely discussed in the United States today (even Usama Bin Laden has reportedly used the phrase), although little consensus has developed on how to translate this idea into useful ends, ways, and means. Funding the long-war is but one aspect of it that must be clarified, but that will remain a fundamental challenge until the war's overarching strategic framework is agreed upon by a majority of American citizens and their leaders. Yet in examining the Cold War and its periods of "hot" conflict, some funding trends are evident for reference.

Figure 7.1 shows how national defense budget outlays during the GWOT compares with periods of "hot" conflict in the Cold War, or heightened tensions as represented by the Reagan-era defense buildup. World War II is also depicted as a point of reference as a case of total war mobilization. Each period is depicted with its actual years of combat, plus one year before and two years after reflecting the transition years. As a percentage of national wealth, GWOT costs have hardly fluctuated (increased only 1 percent) from their level the year prior to the conflict (2000), and compared with other periods of conflict, are significantly less. More telling is Figure 7.2 that essentially examines all the remaining years in the Cold War not covered by Figure 7.1—essentially the "gap" years of relative peace,

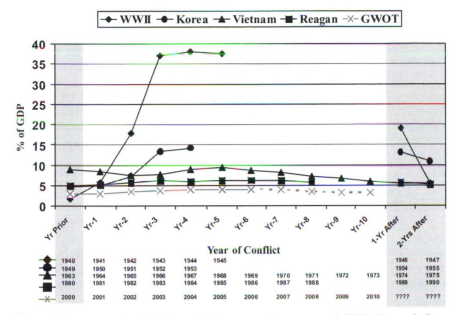

Figure 7.1 Total National Defense Outlays as a Percentage of GDP Years of Conflict/Heightened Tension

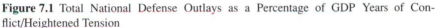

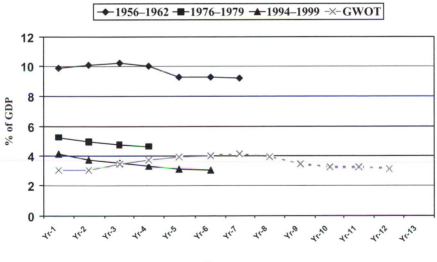

Figure 7.2 Total National Defense Outlays as a Percentage of GDP "Gap" Years Between Conflict/Heightened Tension

when no extended "hot" conflicts occurred. GWOT's hot conflicts, overall level of effort, and all other defense spending combined, only exceed the major defense drawdown of the 1990s by a small (less than half percent) margin; all other periods of peace in the Cold War spent considerably more on defense than the costs of the GWOT today. These figures suggest that the nation has the wealth for greater commitment to the long-war effort if it so chooses. However, two major challenges confront the United States in potentially increasing GWOT spending for the future: a concurrence of fiscal events leading to a potentially unique demand on resources, and a conceptual change in how Americans think about their security needs.

FISCAL ENVIRONMENT

Compared to preceding Cold War periods, the major difference—and danger—is the unique combination of fiscal factors on the horizon. The first collective set of challenges is in the security arena. The demand for security spending in the near future will include: the rising regular DoD budget to support recapitalization and transformation of the force, the significant continued costs of operations in Iraq and Afghanistan, and looming challenges on the homeland security front, all of which will require large sums of money.

The second set of challenges stems from demographic changes and entitlement spending growth triggered by baby-boomer retirement—the first year of which, 2011, is now inside DoD's 6-year fiscal planning window. Growth in entitlement spending for programs like Social Security, Medicare, Medicaid, and so forth will explode in the coming decades. Entitlement programs such as Social Security & Medicare have steadily grown as a share of the budget and GDP, while spending for defense has been on a slow but steady decline since the Korean War. The demand for increased entitlements will quickly outstrip projected national resources to pay for these benefits without some type of major reform or increased revenues. While these challenges have grown, the recent trend has been to suppress spending in other discretionary programs, but with funding growth at or below the rate of inflation in many domestic accounts, eventually pressure may be brought to bear to increase funding in those accounts as well, creating yet another demand for money. Finally, major challenges are the deficit and ever-widening current account and trade imbalances, which have seen the developed world fund much of the U.S. debt. Facing budget pressures of their own, and a U.S. dollar in continuing decline, foreign investors may begin to reduce future bond and treasury bill investment, which could in turn trigger a run on the dollar and severe global economic contractions. Many fiscal challenges face the U.S. in the strategic planning environment for the GWOT that lies ahead. In addition, episodic events like Hurricane Katrina and oil price spikes create further funding demands.

GWOT CONCEPTUAL CHALLENGE

Another fundamental challenge facing the GWOT is conceptual. Every American born between 1920 and 1980—three generations—either spent their entire adult experience, or came to maturation, within the Cold War security framework. For human nature, any significant change is always hard, even more so in an uncertain environment and competitive interest-driven democracy, so significant or radical changes that may be required for the concept of "national security" in the GWOT are difficult.

In the old Cold War paradigm, military planners had to balance the needs of today (maintaining personnel and equipment for current operations) against the needs of tomorrow (research and development, investment, and maintaining attractive career options for increasingly talented and highly trained personnel). While the character and conduct of war, and forces required to fight it, evolved, the basic trends were slow and evolutionary. As the United States fought the Korean and Vietnam Wars, much that was developed and produced in these experiences translated to other Cold War security challenges.

If many of the presumptions regarding what is required to fight successfully in the long-term GWOT are true, and there is still the need to be prepared for more conventional types of fighting, then the United States must prepare for two mutually supporting, but very different, sets of capabilities. In addition to managing the "old paradigm" force management balance, now entirely new requirements must be added. Recently highlighted examples of the capabilities essential for success in the GWOT are: foreign aid and development, information programs, language capability and cultural awareness, greater numbers of special forces, intelligence reform/new capabilities, more homeland security initiatives, a professional reconstruction corps for overseas work, and a better interagency process. If balancing needs was difficult in the Cold War, in the new environment, balancing them—and managing risk—will prove considerably more difficult.

SUMMARY

Every war has its own unique conditions. For better or for worse, war serves as catalyst for many changes, including funding and economic challenges, with fiscal impacts that resonate far beyond the fighting. Korea began in a time of readjustment from total war, international uncertainty, and a desire to focus on domestic concerns. Aside from the direct costs of the war, the conflict instigated an end to the long-running dispute of monetary policy between the Federal Reserve and Treasury Department that in turn created the fundamental conditions for Fed operations today. The war reoriented the economy for sustained Cold War military production, which contributed to the demographic and wealth shifts in the southern and western parts of the country as the new military-industrial complex's infrastructure was established. In the military realm, it fostered a bias favoring technology, especially air and sea power, the essence of defense transformation in the 1950s. The costs associated with heavy ground involvement in Korea provided further impetus for the defense policies that immediately followed the war, that is, President Eisenhower's New Look Strategy.

The gradual involvement in Vietnam spanned a much longer period of time. The heightened period of escalation was overlaid on an aggressive domestic agenda that competed for resources. The combined higher spending drove inflation that contributed to the U.S. balance of payments crisis, end of fixed monetary exchange rates, removal of the United States from the gold standard, and the ultimate death of the Bretton Woods system and its arrangement of international monetary management dating back to World War II. It also redefined and increased the Legislative-Executive tension regarding war powers and the funding support for these relationships—a tension level that remains today. Both conflicts left a legacy of debts and veterans payments that carried forward into the twenty-first century.

It is still too soon for any historical judgments on the GWOT. Perhaps, if and when Americans perceive the threats posed in the GWOT to be truly matters of national survival, some of the tough funding decisions described above will develop a consensus for action. One example is entitlement spending, an area in need of reform regardless of any other external factors—policymakers know it, and even the public has a general awareness of the problems posed by future entitlement spending levels. However, as is often said, entitlements are the third rail in politics—the electrified one—touch it and you are dead. If a greater threat is perceived, maybe entitlements can be touched. Even a modest decrease in entitlement outlays resulting from reforms would make significant increases in funding available to sustain or improve GWOT funding for activities like homeland defense and international aid and assistance. Other issues, like the current levels of annual budget deficits, could be addressed without raising taxes. Today, these developments are unlikely, but if the GWOT becomes the great imperative in the public conscience, it could become the "forcing function" to enable implementation of funding to support the strategy ultimately adopted to prosecute this war.

In that sense, it is "back to the future," and the United States seems figuratively stuck circa late 1940s. Back then, the atomic explosions at Hiroshima and Nagasaki marked the end of World War II and ushered in a new era of national security challenges. While international security was always a concern, the public's priorities were primarily focused on domestic issues. Tax cuts were enacted and the prospects for military funding were bleak. No consensus had formed on how best to bring all the elements of national power and strategic focus cohesively together to produce containment—the 1950 outbreak of war in Korea was required to do that. Today, looking back, 9/11 not only exploded airplanes and buildings, it also exploded some, if not all, of the old notions of Cold War security frameworks and ushered in an era of new security challenges. Today, the fundamental pieces of a strategy to confront these challenges are widely discussed and debated, but no nationwide consensus has developed. Tax cuts are in place and helping spur the economy, but there is concern over rising energy prices, deficits, and demographic development of the looming fiscal crunch from the baby-boom generation's retirement. How all of these issues will fiscally balance, with the likely added demands of a long-war, remain to be seen. However, if 9/11 clarified the end of the Cold War, one must wonder what will be this generation's equivalent of Korea that forges a new funding consensus for another long-term American strategy.

Notes

Chapter 1

1. Extended conflict or war defined herein as conflict with duration of greater than one year. References to the "long-war" are analogous to an overall conflict like the Cold War that persists for decades. In these terms, Korea, Vietnam, Iraq, and Afghanistan would all be considered extended conflicts and the Cold War and the GWOT would be characterized as long-wars.

Chapter 2

1. Russell F. Weigley, *The American Way of War* (Bloomington: Indiana University Press, 1973), xix–xxii.

2. A.C. Pigou, *The Political Economy of War* (New York: The Macmillan Company, 1939), 29–30.

3. Ibid.

4. Supply-side economic advocates might argue that revenues can be raised by cutting taxes (the Laffer Curve effect); however, this author knows of no historical periods of U.S. conflict where taxes were cut and the result was significantly increased revenues that were enough to pay for the conflict or prevent increased deficit spending.

5. Claudia D. Goldin, "War," in *Encyclopedia of American Economic History*, Vol. III, ed. Glenn Porter (New York: Charles Scribner's Sons, 1980), 941.

6. Marc Labonte, *Financing Issues and Economic Effects of Past American Wars*, (Washington, DC: Congressional Research Service, 2001), 2.

7. Goldin, "War," 937.

8. Ibid., 941.

9. "On" or "Off" budget, spending caps, emergency designations, and budget enforcement mechanisms have varied over time. For greater discussion of budget-related terms and definitions, see the Glossary.

Chapter 3

1. A few references, for example: $50 billion is the direct cost cited in Glen Porter, ed. *Encyclopedia of American Economic History* (New York: Charles Scribner's Sons, 1980), s.v. "War," by Claudia Goldin. The Congressional Research Service (CRS) also cites $50 billion with their data taken from the Statistical Abstract of the United States, but notes that the figure is not a precise computation, but rather illustrative of the magnitude of the costs; Stephen Daggett and Nina Serafino, *Costs of Major U.S. Wars and Recent Military Operations* (Washington, DC: Congressional Research Service, 2001), 2, CRS, RS21013. A sample of Internet sources finds $54 billion of direct costs in: The U.S. Civil War Center, *Statistical Summary America's Major Wars*, available at http://www.cwc.lsu.edu/cwc/other/stats/warcost.htm. This site also notes that pension costs ultimately tend to triple this figure. $64 billion in total costs including aid to the Republic of Korea in the estimate given by: Consulate-General of the People's Republic of China in New York, *Korean War: In the View of Cost-Effectiveness*, available at http://www/nyconsulate.prchina.org/eng/xw/t31430.htm.

2. Robert Jervis, "The Impact of the Korean War on the Cold War," *The Journal of Conflict Resolution* 24(4) (December 1980): 567.

3. Ibid., 568.

4. Department of State, Policy Planning Staff, *Résumé of World Situation (6 November 1947)*, Policy Planning Staff Files (PPS/13), in Department of State, *Foreign Relations of the United States, 1947*, vol. I (Washington, DC: GPO, 1947), 770.

5. Ibid., 771.

6. Melvyn P. Leffler, "The American Conception of National Security and the Beginnings of the Cold War, 1945–48," The American Historical Review 89(2) (April 1984): 374.

7. James Forrestal, Letter to the President, July 10, 1948, *Foreign Relations of the United States, 1948*, vol. I, Part II, 592–593 quoted in S. Nelson Drew, ed., *NSC-68 Forging the Strategy of Containment*, with analyses by Paul H. Nitze (Washington, DC: NDU Press, 1994), 23.

8. Jervis, "The Impact of the Korean War on the Cold War," 565.

9. Gabriel Kolko, *Century of War* (New York: The New Press, 1994), 397.

10. Leffler, "The American Conception of National Security and the Beginnings of the Cold War, 1945–48," 376.

11. Jervis, "The Impact of the Korean War on the Cold War," 568.

12. John Lewis Gaddis, *Strategies of Containment* (Oxford: Oxford University Press, 1982), 93–94.

13. Jervis, "The Impact of the Korean War on the Cold War," 568.

14. Leffler, "The American Conception of National Security and the Beginnings of the Cold War, 1945–48," 378. Italics added.

15. Mildred Strunk, "The Quarter's Polls," *The Public Opinion Quarterly* 13(4) (Winter 1949–1950): 182, 192.

16. Mildred Strunk, "The Quarter's Polls," *The Public Opinion Quarterly* 14(3) (Autumn 1950): 596. The poll cited was taken by George Gallup and the American Institute of Public Opinion (AIPO) on March 24, 1950.

17. Mildred Strunk, "The Quarter's Polls," 721. The poll cited was taken by George Gallup and the American Institute of Public Opinion (AIPO) on September 18, 1949.

18. Ibid., 721–722.

19. Ibid., 725. The poll cited was taken by George Gallup and the American Institute of Public Opinion (AIPO) on September 7, 1949.

20. David McCullough, *Truman* (New York: Simon and Schuster, 1992), 785.

21. Congressional Quarterly, *Congress and the Nation, Vol. 1, 1945–1964* (Washington DC: Congressional Quarterly, 1965), 342.

22. Kenyon E. Poole, "Full Employment, Wage Flexibility, and Inflation," *The American Economic Review* 45(2) (May 1955): 586.

23. Mildred Strunk, "The Quarter's Polls," 603.

24. In addition to the specific polls previously cited, to support this conclusion, the author reviewed over 160 different polling questions taken from the Spring of 1949 to the Summer of 1950 (essentially the year prior to the outbreak of the Korean War) on defense issues, foreign affairs focused on communism, the Far East and Russia, and the domestic economy. The views expressed herein reflect the overall consensus and trends in those poll results.

25. George Marshall, *Semiannual Report of the Secretary of Defense, 1 January 1951 to 30 June 1951* (Washington DC: GPO, 1951), 10.

26. See Glossary for definition of TOA and other budget-related terms.

27. Doris Condit, *The Test of War 1950–1953*, History of the Office of the Secretary of Defense, ed. Alfred Goldberg, vol. II (Washington DC: GPO, 1988), 225.

28. Congress, House, Committee on Appropriations, Subcommittee on Defense, *The Supplemental Appropriation Bill for 1951*, 81st Cong., 2nd sess., July 27, 1950, 26–27.

29. Ibid., 106.

30. Ibid., 109.

31. Ibid., 140.

32. Ibid., 222.

33. Condit, *The Test of War 1950–1953*, 227.

34. An example: supplemental funds were dedicated to the Atomic Energy Commission (AEC) to support atomic weapon development, indirectly requiring funds also for the Tennessee Valley Authority (TVA) to support the AEC power requirements of this atomic work.

35. Clayton Knowles, "Republicans Lead in Pennsylvania," *New York Times*, October 15, 1950, 75.

36. James Reston, "Defamation Marks Violent Campaign," *New York Times*, October 31, 1950, 22.

37. "Hanley Says Foes Cause Inflation," *New York Times*, October 19, 1950, 35.

38. Condit, *The Test of War 1950–1953*, 234.

39. The Revenue Act of 1950, (PL 81-814) signed September 23, 1950, "repealed the personal income tax cuts of 1945 and 1948, returning rates to their 1945 level effective Oct. 1; fixed the combined corporate rate at 42 percent of profits over $25,000 in 1950 and at 45 percent in 1951; and accelerated payment of corporate taxes over a 5-year span. The law also reinstated a World War II provision for accelerated depreciation of emergency facilities; revised loss carry-over provisions to limit carry-backs to 1 year and extended carry-forwards to 5 years; denied capital gains treatment to stockholders of collapsible corporations; and made the unrelated business income of tax-exempt organizations subject to tax." It also imposed a 10 percent excise tax on television sets and home freezers (attempting to help the electronics and steel industries shift emphasis to defense production)

and created tax exemptions for military members serving in combat zones. Congressional Quarterly, *Congress and the Nation* 410.

40. Congress, House, Committee on Appropriations, Subcommittee on National Defense, *Second Supplemental Appropriation Bill for 1951*, 81st Cong., 2nd sess., December 1, 1950, 15.

41. Ibid., 17.

42. Ibid., 21.

43. Congress, House, Committee on Appropriations, Subcommittee on National Defense, *Second Supplemental Appropriation Bill for 1951*, 81st Cong., 2nd sess., December 4, 1950, 53.

44. Ibid., 54.

45. Ibid., 55

46. Ibid., 18.

47. Ibid., 58–59.

48. Unrelated costs fell from approximately 2 percent to fewer than 1 percent of the second supplemental and therefore do not appear on the second pie chart.

49. Both Foreign Aid and Unrelated costs fell below 1 percent of the second supplemental and therefore do not appear on the second pie chart.

50. Ibid., 27.

51. Congress, *The Defense Production Act of 1950*, 81st Cong., 2nd sess., H.R. 9176, PL 81-774, (September 8, 1950), various.

52. Ibid., 6.

53. Congress, House, Committee on Appropriations, *Third Supplemental Appropriation Bill, 1951*, Report to accompany H.R. 3587, 82nd Cong., 1st sess., 1951, Report No. 298, 35.

54. Condit, *The Test of War 1950–1953*, 241.

55. George Marshall, Semiannual Report of the Secretary of Defense, 1 July 1950 to 31 December 1950 (Washington DC: GPO, 1951), 4.

56. Documented accounts of inflation by the Services ranged from 5–8 percent on the low end, to the 30–40 percent range for selected goods such as military radio sets and other electronic equipment.

57. Deficiency spending is when obligations for goods and services are made without having the congressionally approved authority or appropriations to cover the costs.

58. Congress, Senate, Committee on Appropriations, *Fourth Supplemental Appropriation Bill, 1951*, Report to accompany H.R. 3842, 82nd Cong., 1st sess., 1951, Report No. 329, 5.

59. Ibid.

60. Congress, Senate, Committee on Appropriations, Subcommittee of the Department of Defense, *Department of Defense Appropriations for 1953*, 82nd Cong., 2nd sess., February 4, 1952, 26–27.

61. Insert for the Congressional Record, dated March 28, 1952, prepared by Assistant Secretary of Defense (Comptroller) W.J. McNeil for the House hearing: Congress, House, Committee on Appropriations, Subcommittee for the Department of Defense, *Department of Defense and Related Independent Agencies Appropriations for 1953*, 82nd Cong., 2nd sess., March 26, 1952, 33.

62. As the lead Service on the ground in Korea, the Army funded common support items like food and ammunition for use in Korea by the Marine Corps.

63. Congress, Senate, Committee on Appropriations, Subcommittee for the Department of Defense, *Department of Defense Appropriations for 1953*, 82nd Cong., 2nd sess., June 11, 1952, 891. Statement made by Karl R. Bendetsen, Under Secretary of the Army in response to questioning regarding budget planning assumptions.

64. Congress, Senate, Committee on Appropriations, Subcommittee for the Department of Defense, *Department of Defense Appropriations for 1953*, 82nd Cong., 2nd sess., April 30, 1952, 232–233.

65. Congress, *Department of Defense Appropriation Act, 1952*, 82nd Cong., 1st sess., H.R. 5054, PL 82-179, (October 18, 1951), 26–27. Congress, *Department of Defense Appropriation Act, 1953*, 82nd Cong., 2nd sess., H.R. 7391, PL 82-488, (July 10, 1952), 19.

66. The FY54 budget request was formulated in mid-to-late calendar year 1952, and submitted to Congress in early calendar year 1953. The Korean War cease-fire occurred on July 27, 1953. Ammunition was the one major item where Korean War consumption rates far exceeded peacetime requirements and it was appropriations in this category where additional funding was included in the FY54 baseline budget request. Statements made by W.J. McNeil, Assistant Secretary of Defense (Comptroller) in: Congress, House, Committee on Appropriations, Subcommittee for the Department of Defense, *Department of Defense and Related Agencies, Appropriations for 1954*, 83rd Cong., 1st sess., February 24, 1953, 48–49. Another addition was for equipping Republic of Korea Army divisions. Based on statements from Secretary of Defense Charles Wilson, the total for the two purposes included in the budget was estimated between $1.8–$2.0 billion. Congress, House, Committee on Appropriations, Subcommittee for the Department of Defense, *Department of Defense Appropriations for 1954*, 83rd Congress, 1st sess., May 19, 1953, 5–6. This amount may actual be slightly below the total included in the FY54 submit based upon Secretary of the Army, Robert Stevens claim that approximately $2.5 billion was included in the Army budget submission. Congress, Senate, Committee on Appropriations, Subcommittee for the Department of Defense, *Department of Defense Appropriations for 1954*, 83rd Cong., 1st sess., June 2, 1953, 112–113. Given that these modified budget estimates were done in a matter of days after inauguration of the new Administration, it is not surprising there is a slight difference in the estimates quoted by different officials.

67. Several examples exist where Assistant Secretary of Defense (Comptroller) W.J. McNeil in FY52 and Secretary of Defense R.A. Lovett in FY53 testified the increased force levels and corresponding troop pay would " ... go on whether Korea is in its present state, or not." The assumption was overall increased force levels were necessary to counter the communist threat regardless of the location (although generally assumed to be Europe) and duration of particular conflicts—an assumption that proved incorrect.

68. The 5-year (FY56–60) period is a reasonably steady state end strength baseline to compare against. During this period, the same Administration was in place, there were no extended periods of hot conflict, and it was post-Korea and pre-Vietnam in terms of personnel demobilization and mobilization respectively.

69. The explanation of excess end strength and costing was provided in the proceeding section on Other Costs. It is widely accepted that the tax increases sought by President Truman to pay for the Korean War covered the full cost of the war. Examining the amounts that tax revenues increased from FY50 through FY53, considering the actual direct, mixed, and indirect war costs, and the FY52–53 federal budget deficits, it is evident taxes did not

fully pay for the war. Using the fair share of national defense and veterans spending applied to the same year's federal budget deficits, an estimate was made for the assumed portion of the war financed through deficits. Interest calculations were done using the reported interest rates and percentage composition of interest bearing government securities issued in FY52–53. It was assumed that all of these securities were held to their full maturity dates. The VA costs shown are strictly the calculated payments for compensation and pensions attributable to Korean War veterans and do not include other VA health care and benefit costs they might have generated.

70. Rough approximation for appropriated funds for the war breaks down with 50 percent for investment, 30 percent for manpower, and 20 percent for operations and maintenance. These figures do not include the added costs shown above for long-term veterans costs and calculated excess manpower—if those are included, manpower funding becomes the dominant share of the war appropriations.

71. Aaron L. Friedberg, *In the Shadow of the Garrison State* (Princeton: Princeton University Press, 2000), 115.

72. U.S. President, *Public Papers of the Presidents of the United States* (Washington, DC: Office of the Federal Register, National Archives and Records Service, 1960), Dwight D. Eisenhower, 1960, 1305–1040.

Chapter 4

1. Cost estimates developed from a variety of sources. DoD costs of military advisors developed from Murray L. Weidenbaum, *Economic Impact of the Vietnam War* (Washington, DC: Georgetown University Center for Strategic Studies, 1967), 4.; Anthony S. Campagna, *The Economic Consequences of the Vietnam War* (New York: Praeger, 1991), 3–5; Foreign aid estimates developed from Leonard B. Taylor, *Financial Management of the Vietnam Conflict 1962–1972* (Washington, DC: Department of the Army, 1974), 23; and U.S. Department of State, *American Foreign Policy Documents 1950–1955* (Washington, DC: GPO, 1956), various.

2. Michael Beschloss, *Reaching for Glory Lyndon Johnson's Secret White House Tapes, 1964–1965* (New York: Touchstone Books, 2001), 310.

3. Ibid., 311–312.

4. H.R. McMaster, *Dereliction of Duty Lyndon Johnson, Robert McNamara, The Joint Chiefs of Staff, and the Lies That Led to Vietnam* (New York: Harper Collins Publishers, 1997), 308–321. This protection of the Great Society Programs at the expense of honesty surrounding the Vietnam cost estimates in the Spring and Summer of 1965 is noted by McMaster from sources like Secretary of Defense Robert McNamara, Presidential aide Jack Valenti, Commandant of the Marine Corps General Wallace Greene, and Deputy Secretary of Defense Cyrus Vance.

5. Ibid., 312–313.

6. Some of the most vocal Republicans pushing for the Administration to reveal requirements and request specific funds for Vietnam were: Reps. Gerald Ford of Michigan, Melvin Laird of Wisconsin, Glenard Lipscomb of California, William Minshall of Ohio, and Senator Everett Dirksen of Illinois.

7. Congress, Senate, Committee on Appropriations, Subcommittee on Department of Defense, *Department of Defense Appropriations for Fiscal Year 1966*, 89th Cong., 1st sess., August 4, 1965, 761.

8. Charles L. Schultze, Director of the Bureau of the Budget Memo to President Lyndon B. Johnson as submitted to Congress and incorporated in the record of: Congress, Senate, Committee on Appropriations, Subcommittee on Department of Defense, *Department of Defense Appropriations for Fiscal Year 1966*, 89th Cong., 1st sess., August 4, 1965, 733.

9. The 23,500 troop level cited by Secretary McNamara is taken from: Congress, Senate, Committee on Armed Services and Committee on Appropriations, Subcommittee on Department of Defense, *Military Authorizations and Defense Appropriations for Fiscal Year 1966*, 89th Cong., 1st sess., February 24, 1965, 16. The 75,000 troop level cited by Secretary McNamara is taken from: Congress, Senate, Committee on Appropriations, Subcommittee on Department of Defense, *Department of Defense Appropriations for Fiscal Year 1966*, 89th Cong., 1st sess., August 4, 1965, 767.

10. The 125,000 troop level cited by Secretary McNamara is taken from: Congress, Senate, Committee on Appropriations, Subcommittee on Department of Defense, *Department of Defense Appropriations for Fiscal Year 1966*, 89th Cong., 1st sess., August 4, 1965, 767. The $1.3 billion cost estimate derived by author from the previous discussion in the *Vietnam Introduction* of U.S. military advisor cost in Vietnam during this period estimated at $25,000 per soldier per year.

11. Congress, Senate, Committee on Appropriations, Subcommittee on Department of Defense, *Department of Defense Appropriations for Fiscal Year 1966*, 89th Cong., 1st sess., August 4, 1965, 767–768.

12. Carl von Clausewitz, *On War*, trans. Michael Howard and Peter Paret (Princeton: Princeton University Press, 1976), 88.

13. McMaster, 316. Revelation of this conversation and the $1 billion was in a Memorandum for the Record written by General Greene documenting his evening meeting with Secretary Nitze on July 23, 1965.

14. Ibid.

15. Congress, Senate, Committee on Armed Services and Committee on Appropriations, Subcommittee on Department of Defense, *Military Authorizations and Defense Appropriations for Fiscal Year 1967*, 89th Cong., 2nd sess., February 23, 1966, 6.

16. Ibid., 10.

17. Testimony by Major General F.J. Chesarek, Assistant Deputy Chief of Staff for Logistics (Programs) to: Congress, House, Committee on Appropriations, Subcommittee on Department of Defense, *Department of Defense Appropriations for 1966, Part 4 Procurement*, 89th Cong., 1st sess., March 22, 1965, 155–156. Also in testimony by Major General F.J. Chesarek, Assistant Deputy Chief of Staff for Logistics (Programs) to: Congress, Senate, Committee on Appropriations, Subcommittee on Department of Defense, *Department of Defense Appropriations, 1966*, 89th Cong, 1st sess., July 14, 1965, 122. General Chesarek repeatedly testified that Army budget development included requirements with assumed monthly loss rates of various aircraft in Vietnam based upon available data from experience in the field and levels of activity at the time. Army calculations did not incorporate increased loss rates resulting from later escalation of U.S. efforts in Vietnam, but even the level of budget planning General Chesarek indicated was counter to Secretary McNamara's congressional testimony a year later.

18. Congress, Senate, Committee on Armed Services and Committee on Appropriations, Subcommittee on Department of Defense, *Military Authorizations and Defense Appropriations for Fiscal Year 1967*, 89th Cong., 2nd sess., February 23, 1966, 12–13.

19. Congress, Senate, *Armed Forces Supplemental Appropriation Authorization, 1967*, 90th Cong., 1st sess., S. 665, PL90-5, March 16, 1967, 80 STAT 275, Sec. 401.

20. Congress, Senate, Committee on Armed Services and Committee on Appropriations, Subcommittee on Department of Defense, *Military Authorizations and Defense Appropriations for Fiscal Year 1968*, 90th Cong., 1st sess., January 26, 1967, 265.

21. Leonard B. Taylor, *Financial Management of the Vietnam Conflict 1962–1972* (Washington, DC: GPO, 1974), 28–29.

22. Congress, Senate, Committee on Armed Services and Committee on Appropriations, Subcommittee on Department of Defense, *Supplemental Defense Appropriations and Authorizations for Fiscal Year 1967*, 90th Cong., 1st sess., January 23, 1967, 10.

23. Ibid.

24. Ibid., 18–19.

25. Ibid., 11.

26. President, The Budget Message, "The President's Message to the Congress Transmitting the Budget for Fiscal Year 1967," *Weekly Compilation of Presidential Documents* 2(4) (January 24, 1966): 82–94; President, The Budget Message, "The President's Message to the Congress Transmitting the Budget for Fiscal Year 1968," *Weekly Compilation of Presidential Documents* 3(4) (January 24, 1967): 84–97.

27. President, The Budget Message, "The President's Message to the Congress Transmitting the Budget for Fiscal Year 1969," *Weekly Compilation of Presidential Documents* 4(5) (January 29, 1968): 148–164.

28. President, The Budget Message, "The President's Message to the Congress Transmitting the Budget for Fiscal Year 1970," *Weekly Compilation of Presidential Documents* 5(3) (January 20, 1969): 70–90.

29. Congress, Senate, Committee on Appropriations, Subcommittee on Department of Defense, *Department of Defense Appropriations for Fiscal Year 1969*, 90th Cong., 2nd sess., May 7, 1968, 263.

30. Congress, Senate, Committee on Appropriations, Subcommittee on Department of Defense, *Department of Defense Appropriations for Fiscal Year 1969*, 90th Cong., 2nd sess., May 10, 1968, 772.

31. Congress, Senate, Committee on Appropriations, Subcommittee on Department of Defense, *Department of Defense Appropriations for Fiscal Year 1970*, 91st Cong., 1st sess., December 9, 1969, 58.

32. Congress, Senate, Committee on Appropriations, Subcommittee on Department of Defense, *Department of Defense Appropriations for Fiscal Year 1970*, 91st Cong., 1st sess., December 9, 1969, 65.

33. Ibid., 63

34. Robert P. Mayo, Director of the Bureau of the Budget memorandum included in the congressional record: Congress, Senate, Committee on Appropriations, Subcommittee on Department of Defense, *Department of Defense Appropriations for Fiscal Year 1970*, 91st Cong., 1st sess., June 10, 1969, 154.

35. Congress, House, *Second Supplemental Appropriations Act, 1970*, 91st Cong., 2nd sess., H.R. 17399, PL91-305, July 6, 1970, 84 STAT 376-407.

36. Congress, Senate, Committee on Appropriations, Subcommittee on Department of Defense, *Department of Defense Appropriations for Fiscal Year 1970*, 91st Cong., 1st sess., June 12, 1969, 170–171.

37. Congress, Senate, Committee on Appropriations, Subcommittee on Department of Defense, *Department of Defense Appropriations for Fiscal Year 1971*, 91st Cong., 2nd sess., April 16, 1970, 594–603.

38. Congress, House, *Continuing Appropriations, 1974*, 93rd Cong., 1st sess., H.J. Res. 636, PL93-52, July 1, 1973, 87 STAT 134.

Chapter 5

1. George W. Bush, Address to a Joint Session of Congress, U.S. Capitol, Washington, DC, September 20, 2001.

2. Institute for Defense Analysis, Contingency Operations Support Tool (COST) Manual, (Alexandria: IDA, 2004).

3. More detailed notes from the COST Manual: COST contains default cost factors and management factors, along with a user-supplied description of the contingency, to estimate the cost of an operation. COST uses a specific Cost Breakdown Structure (CBS) to estimate costs. The CBS used by the COST model is the same structure used by the military services and defense agencies for reporting actual costs of contingency operations to the Defense Finance and Accounting Service (DFAS).
COST is preloaded with standard cost and management factors that are used in equations to produce the estimates. Users can review and change any of the factors used for a calculation. All COST calculations produce incremental costs; costs that are over and above budgeted peacetime operation costs.
COST incorporates appropriate algorithms to compute the cost of each element in the cost breakdown structure. Users can review these algorithms at any time to verify the calculations or to determine which factors were used to produce an estimate. Users can change the factors and recalculate an estimate to see the effect of the change.
COST needs a minimum amount of information from the user to develop a preliminary or planning estimate. Once that information is entered, a baseline cost estimate can be calculated. It is easy to adjust the estimate as plans for and assumptions about the operation become better known.

4. Congress, House, 2001 *Emergency Supplemental Appropriations Act for Recovery from and Response to Terrorist Attacks on the United States*, 107th Cong., 1st sess., H.R. 2888, PL107-38, 18 September 2001, 115 STAT. 220.

5. Amy Belasco and Larry Nowles, *Combating Terrorism: 2001 Congressional Debate on Emergency Supplemental Allocations*, CRS RL31187 (Washington, DC: GPO, 2002), 2.

6. Ibid., 5–8. The categories listed were defined by CRS as: *Defense*—paying for military operations in Afghanistan and related areas, activating reservists for base security as well as wartime responsibilities, enlarging munitions stockpiles and more reconnaissance and surveillance, repair, and renovation of the Pentagon, and support for nations working with the United States to combat terrorism worldwide. *Bioterrorism*—countering potential biological, disease, and chemical threats to civilian populations. *Humanitarian Assistance*—USAID operations in Afghanistan, food and refugee relief in Central Asia, together with *International Security Assistance*—Economic Support Fund (ESF) grants and financing sales of U.S. military equipment and support of counternarcotics and law enforcement activities to "front-line" states cooperating with the United States. in the war on terrorism, and peacekeeping operations in Afghanistan. *Investigation and Law Enforcement*—agency investigative and law enforcement work and initiatives following the September 11

attacks. *Preparedness*—training, technical assistance, and other activities aimed at strengthening the capacity to respond to future terrorist events. *Public Diplomacy*—enhanced U.S. broadcasts and media outreach capabilities to the people in Central and Southwest Asia. *Recovery*—debris removal, repair, replacement, or rebuilding of damaged equipment and infrastructure (including utilities and mass transit), and relocation of dislocated offices and workers (excluding Pentagon repairs). *Security of Infrastructure/Personnel*—strengthened security at critical U.S. facilities worldwide (excluding DoD facilities) and evacuation of overseas personnel. *Security of Aviation Facilities*—enhanced security at U.S. airports and on board aircraft (excluding DoD funding to station National Guard personnel at airports). *Victim Relief*—assistance to individuals, families, and businesses directly and indirectly affected by the September 11 attacks.

7. Belasco and Nowles, Combating Terrorism, 5.

8. Normally, shifting significant amounts of appropriations between accounts requires a reprogramming action, and depending upon the amount of money involved, may be at the discretion of the agency or may require notification and prior approval by Congress. When DERF was created in 1989, it was originally envisioned as a flexible account for DoD to use when responding to events like natural disasters.

9. See Appendix 1 for further explanation of the BEA.

10. Because of the late fiscal year approval, most of the funding was extended upon enactment beyond the current fiscal year.

11. Belasco and Nowles, Supplemental Appropriations for FY2002, 23.

12. Under Secretary of Defense (Comptroller), *Defense Emergency Response Fund FY2002 Execution Report*, Unpublished Briefing Papers, September 2002.

13. Congress, House, 2002 *Supplemental Appropriations Act for Further Recovery From and Response to Terrorist Attacks on the United States*, 107th Cong., 2nd sess., H.R. 4775, P.L. 107-206, August 2, 2002, Sec. 603, 116 STAT. 859.

14. See Appendix 1 for further discussion of PAY-GO rules, debt ceilings, and other budget related terminology.

15. Dov Zakheim, "Time Is Running Out On Supplemental Budget," *The Hill*, July 17, 2002.

16. FY51–52 supplementals for Korea were more if adjusted for inflation and the FY66–67 supplementals for Vietnam were comparable when adjusted for inflation.

17. Congressional Quarterly, *CQ Almanac Backgrounder: Fiscal 2003 Iraq Supplemental Appropriations*, Budget Tracker News, (Washington, DC: Congressional Quarterly), June 2, 2004.

18. Ibid.

19. Congress, *An Act Making Emergency Wartime Supplemental Appropriations for the Fiscal Year 2003, and for Other Purposes*, 108th Cong., 1st sess., H.R. 1559, P.L. 108-11, (April 16, 2003), 117 STAT. 569. Section 1313 specifically stated: "As of October 31, 2003, all balances of funds remaining in the 'Defense Emergency Response Fund' shall be transferred to, and merged with, the 'Iraq Freedom Fund,' and shall be available for the same purposes, and under the same terms and conditions, as funds appropriated to the 'Iraq Freedom Fund' in this chapter."

20. The funds to address Iraqi oil well fires and oil infrastructure in the 2003 Supplemental were designated as the NRRRF—National Resource Risk Remediation Fund.

21. Dov Zakheim, "Transcript of Under Secretary of Defense (Comptroller) Briefing," Department of Defense, Washington, DC, April 16, 2003, available at http://www.defenselink.mil/transcripts/2003/tr20030416-0111.html.

22. See Appendix 1 for discussion of transfer authorities.

23. Dov Zakheim, Under Secretary of Defense (Comptroller), "Press Conference/Briefing," Department of Defense, Washington, DC, February 3, 2003, available at http://www/defenselink.mil/transcripts/2003/t02032003_t0203budget.html.

24. Congressional Quarterly, *CQ Almanac Backgrounder: Fiscal 2003 Iraq Supplemental Appropriations*, Budget Tracker News, (Washington, DC: Congressional Quarterly), June 2, 2004.

25. Congress, House, *Department of Defense Appropriation Act, Fiscal Year 2004*, 108th Cong., 2nd sess., H.R. 2658, P.L. 108-87, September 30, 2003, Sec. 8128. Exact amount of rescission was $3,490,000,000.

26. Office of the Chairman of the Joint Chiefs of Staff, Directorate for Force Structure, Resources and Assessments (J8), Program and Budget Analysis Division (PBAD), Unclassified Working Papers, September 9, 2003.

27. Department of Defense, Office of the Under Secretary of Defense (Comptroller), *FY 2004 Supplemental Request for Operation Iraqi Freedom (OIF), Operation Enduring Freedom (OEF), Operation Noble Eagle (ONE)* (Washington, DC: U.S. Department of Defense, 2003), 3.

28. Congress, *An Act Making Emergency Supplemental Appropriations for Defense and for the Reconstruction of Iraq and Afghanistan for the Fiscal Year Ending September 30, 2004, and for Other Purposes*, 108th Cong., 1st sess., H.R. 3289, PL 108-106, November 6, 2003, 117 STAT.

29. Seized assets were comprised of the large stashes of currency found by coalition forces throughout the country after the invasion. Vested assets were those Iraqi government assets that were frozen in various international financial institutions after the 1990 Iraqi invasion of Kuwait and subsequently released to the CPA for the benefit of Iraq and the Iraqi people.

30. Congress, *An Act Making Emergency Supplemental Appropriations for Defense and for the Reconstruction of Iraq and Afghanistan for the Fiscal Year Ending September 30, 2004, and for Other Purposes*, 108th Cong., 1st sess., H.R. 3289, PL 108-106, Title I, Chapter I, November 6, 2003, 117 STAT. 1210.

31. Ibid., Sec. 1101, 117 STAT. 1213.

32. Ibid., Sec. 1301, 117 STAT. 1221.

33. Ibid., Sec. 1107, 117 STAT. 1214

34. There were several statements to suggest Iraqi oil profits would be able to support and sustain reconstruction and a new sovereign government. From those proposing the loan structure on this argument, perhaps the most often repeated quote was that of then Deputy Defense Secretary Paul Wolfowitz, "[regarding use of oil revenues] . . . we are dealing with a country that can really finance its own reconstruction and relatively soon." Congress, House, Committee on Appropriations, Subcommittee on Defense, *FY 2004 Appropriations: Hearing before the Committee on Appropriations, Subcommittee on Defense*, 108th Cong., 1st sess., March 27, 2003.

35. The Administration proposed to allow these benefits to expire at the end of calendar year 2003 and begin paying increased Hardship Duty Pay (HDP) only to those troops directly participating inside Iraq, Afghanistan, and other specifically designated

locations. This change would have resulted in selected members who currently received the IDP/FSA increased rates to experience a reduction as of December 31, 2003.

36. DoD had a total of $440 billion available in FY04—$375 billion appropriated in the FY 2004 Appropriations Act and $65 billion appropriated in the FY 2004 Emergency Supplemental Appropriation Act—upon which to draw against for additional war costs if Congress granted the appropriate authorities.

37. Government Accountability Office, Fiscal Year 2004 Costs for the Global War on Terrorism Will Exceed Supplemental, Requiring DOD to Shift Funds from Other Uses, GAO-04-915 (Washington, DC: GPO, 2004), 3.

38. Congress, House, *Department of Defense Appropriations Act, 2005*, 108th Cong., 2nd sess., H.R. 4613, P.L. 108-287, August 5, 2004, Sec. 9001, 118 STAT. 1006.

39. The purpose of CERP is to enable military commanders to respond to urgent humanitarian relief and reconstruction requirements within their areas of responsibility by carrying out programs that will immediately assist the local populace. The program started in FY03 in Iraq using seized and vested Iraqi assets, was later expanded to include the use of U.S. appropriated funds, and the Bridge Supplemental authorized the expansion of the program for use in Afghanistan.

40. When the FY05 supplemental was submitted in February 2005, of the prior year $18.4 billion Iraqi reconstruction funds, $3 billion had been executed through disbursements and approximately $10.9 billion was obligated for various projects.

41. Congress, *An Act Making Emergency Supplemental Appropriations for Defense the Global War on Terror, and Tsunami Relief, for the Fiscal Year Ending September 30, 2005, and for Other Purposes*, 109th Cong., 1st sess., H.R. 1268, PL 109-13, May 11, 2005, Sec. 1024, 119 STAT. 252.

42. Congress, *An Act Making Appropriations for Department of Defense for the Fiscal Year Ending September 30, 2004, and for Other Purposes*, 108th Cong., 1st sess., H.R. 2658, PL 108-87, September 30, 2003, Sec. 8139, 117 STAT. 1107. Senate Amendment vote no. 286 adopted 81-15; (R) 36-15, (D) 44-0, (I) 1-0. Congress, *An Act Making Appropriations for Department of Defense for the Fiscal Year Ending September 30, 2005, and for Other Purposes*, 108th Cong., 2nd sess., H.R. 4613, PL 108-287, August 5, 2004, Sec. 8138, 118 STAT. 1002-1003. Senate Amendment vote no. 147 adopted 89-9; (R) 41-9, (D) 47-0, (I) 1-0. Congress, *An Act Making Emergency Supplemental Appropriations for Defense the Global War on Terror, and Tsunami Relief, for the Fiscal Year Ending September 30, 2005, and for Other Purposes*, 109th Cong., 1st sess., H.R. 1268, PL 109-13, May 11, 2005, Sec. 1024, 119 STAT. 252. Senate Amendment no. 464, Senate vote no. 96 adopted 61-31 (5 not presented recorded statements indicated they would have voted yes if present for 66 total votes and House motion to instruct their conferees to accept the Senate language, vote no. 133, passed 417-4.

43. Ibid., Title I., 119 STAT. 235–119 STAT. 237.

44. Ibid., Title II, Chap. 2.

45. Congressional Budget Office, *Federal Funding for Homeland Security: An Update*, (Washington, DC: GPO, 2005), 1.

46. Government Accountability Office, *Combating Terrorism: Determining and Reporting Federal Funding Data*, (Washington, DC: GPO, 2006), 4–5.

47. CBO, *Federal Funding for Homeland Security*, 2. Note: CBO analysis did not include offsetting collections from fee-funded activities (example would be increased security

fees charged for air travel); GAO analysis does include this revenue and reflects them as offsetting costs.

48. George W. Bush, "State of the Union Address," U.S. Capitol, Washington, DC, January 28, 2002.

49. Peter Pace, "Posture Statement of the Chairman of the Joint Chiefs of Staff," before Congress, Senate, Committee on Armed Services, 109th Cong., 2nd sess., February 7, 2006.

Chapter 6

1. Clausewitz, Carl von. *On War*. Translated by Michael Howard and Peter Paret. Princeton: Princeton University Press, 1976, 86.

2. Congress, House, Committee on Appropriations, Subcommittee on Department of Defense, *The Supplemental Appropriation Bill for 1951*, 81st Cong., 2nd sess., July 25, 1950, 9–10.

3. Congress, House, Committee on Appropriations, Subcommittee on Department of Defense, *Second Supplemental Appropriation Bill for 1951*, 81st Cong., 2nd sess., December 1, 1950, 16.

4. Congress, Senate, Committee on Appropriations, Subcommittee on Department of Defense, *Department of Defense Appropriations Bill, 1953*, 83th Cong., 1st sess., February 4, 1952, 27.

5. Congress, Senate, Committee on Armed Services, Committee on Appropriations, Subcommittee on Department of Defense, *Supplemental Defense Appropriations and Authorizations for Fiscal Year 1967*, 90th Cong., 1st sess., January 23, 1967, 8. Secretary McNamara was quoting his own previous testimony to the same committees from a year earlier when testifying on the FY67 baseline budget request for DoD and FY66 Supplemental request for Southeast Asia operations.

6. Congress, Senate, Committee on Armed Services, *Posture Hearing FY2006 Budget: Defense*, 109th Cong., 1st sess., February 17, 2005.

7. William Matthews, "Shadow Budget," *Armed Forces Journal* 143(9) (April 2006): 10.

8. Department of Commerce, *Statistical Abstract of the United States*, (Washington, DC: 1951–2003 series), various pages each volume.

9. James L. Clayton, "The Fiscal Cost of the Cold War to the United States: The First 25 Years, 1947–1971," *The Western Political Quarterly* 25 (September 1972): 388.

10. Clausewitz, Carl von. *On War*. Translated by Michael Howard and Peter Paret. Princeton: Princeton University Press, 1976, 92.

Glossary

302(b) Allocations: The Budget Resolution gives the Appropriations Committees their overall allocation of spending authority. The Appropriations Committees then divide that amount among the 13 subcommittees in each House that share responsibility for the various departments of the Government. These are called the 302(b) allocations.

Appropriation: The amount of funding Congress provides for a federal program to spend in a given year. Legislative language sometimes set the terms under which funds may be spent.

Authorization: Legislation that establishes or continues a federal program or agency, specifies its general goals and conduct, and usually sets a ceiling on the amount of money that can be appropriated for it. Appropriators may not exceed the amount authorized for a given program, but are under no obligation to fully or even partially fund the program.

Budget Authority (BA): Authority to enter into obligations that will result in immediate or future outlays involving federal funds.

Budget Enforcement Act (BEA): Passed in 1990, it established caps on discretionary spending in the three categories of federal spending—defense, domestic, and international. It also prohibited transfers between these categories. The Act expired in 2002.

Definitions compiled and adapted from several sources including:

(1) DoD Financial Management Regulation Volume 3, Chapter 6, available at http://72.14.207. 104/search?q=cache:kc00xzoBVGAJ:www.dod.mil/comptroller/fmr/03/03arch/03_06.pdf+ Define+dod+reprogramming+requirements&hl=en&gl=us&ct=clnk&cd=5.

(2) National Priorities Project, available at http://www.nationalpriorities.org/index.php?option= com_content&task=view&id=74&Itemid=110#c.

(3) Author-defined terms from common practice.

Capped Entitlement: An entitlement on which an overall annual funding limit is placed and funding is distributed by formula.

Cash Flow: Practice of moving funds apportioned for later in the fiscal year spending to earlier periods in order to cover costs. Usually done in the manpower and operations and maintenance accounts to pay for ongoing operations, it often entails spending funds designated for the third and fourth quarter earlier in the fiscal year.

Categorical Grant: An allocation of funds for a particular programmatic purpose.

Concurrent Budget Resolution: A budget resolution passed by both Houses of Congress but not signed by the President. The annual budget resolution presents both fiscal aggregates such as total budget authority, outlays and deficit, and a subdivision of spending by functional category for the year. May also include binding instructions on the level of savings each committee must produce (see reconciliation).

Congressional Budget Office (CBO): A legislative agency that assists Congress in the preparation of the budget and analyzes budget-related issues. CBO is responsible for estimating the budgetary effects of all spending and revenue bills.

Constant Dollars (CY$): If something is said to be in *constant dollars*, it means that it has been controlled for inflation. In other words, if a graph shows spending from 1980–2002, and says *in constant 2002 dollars*, it means that every value has been adjusted to reflect the amount it *would be* in the year 2002.

Continuing Resolution: Legislation that extends appropriations for specific ongoing programs when the regular appropriation has not been enacted by the beginning of the fiscal year (October 1).

Current Dollars: See **Then Year Dollars.**

Debt: The total accumulated amount of money the federal government has borrowed to make up shortfalls in revenue (currently in the trillions of dollars). There are three basic measures of the federal debt:

> **Debt Held by the Public:** Federal debt held by all investors outside the federal government, including individuals, corporations, state or local governments, the Federal Reserve banking system, and foreign governments. When the debt held by the Federal Reserve is excluded, the remaining amount is referred to as privately held debt.

> **Debt Held by Government Accounts:** Federal debt held by the federal government itself. Most of this debt is held by trust funds, such as Social Security.

> **Gross Debt:** The total amount of outstanding federal debt, whether issued by the Treasury or other agencies and held by the public or federal government accounts.

> **Debt Ceiling:** A statutory limit imposed on the total outstanding federal debt. The ceiling can be raised or lowered through an act of Congress.

Deficit: The amount by which the government's spending exceeds its revenues in a single fiscal year.

> **Unified Deficit:** The most commonly used measure of the federal deficit. It includes all federal spending and all federal revenues.

> **Federal Funds Ceiling:** A measure of the federal deficit that excludes the spending and revenue totals of federal government trust funds such as Social Security.

Discretionary Programs: Programs funded by annual congressional appropriations bills, except for "appropriated entitlements" such as veterans' compensation. Under the Budget Enforcement Act, these expenditures are capped.

Discretionary Spending Cap: Limits placed on the total amount of budget authority and outlays for discretionary programs Congress can provide in a given fiscal year.

Emergency Appropriations: An exception to the budget "caps," allowing the limit to be raised by the amount of the emergency appropriation. There are no precise definitions of what constitutes an "emergency," and it has included things like natural disasters, September 11, "Y2K," etc. In mandatory (see "mandatory spending") programs, the emergency designation would exempt the spending from pay-as-you-go (see "pay-as-you-go") requirements.

End Strength: The congressional authorized size of military personnel required for each of the Services as of the last day of the designated fiscal year.

Entitlement: Program mandating the payment of benefits to any person meeting eligibility requirements established by statute. The amount spent is not controlled by annual congressional appropriations. Entitlement programs include Social Security, Medicare, and Medicaid.

Fiscal Year (FY): The federal government's accounting period, which begins October 1 and ends September 30. NOTE: During the Korean and Vietnam conflicts, the FY started July 1 and ended June 30.

Gross Domestic Product (GDP): The value of all finished goods and services produced in a country during a given period. GDP serves as the principal measure of the size of a country's economy.

Inflation: The general rise in the price level, usually expressed on an annual basis. For example, a rate of inflation of 3 percent means that the general price level, as measured by a basket of goods, is 3 percent higher than last year. It does not mean that every single good or service has increased by 3 percent. Some may have increased more while some may have even decreased.

Mandatory Spending: Federal spending on entitlement programs and interest on the national debt. Mandatory spending accounts for approximately two-thirds of all federal spending.

"Off-Budget": Spending or revenues excluded from the budget totals by law. Social Security and the Postal Service are "off-budget." "Off-budget" spending is excluded from budget caps, sequestration, and "pay-as-you-go" requirements.

Omnibus Bill: The package that results when a number of bills on related topics are combined into a single bill for floor action. Often the jurisdictions of several committees are involved.

"On-Budget": Federal budget totals excluding "off-budget" programs. The "Unified" budget is the presentation of the Federal budget in which revenues from all sources and outlays to all activities are consolidated.

Outlay: Payment actually made by the federal government. This differs from budget authority in that it reflects money the federal government actually spends, not the amount that has been appropriated by Congress. Many times in a given year outlays are often less than the budget authority granted by Congress.

Pay-As-You-Go (a.k.a.: Pay-Go): A provision of the now-expired Budget Enforcement Act of 1990. Pay-Go required that any entitlement or tax proposal include provisions for financing. Raising new revenue or cutting existing entitlement programs must pay for new entitlements or changes to the tax code. Thus, under the Pay-Go provision of the BEA changes in entitlement programs or revenues had to be deficit neutral.

President's Budget: The President is required to submit a budget request each year by the first week in February. This budget request is produced in great detail resulting in six volumes of information and reflects a process of consulting between the agencies and the Office of Management and Budget, but ultimately reflects the priorities of the current administration.

Reconciliation: The process used by Congress to amend tax and entitlement programs to meet the instructions in the budget resolution regarding outlay and revenue targets. Reconciliation legislation has served recently as the primary vehicle for deficit reduction measures. "Reconciliation" has recently been used to insure the passage of tax cuts, that is, reconciliation instructions were included in the FY 2004 Resolution requiring passage of a specified amount as tax cut legislation.

Rescission: A statutory mid-year reduction or cancellation in previously appropriated funds. The President submits a rescission request to Congress, specifying the amount of the cut and estimating the impact. Congress then has 45 days to pass a bill allowing the cut in spending. If Congress does not pass a bill in that period of time, the rescission request is considered refused.

Revenue: Funds collected from the public that come about from government's exercise of its sovereign or governmental powers, including taxes, customs duties, fees, and fines.

Sequestration: Pursuant to the Gramm-Rudman-Hollings Act (the 1985 deficit reduction law); a procedure created by law to automatically cut spending (across-the-board) if, for a given fiscal year, discretionary appropriations exceed the discretionary spending limits or enacted legislation affecting mandatory spending and receipts increases the deficit or reduces the surplus. Sequestered funds are permanently canceled.

Supplemental Appropriations: An act to provide funds for an agency or program in addition to a regular appropriations bill usually reserved for circumstances that cannot wait for the next normal appropriations cycle.

Surplus: The amount by which revenues exceed outlays.

Then Year (TY$) Dollars: When money amounts are in *then year or current dollars*, it means that they have not been adjusted to take inflation into account.

Total Obligation Authority (TOA): Congressionally approved budget authority (BA), plus or minus financing and receipts or other adjustments. In the Defense Department, this is the amount of funds often referred to in any given year as the "top-line" for the budget. Examples why TOA may differ from BA, include: BA lapsing before obligations were incurred, Legislation transferring unobligated balances, Reappropriations (the extension of availability of previously appropriated funds), Rescissions (Congressional action canceling new budget authority or unobligated balances), or Net Offsetting Receipts (collections from the public that arise out of the business-type or market-oriented activities of the Government and are deposited in receipt accounts).

Transfer Authority: A grant by Congress to a department or agency to be able to shift funds from one appropriation to another within specified limits. A broad authority over an entire spending bill is usually referred to as General Transfer Authority (GTA). These authorities can also be structured with more limits, or confined to specified accounts and are then usually called Special Transfer Authorities.

Trust Funds: Government accounts for revenues and spending designated for specific purposes. The Social Security Trust Fund is one example. Even though the surplus trust fund revenue is spent, an accounting of how much the Trust Fund is owed is made.

Selected Bibliography

GENERAL

Books

Clausewitz, Carl von. *On War*. Translated by Michael Howard and Peter Paret. Princeton: Princeton University Press, 1976.

Goldin, Claudia D. "War," 1980. In *Encyclopedia of American Economic History*, ed. Glenn Porter. New York: Charles Scribner's Sons, 1980.

Holsti, Ole R. *Public Opinion and American Foreign Policy*. Ann Arbor: University of Michigan Press, 1996.

Lee, Steven Hugh. *Outposts of Empire: Korea, Vietnam and the Origins of the Cold War in Asia, 1949–1954*. Quebec: McGill-Queen's University Press, 1995.

Pigou, A.C. *The Political Economy of War*. New York: The Macmillan Company, 1939.

Sobel, Richard. *The Impact of Public Opinion on U.S. Foreign Policy Since Vietnam*. New York: Oxford University Press, 2001.

Weigley, Russell F. *The American Way of War*. Bloomington: Indiana University Press, 1973.

Government Publications

Congressional Budget Office. *The Budget and Economic Outlook: An Update*. Washington, DC: GPO, August 2002.

Congressional Research Service. *Costs of Major U.S. Wars and Recent Military Operations*, CRS RS21013, by Stephen Daggett and Nina Serafino. Washington, DC: GPO, 2001.

———. *Financing Issues and Economic Effects of Past American Wars*, by Marc Labonte. Washington, DC: GPO, 2001.

Office of Management and Budget. *Historical Tables of the Fiscal Year 2007 Budget*. Washington, DC: GPO, 2006.

U.S. Department of Commerce. Bureau of the Census. *Statistical Abstract of the United States 1951*. Washington, DC: GPO, 1951.

————. *Statistical Abstract of the United States 1953*. Washington, DC: GPO, 1953.

————. *Statistical Abstract of the United States 1954*. Washington, DC: GPO, 1954.

————. *Statistical Abstract of the United States 1955*. Washington, DC: GPO, 1955.

————. *Statistical Abstract of the United States 1956*. Washington, DC: GPO, 1956.

————. *Statistical Abstract of the United States 1957*. Washington, DC: GPO, 1957.

————. *Statistical Abstract of the United States 1962*. Washington, DC: GPO, 1962.

————. *Statistical Abstract of the United States 1964*. Washington, DC: GPO, 1964.

————. *Statistical Abstract of the United States 1966*. Washington, DC: GPO, 1966.

————. *Statistical Abstract of the United States 1967*. Washington, DC: GPO, 1967.

————. *Statistical Abstract of the United States 1968*. Washington, DC: GPO, 1968.

————. *Statistical Abstract of the United States 1969*. Washington, DC: GPO, 1969.

————. *Statistical Abstract of the United States 1970*. Washington, DC: GPO, 1970.

————. *Statistical Abstract of the United States 1971*. Washington, DC: GPO, 1971.

————. *Statistical Abstract of the United States 1973*. Washington, D.C.: GPO, 1973.

————. *Statistical Abstract of the United States 1975*. Washington, D.C.: GPO, 1975.

————. *Statistical Abstract of the United States 1977*. Washington, D.C.: GPO, 1977.

————. *Statistical Abstract of the United States 1978*. Washington, D.C.: GPO, 1978.

————. *Statistical Abstract of the United States 1979*. Washington, D.C.: GPO, 1979.

————. *Statistical Abstract of the United States 1981*. Washington, D.C.: GPO, 1981.

————. *Statistical Abstract of the United States 1985*. Washington, D.C.: GPO, 1985.

————. *Statistical Abstract of the United States 1988*. Washington, DC: GPO, 1988.

————. *Statistical Abstract of the United States 1990*. Washington, DC: GPO, 1990.

————. *Statistical Abstract of the United States 1992*. Washington, DC: GPO, 1992.

————. *Statistical Abstract of the United States 1993*. Washington, DC: GPO, 1993.

————. *Statistical Abstract of the United States 1995*. Washington, DC: GPO, 1995.

————. *Statistical Abstract of the United States 1999*. Washington, DC: GPO, 1999.

————. *Statistical Abstract of the United States 2000*. Washington, DC: GPO, 2000.

————. *Statistical Abstract of the United States 2001*. Washington, DC: GPO, 2001.

————. *Statistical Abstract of the United States 2003*. Washington, DC: GPO, 2003.

U.S. Department of Defense. Office of the Under Secretary of Defense (Comptroller). *National Defense Budget Estimates for Fiscal Year 2006*. Washington DC: GPO, 2005.

Journals

Clayton, James L. "The Fiscal Cost of the Cold War to the United States: The First 25 Years, 1947–1971." *The Western Political Quarterly* 25(3) (September 1972): 375–395.

Cohen, Eliot A. "Constraints on America's Conduct of Small Wars." *International Security* 9(2) (Autumn 1984): 151–181.

Fordham, Benjamin O. "Economic Interests, Party, and Ideology in Early Cold War Era U.S. Foreign Policy." *International Organization* 52(2) (Spring 1998): 359–396.

Hansen, Alvin H. "Monetary Policy and the Control of Inflation." *The Review of Economics and Statistics* 33(3) (August 1951): 191–194.

Makinen, G.E. "Economic Stabilization in Wartime: A Comparative Case Study of Korea and Vietnam." *The Journal of Political Economy* 79(6) (November–December 1971): 1216–1243.

Mintz, Alex, and Chi Huang. "Guns versus Butter: The Indirect Link." *American Journal of Political Science* 35(3) (August 1991): 738–757.

Mueller, Eva. "Consumer Reactions to Inflation." *The Quarterly Journal of Economics* 73(2) (May 1959): 246–262.

Page, Benjamin I., and Robert Y. Shapiro. "Changes in Americans' Policy Preferences, 1935–1979." *The Public Opinion Quarterly* 46(1) (Spring 1982): 24–42.

Rockoff, Hugh. "Price and Wage Controls in Four Wartime Periods." *The Journal of Economic History* 41(2) (June 1981): 381–401.

Russett, Bruce. "Doves, Hawks, and U.S. Public Opinion." *Political Science Quarterly* 105(4) (Winter 1990/1991): 515–538.

Samuelson, Paul A., Charles R. Whittlesey, Lawrence H. Seltzer, Milton Friedman, Roland I. Robinson, Charles J. Hitch, George L. Bach, Herbert Stein, Lester V. Chandley, E.A. Goldenweiser, Alvin H. Hansen, Richard Musgrave, and Jocob Viner. "Monetary Policy to Combat Inflation." *The American Economic Review* 42(3) (June 1952): 384–391.

Turner, Robert F. "Truman, Korea, and the Constitution: Debunking the 'Imperial President' Myth." *Harvard Journal of Law and Public Policy* 19(2) (Winter 1996): 533.

Wallis, John Joseph. "American Government Finance in the Long Run: 1790 to 1990." *The Journal of Economic Perspectives* 14(1) (Winter 2000): 61–82.

KOREAN WAR

Books

Brune, Lester H., ed. *The Korean War Handbook of the Literature and Research*. Westport: Greenwood Press, 1996.

Condit, Doris. *History of the Office of the Secretary of Defense, Vol. II: The Test of War 1950–1953*, ed. Alfred Goldberg. Washington DC: GPO, 1988.

Congressional Quarterly. *Congress and the Nation, Vol. I, 1945–1964*. Washington, DC: Congressional Quarterly, 1965.

Drew, S. Nelson, ed. *NSC-68 Forging the Strategy of Containment*. With Analyses by Paul H. Nitze. Washington, DC: NDU Press, 1994.

Eisenhower, Dwight D. *Mandate for Change*. New York: Doubleday & Company, Inc., 1963.

Friedberg, Aaron L. *In the Shadow of the Garrison State*. Princeton: Princeton University Press, 2000.

Friedman, Milton and Anna Jacobson Schwartz. *A Monetary History of the United States 1867–1960*. Princeton: Princeton University Press, 1963.

Gaddis, John, Lewis. *Strategies of Containment*. Oxford: Oxford University Press, 1982.

———. *The United States and the Origins of the Cold War*. New York: Columbia University Press, 1972.

Holmans, A.E. *United States Fiscal Policy 1945–1959*. Oxford: Oxford University Press, 1961.

Huston, James A. *Guns and Butter, Powder and Rice: U.S. Army Logistics in the Korean War*. Selinsgrove: Susquehanna University Press, 1989.

Kolko, Gabriel. *Century of War*. New York: The New Press, 1994.

Leighton, Richard M. *Strategy, Money, and The New Look 1953–1956, Vol. III: History of the Office of the Secretary of Defense*, ed. Alfred Goldberg. Washington DC: GPO, 2001.

McCullough, David. *Truman*. New York: Simon and Schuster, 1992.

Government Archives

National Archives of the United States II, College Park, MD:

Records Group 51, Records of the Bureau of the Budget Series (47.8 Series): Budgetary Administration For Defense Activities, Korean Emergency Period, 1950–1953 (51.27).

Supplemental and Deficiency Budget Estimates for the National Military Establishment and Department of Defense, 1953–1961 (51.14c).

Annual Budget Estimates for the National Military Establishment and Department of Defense, 1953–1961 (51.14b).

Budgetary Administration in National Military Establishment, FY 1949–1952 (47.8c).

Government Publications

U.S. Congress. *Official Congressional Directory*. Washington, DC: GPO, 1951.

U.S. Department of Defense. *Semiannual Report of the Secretary of Defense, 1 July 1950 to 31 December 1950*, by George Marshall. Washington DC: GPO, 1951.

U.S. Department of Defense. *Semiannual Report of the Secretary of Defense, 1 January 1951 to 30 June 1951*, by George Marshall. Washington DC: GPO, 1951.

U.S. Department of State. *Foreign Relations of the United States, 1947, Volume I*. Washington, DC: GPO, 1947.

U.S. President. *Public Papers of the Presidents of the United States*, Dwight D. Eisenhower. Washington, DC: Office of the Federal Register, National Archives and Records Service, 1960–1961. Dwight D. Eisenhower, 1960.

Journals

Brockie, Melvin D., "Debt Management and Economic Stabilization." *The Quarterly Journal of Economics* 68(4) (November 1954): 613–628.

Fellner, William J. "Postscript on War Inflation: A Lesson from World War II." *The American Economic Review* 37(1) (March 1947): 76–91.

Jervis, Robert. "The Impact of the Korean War on the Cold War." *The Journal of Conflict Resolution* 24(4) (December 1980): 567.

Jones, Byrd, L. "The Role of Keynesians in Wartime Policy and Postwar Planning, 1940–1946." *American Economic Review* 62(2) (May 1972): 125–133.

Leffler, Melvyn P. "The American Conception of National Security and the Beginnings of the Cold War, 1945–48." *The American Historical Review* 89(2) (April 1984): 374.

Mueller, John E. "Trends in Popular Support for the Wars in Korea and Vietnam." *The American Political Science Review* 65(2) (June 1971): 358–375.

Ohanian, Lee E. "The Macroeconomic Effects of War Finance in the United States: World War II and the Korea War." *The American Economic Review* 87(1) (March 1997): 23–40.

Poole, Kenyon, E. "Full Employment, Wage Flexibility, and Inflation." *The American Economic Review* 45(2) (May 1955): 586.

Strunk, Mildred. "The Quarter's Polls." *The Public Opinion Quarterly* 13(4) (Winter 1949–1950): 182, 192, 721.

———. "The Quarter's Polls." *The Public Opinion Quarterly* 14(3) (Autumn 1950): 596, 603.

Suchman, Edward A., Rose K. Goldsen, and Robin M. Williams, Jr. "Attitudes Towards the Korea War." *The Public Opinion Quarterly* 17(2) (Summer 1953): 171–184.

Warburton, Clark. "A Hedge Against Inflation." *Political Science Quarterly* 67(1) (March 1952): 1–17.

Legislation and Related Documents

Hearings, Debates, and Committee Reports

U.S. Congress. House. Committee on Appropriations, Subcommittee on National Defense. *The Supplemental Appropriation Bill for 1951*, 81st Cong., 2nd sess., July 25, 1950.

———. Committee on Appropriations. Subcommittee on National Defense. *The Supplemental Appropriation Bill for 1951*. 81st Cong., 2nd sess., July 27, 1950.

———. Committee on Appropriations. Subcommittee on National Defense. *Second Supplemental Appropriation Bill for 1951*. 81st Cong., 2nd sess., December 1, 1950.

———. Committee on Appropriations. Subcommittee on National Defense. *Second Supplemental Appropriation Bill for 1951*. 81st Cong., 2nd sess., December 4, 1950.

———. Committee on Appropriations. *Third Supplemental Appropriation Bill, 1951*. Report to accompany H.R. 3587, Report no. 298. 82nd Cong., 1st sess., April 6, 1951.

———. Committee on Appropriations. *Third Supplemental Appropriation Bill, 1951*. Conference Report to accompany H.R. 3587, Report no. 484. 82nd Cong., 1st sess., May 18, 1951.

———. Committee on Appropriations. Special Subcommittee on Emergency Defense Appropriations. *Third Supplemental Appropriation Bill, 1951*. 82nd Cong., 1st sess., March 7, 1951.

———. Committee on Appropriations. Special Subcommittee on Emergency Defense Appropriations. *Third Supplemental Appropriation Bill, 1951*. 82nd Cong., 1st sess., March 14, 1951.

———. Committee on Appropriations. Special Subcommittee on Emergency Defense Appropriations. *Third Supplemental Appropriation Bill, 1951*. 82nd Cong., 1st sess., March 15, 1951.

———. Committee on Appropriations. *Fourth Supplemental Appropriation Act, 1951*. Report to Accompany H.R. 3842, Report no. 377. 82nd Cong., 1st sess., April 25, 1951.

———. Committee on Appropriations. Subcommittee on National Defense. *Department of Defense Appropriation Act, 1953*. 82nd Cong., 2nd sess., January 22, 1952.

———. Committee on Appropriations. Subcommittee for the Department of Defense. *Department of Defense and Related Independent Agencies Appropriations for 1953*. 82nd Cong., 2nd sess., March 26, 1952.

————. Committee on Appropriations. *Department of Defense Appropriation Act, 1953,* Report to Accompany H.R. 7391, Report no. 1685. 82nd Cong., 2nd sess., April 3, 1952.

————. Committee on Appropriations. *Supplemental Appropriation Act, 1953.* Report to Accompany H.R. 8370, Report no. 2316. 82nd Cong., 2nd sess., June 26, 1952.

————. Committee on Appropriations. *Urgent Deficiency Appropriation Act, 1952.* Conference Report to Accompany H.R. 7860, Report no. 2343. 82nd Cong., 2nd sess., June 27, 1952.

————. Committee on Appropriations. *Department of Defense Appropriation Act, 1953,* Conference Report to Accompany H.R. 7391, Report no. 2483. 82nd Cong., 2nd sess., July 4, 1952.

————. Committee on Appropriations. *Department of Defense Appropriation Act, 1953,* Conference Report to Accompany H.R. 7391, Report no. 2495. 82nd Cong., 2nd sess., July 5, 1952.

————. Committee on Appropriations. *Second Supplemental Appropriation Bill, 1953.* Report to Accompany H.R. 3053, Report no. 46. 83rd Cong., 1st sess., February 16, 1953.

————. Committee on Appropriations. Subcommittee for the Department of Defense. *Department of Defense and Related Agencies, Appropriations for 1954.* 83rd Cong., 1st sess., February 24, 1953.

————. Committee on Appropriations. Subcommittee for the Department of Defense. *Department of Defense Appropriations for 1954.* 83rd Congress, 1st sess., May 19, 1953.

U.S. Congress. Senate. Committee on Appropriations. *Third Supplemental Appropriation Bill, 1951.* Report to accompany H.R. 3587, Report no. 302. 82nd Cong., 1st sess., April 30, 1951.

————. Committee on Appropriations. *Third Supplemental Appropriation Bill, 1951.* 82nd Cong., 1st sess., March 28, 1951.

————. Committee on Appropriations. *Third Supplemental Appropriation Bill, 1951.* 82nd Cong., 1st sess., March 29, 1951.

————. Committee on Appropriations. *Fourth Supplemental Appropriation Bill, 1951.* Report to accompany H.R. 3842, Report no. 329. 82nd Cong., 1st sess., May 22, 1951.

————. Joint Committee on the Economic Report. *Monetary Policy and the Management of the Public Debt.* Replies to Questions. Document no. 123, Part 1. 82nd Cong., 2nd sess., February 20, 1952.

————. Committee on Appropriations. Subcommittee for the Department of Defense. *Department of Defense Appropriations for 1952.* 82nd Cong., 1st sess., June 7, 1952.

————. Committee on Appropriations. Subcommittee for the Department of Defense. *Department of Defense Appropriations for 1952.* 82nd Cong., 1st sess., June 11, 1952.

————. Committee on Appropriations. Subcommittee for the Department of Defense. *Department of Defense Appropriations for 1952.* 82nd Cong., 1st sess., August 8, 1952.

————. Committee on Appropriations. Subcommittee for the Department of Defense. *Department of Defense Appropriations for 1953.* 82nd Cong., 2nd sess., February 4, 1952.

————. Committee on Appropriations. Subcommittee for the Department of Defense. *Department of Defense Appropriations for 1953.* 82nd Cong., 2nd sess., April 30, 1952.

————. Committee on Appropriations. Subcommittee for the Department of Defense. *Department of Defense Appropriations for 1953*. 82nd Cong., 2nd sess., June 11, 1952.

————. Committee on Appropriations. *Urgent Deficiency Appropriation Act, 1952*. Report to Accompany H.R. 7860, Report no. 1780. 82nd Cong., 2nd sess., June 17, 1952.

————. Committee on Appropriations. *Department of Defense Appropriation Act, 1953*, Report to Accompany H.R. 7391, Report no. 1861. 82nd Cong., 2nd sess., June 27, 1952.

————. Committee on Appropriations. *Second Supplemental Appropriation Act, 1953*. Report to Accompany H.R. 3053, Report no. 48. 83rd Cong., 1st sess., February 27, 1953.

————. Committee on Appropriations. Subcommittee for the Department of Defense. *Department of Defense Appropriations for 1954*. 83rd Cong., 1st sess., June 2, 1953.

Public Laws

U.S. Congress. *Defense Production Act of 1950*. 81st Cong., 2nd sess., H.R. 9176, P.L. 81-774, September 8, 1950.

————. *Supplemental Appropriation Act, 1951*. 81st Cong., 2nd sess., H.R. 9526, P.L. 81-843, September 27, 1950.

————. *Second Supplemental Appropriation Act, 1951*. 81st Cong., 2nd sess., H.R. 9920, P.L. 81-911, January 6, 1951.

————. *Third Supplemental Appropriation Act, 1951*. 82nd Cong., 1st sess., H.R. 3587, P.L. 82-45, June 2, 1951.

————. *Fourth Supplemental Appropriation Act, 1951*. 82nd Cong., 1st sess., H.R. 3842, P.L. 82-43, May 31, 1951.

————. *Department of Defense Appropriation Act, 1952*. 82nd Cong., 1st sess., H.R. 5054, P.L. 82-179, October 18, 1951.

————. *Supplemental Appropriation Act, 1952*. 82nd Cong., 1st sess., H.R. 5215, P.L. 82-253, November 1, 1951.

————. *Second Supplemental Appropriation Act, 1952*. 82nd Cong., 1st sess., H.R. 5650, P.L. 82-254, November 1, 1951.

————. *An Act to Increase Income Limitations Governing the Payment of Pension to Certain Veterans and their Dependents*. 82nd Cong., 2nd sess., H.R. 4387, P.L. 82-357, May 23, 1952.

————. *Third Supplemental Appropriation Act, 1952*. 82nd Cong., 2nd sess., H.R. 6947, P.L. 82-375, June 5, 1952.

————. *Urgent Deficiency Appropriation Act, 1952*. 82nd Cong., 2nd sess., H.R. 7860, P.L. 82-431, June 30, 1952.

————. *Department of Defense Appropriation Act, 1953*, 82nd Cong., 2nd sess., H.R. 7391, P.L. 82-488, July 10, 1952.

————. *Supplemental Appropriation Act, 1953*. 82nd Cong., 2nd sess., H.R. 8370, P.L. 82-547, July 15, 1952.

————. *Second Supplemental Appropriation Act, 1953*. 83rd Cong., 1st sess., H.R. 3053, P.L. 83-11, March 28, 1953.

————. *Third Supplemental Appropriation Act, 1953*. 83rd Cong., 1st sess., H.R. 4664, P.L. 83-59, June 15, 1953.

Newspapers and Periodicals

Childs, Marquis. "Divisions On Trial." *Washington Post*, February 24, 1951, 9.

"Hanley Says Foes Cause Inflation." *New York Times*, October 19, 1950, 35.

Knowles, Clayton. "Republicans Lead in Pennsylvania." *New York Times*, October 15,1950, 75.

Leviero, Anthony. "U.S. Output Vital." *New York Times*, July 27, 1950, 1.

Reston, James. "Defamation Marks Violent Campaign." *New York Times*, October 31, 1950, 22.

"Senators Bid Johnson Itemize War Needs." *New York Times*, July 10, 1950, 6.

On-line Sources

Consulate-General of the People's Republic of China in New York. *Korean War: In the View of Cost-Effectiveness*. Available at http://www.nyconsulate.prchina.org/eng/xw/t31430.htm. Accessed on November 22, 2005.

The U.S. Civil War Center. *Statistical Summary America's Major Wars*. Available at http://www.cwc.lsu.edu/cwc/other/stats/warcost.htm. Accessed on November 22, 2005.

Other Documents

Pierpaoli, Paul George. "The Price of Peace: The Korean War Mobilization and Cold War Rearmament, 1950–1953." Ph.D. diss., Ohio State University, 1995.

VIETNAM WAR
Books

Beschloss, Michael. *Reaching for Glory Lyndon Johnson's Secret White House Tapes, 1964–1965*. New York: Touchstone Books, 2001.

Campagna, Anthony S. *The Economic Consequences of the Vietnam War*. New York: Praeger, 1991.

Committee for Economic Development. Research and Policy Committee. *The National Economy and the Vietnam War*. New York: Committee for Economic Development, 1968.

Copps, John A., ed. *The Cost of Conflict*. Ann Arbor: University of Michigan Press, 1968.

Lewy, Guenter. *America in Vietnam*. Oxford: Oxford University Press, 1978.

McMaster, H.R. *Dereliction of Duty Lyndon Johnson, Robert McNamara, The Joint Chiefs of Staff, and the Lies That Led to Vietnam*. New York: Harper Collins Publishers, 1997.

Weidenbaum, Murray L. *Economic Impact of the Vietnam War*. Washington, DC: Georgetown University Center for Strategic Studies, 1967.

Government Publications

Congressional Budget Office. Staff Working Paper. *Supplemental Appropriations in the 1970s*. Washington, DC: GPO, 1981.

U.S. Department of Defense. Department of the Army. *Financial Management of the Vietnam Conflict 1962–1972*, by Leonard B. Taylor. Washington, DC: GPO, 1974.

U.S. Department of State. *American Foreign Policy Documents 1950–1955*. Washington, DC: GPO, 1956.

U.S. President. The Budget Message. "The President's Message to the Congress Transmitting the Budget for Fiscal Year 1967." *Weekly Compilation of Presidential Documents* (January 24, 1966) vol. 2, no. 4, p. 82–94.

———. The Budget Message. "The President's Message to the Congress Transmitting the Budget for Fiscal Year 1968." *Weekly Compilation of Presidential Documents* (January 24, 1967) vol. 3, no. 4, p. 84–97.

———. The Budget Message. "The President's Message to the Congress Transmitting the Budget for Fiscal Year 1969." *Weekly Compilation of Presidential Documents* (January 29, 1968) vol. 4, no. 5, p. 148–164.

———. The Budget Message. "The President's Message to the Congress Transmitting the Budget for Fiscal Year 1970." *Weekly Compilation of Presidential Documents* (January 20, 1969) vol. 5, no. 3, p. 70–90.

———. Letter to Congress. "Supplemental Appropriations in Support of Southeast Asia." *Weekly Compilation of Presidential Documents* (January 24, 1966) vol. 2, no. 3, p. 60.

———. Letter to Congress. "Supplemental Appropriations for Vietnam." *Weekly Compilation of Presidential Documents* (January 30, 1967) vol. 3, no. 4, p. 97–98.

———. News Conference. "Report to the Nation Following a Review of U.S. Policy in Viet-Nam." *Weekly Compilation of Presidential Documents* (August 2, 1965) vol. 1, no. 1, p. 15–19.

Journals

Galper, Harvey. "The Impacts of the Vietnam War on Defense Spending: A Simulation Approach." *The Journal of Business* 424 (October 1969): 401–415.

Kramer, Helmut and Helfried Bauer. "Imperialism, Intervention Capacity, and Foreign Policy Making: On the Political Economy of the US Intervention in Indochina." *Journal of Peace Research* 9(4) (1972): 285–302.

Kurth, James R. "The Political Economy of Weapons Procurement: The Follow-On Imperative." *American Economic Review* 62(2) (May 1972): 304–311.

Melman, Seymour. "Ten Propositions on the War Economy." *American Economic Review* 62(2) (May 1972): 312–318.

Mueller, John E. "Trends in Popular Support for the Wars in Korea and Vietnam." *The American Political Science Review* 652 (June 1971): 358–375.

Oi, Walter Y. "The Economic Cost of the Draft." *The American Economic Review* 57(2) (May 1967): 39–62.

Schreiber, E.M. "Anti-War Demonstrations and American Public Opinion on the War in Vietnam." *The British Journal of Sociology* 27(2) (June 1976): 225–236.

Wolf, Charles. "The Logic of Failure A Vietnam Lesson." *The American Behavioral Scientist* 15(6) (July/August 1972): 929–937.

Legislation and Related Documents

Hearings, Debates, and Committee Reports

U.S. Congress. House. Committee on Appropriations. Subcommittee on Department of Defense. *Department of Defense Appropriations for 1966, Part 4 Procurement*. 89th Cong., 1st sess., March 22, 1965.

U.S. Congress. Senate. Committee on Armed Services. Committee on Appropriations. Subcommittee on Department of Defense. *Military Authorizations and Defense Appropriations for Fiscal Year 1966*. 89th Cong., 1st sess., February 24, 1965.

———. Committee on Appropriations. Subcommittee on Department of Defense. *Department of Defense Appropriations, 1966*. 89th Cong, 1st sess., July 14, 1965.

———. Committee on Appropriations. Subcommittee on Department of Defense. *Department of Defense Appropriations, 1966*. 89th Cong, 1st sess., July 16, 1965.

———. Committee on Appropriations. Subcommittee on Department of Defense. *Department of Defense Appropriations, 1966*. 89th Cong, 1st sess., July 22, 1965.

———. Committee on Appropriations. Subcommittee on Department of Defense. *Department of Defense Appropriations for Fiscal Year 1966*. 89th Cong., 1st sess., August 4, 1965.

———. Committee on Armed Services. Committee on Appropriations. Subcommittee on Department of Defense. *Military Authorizations and Defense Appropriations for Fiscal Year 1967*. 89th Cong., 2nd sess., February 23, 1966.

———. Committee on Appropriations. *Supplemental Defense Appropriations Bill, 1966*. 89th Cong., 2nd sess., Report to Accompany H.R. 13546, Report no. 1074, March 17, 1966.

———. Committee on Armed Services. Committee on Appropriations. Subcommittee on Department of Defense. *Supplemental Defense Appropriations and Authorizations for Fiscal Year 1967*. 90th Cong., 1st sess., January 23, 1967.

———. Committee on Armed Services. Committee on Appropriations. Subcommittee on Department of Defense. *Military Authorizations and Defense Appropriations for Fiscal Year 1968*. 90th Cong., 1st sess., January 26, 1967.

———. Committee on Appropriations. Subcommittee on Department of Defense. *Department of Defense Appropriations for Fiscal Year 1969*. 90th Cong., 2nd sess., May 6, 1968.

———. Committee on Appropriations. Subcommittee on Department of Defense. *Department of Defense Appropriations for Fiscal Year 1969*. 90th Cong., 2nd sess., May 7, 1968.

———. Committee on Appropriations. Subcommittee on Department of Defense. *Department of Defense Appropriations for Fiscal Year 1969*. 90th Cong., 2nd sess., May 9, 1968.

———. Committee on Appropriations. Subcommittee on Department of Defense. *Department of Defense Appropriations for Fiscal Year 1969*. 90th Cong., 2nd sess., May 10, 1968.

———. Committee on Appropriations. Subcommittee on Department of Defense. *Department of Defense Appropriations for Fiscal Year 1969*. 90th Cong., 2nd sess., May 15, 1968.

———. Committee on Appropriations. Subcommittee on Department of Defense. *Department of Defense Appropriations for Fiscal Year 1970*. 91st Cong., 1st sess., June 10, 1969.

———. Committee on Appropriations. Subcommittee on Department of Defense. *Department of Defense Appropriations for Fiscal Year 1970*. 91st Cong., 1st sess., June 12, 1969.

———. Committee on Appropriations. Subcommittee on Department of Defense. *Department of Defense Appropriations for Fiscal Year 1970*. 91st Cong., 1st sess., December 9, 1969.

————. Committee on Armed Services. Committee on Appropriations. Subcommittee on Department of Defense. *Department of Defense Appropriations for Fiscal Year 1971.* 91st Cong., 2nd sess., February 20, 1970.

————. Committee on Appropriations. Subcommittee on Department of Defense. *Department of Defense Appropriations for Fiscal Year 1971.* 91st Cong., 2nd sess., April 16, 1970.

————. Committee on Appropriations. Subcommittee on Department of Defense. *Department of Defense Appropriations for Fiscal Year 1971.* 91st Cong., 2nd sess., November 20, 1970.

————. Committee on Appropriations. Subcommittee on Department of Defense. *Department of Defense Appropriations for Fiscal Year 1972.* 92nd Cong., 1st sess., March 22, 1971.

————. Committee on Appropriations. Subcommittee on Department of Defense. *Department of Defense Appropriations for Fiscal Year 1973.* 92nd Cong., 2nd sess., February 24, 1972.

————. Committee on Appropriations. Subcommittee on Department of Defense. *Department of Defense Appropriations for Fiscal Year 1974.* 93rd Cong., 1st sess., March 26, 1973.

————. Committee on Appropriations. Subcommittee on Department of Defense. *Department of Defense Appropriations for Fiscal Year 1974.* 93rd Cong., 1st sess., March 29, 1973.

————. Committee on Appropriations. Subcommittee on Department of Defense. *Department of Defense Appropriations for Fiscal Year 1975.* 93rd Cong., 2nd sess., March 5, 1974.

Public Laws

U.S. Congress. *Military Construction Authorization Act, 1965.* 88th Cong., 2nd sess., H.R. 10300, P.L. 88-390, August 1, 1964.

————. *Military Construction Appropriation Act, 1965.* 88th Cong., 2nd sess., H.R. 11369, P.L. 88-576, September 2, 1964.

————. *Supplemental Appropriations for 1965.* 89th Cong., 1st sess., H.J. Res. 447, P.L. 89-18, May 6, 1965.

————. *Military Construction Authorization Act, 1966.* 89th Cong., 1st sess., H.R. 10775, P.L. 89-188, September 16, 1965.

————. *Military Construction Appropriation Act, 1966.* 89th Cong., 1st sess., H.R. 10323, P.L. 89-202, September 25, 1965.

————. *Department of Defense Appropriation Act, 1966.* 89th Cong., 1st sess., H.R. 9221, P.L. 89-213, September 29, 1965.

————. *Foreign Assistance Act of 1961; Amendments.* 89th Cong., 2nd sess., H.R. 12169, P.L. 89-371, March 18, 1966.

————. *Supplemental Defense Appropriation Act, 1966.* 89th Cong., 2nd sess., H.R. 13546, P.L. 89-374, March 25, 1966.

————. *Armed Forces Appropriation Authorization, 1967; Military Pay Increase.* 89th Cong., 2nd sess., S. 2950, P.L. 89-501, July 13, 1966.

————. *Military Construction Authorization Act, 1967.* 89th Cong., 2nd sess., S. 3105, P.L. 89-568, September 12, 1966.

———. *Foreign Assistance Act of 1966.* 89th Cong., 2nd sess., H.R. 15750, P.L. 89-583, September 19, 1966.

———. *Department of Defenses Appropriation Act, 1967.* 89th Cong., 2nd sess., H.R. 15941, P.L. 89-687, October 15, 1966.

———. *Foreign Assistance and Related Agencies Appropriation Act, 1967.* 89th Cong., 2nd sess., H.R. 17788, P.L. 89-691, October 15, 1966.

———. *Military Construction Appropriation Act, 1967.* 89th Cong., 2nd sess., H.R. 17637, P.L. 89-744, November 2, 1966.

———. *Armed Forces Supplemental Appropriation Authorization, 1967.* 90th Cong., 1st sess., S. 665, P.L. 90-5, March 16, 1967.

———. *Supplemental Defense Appropriation Act, 1967.* 90th Cong., 1st sess., H.R. 7123, P.L. 90-8, April 4, 1967.

———. *Second Supplemental Appropriation Act, 1967.* 90th Cong., 1st sess., H.R. 9481, P.L. 90-21, May 29, 1967.

———. *Armed Forces Appropriation Authorization, 1968.* 90th Cong., 1st sess., S. 666, P.L. 90-22, June 5, 1967.

———. *Department of Defenses Appropriation Act, 1968.* 90th Cong., 1st sess., H.R. 10738, P.L. 90-96, September 29, 1967.

———. *Military Construction Authorization Act, 1968.* 90th Cong., 1st sess., H.R. 11722, P.L. 90-110, October 21, 1967.

———. *Foreign Assistance Act of 1967.* 90th Cong., 1st sess., S. 1872, P.L. 90- 137, November 14, 1967.

———. *Military Construction Appropriation Act, 1968.* 90th Cong., 1st sess., H.R. 13606, P.L. 90-180, December 8, 1967.

———. *Continuing Appropriations, 1968.* 90th Cong., 1st sess., H.J. Res. 888, P.L. 90-218, December 18, 1967.

———. *Foreign Assistance and Related Agencies Appropriation Act, 1968.* 90th Cong., 2nd sess., H.R. 13893, P.L. 90-249, January 2, 1968.

———. *Second Supplemental Appropriation Act, 1968.* 90th Cong., 2nd sess., H.R. 17734, P.L. 90-392, July 9, 1968.

———. *Military Construction and Reserve Forces Facilities Authorization Acts, 1969.* 90th Cong., 2nd sess., H.R. 16703, P.L. 90-408, July 21, 1968.

———. *Armed Forces Appropriation Authorization, 1969.* 90th Cong., 2nd sess., S. 3293, P.L. 90-500, September 20, 1968.

———. *Military Construction Appropriation Act, 1969.* 90thCong., 2nd sess., H.R. 18785, P.L. 90-513, September 26, 1968.

———. *Department of Defense Appropriation Act, 1969.* 90th Cong., 2nd sess., H.R. 18707, P.L. 90-580, October 17, 1968.

———. *Foreign Assistance and Related Agencies Appropriation Act, 1969.* 90th Cong., 2nd sess., H.R. 19908, P.L. 90-581, October 17, 1968.

———. *Supplemental Appropriation Act, 1969.* 90th Cong., 2nd sess., H.R. 20300, P.L. 90-608, October 21, 1968.

———. *Second Supplemental Appropriations Act, 1969.* 91st Cong., 1st sess., H.R. 11400, P.L. 91-47, July 22, 1969.

———. *Independent Offices and Department of Housing and Urban Development Appropriation Act, 1970.* 91st Cong., 1st sess., H.R. 12307, P.L. 91-126, November 26, 1969.

———. *Military Construction Authorization Act, 1970.* 91st Cong., 1st sess., H.R. 13018, P.L. 91-142, December 5, 1969.

———. *Military Construction Appropriation Act, 1970.* 91st Cong., 1st sess., H.R. 14751, P.L. 91-170, December 29, 1969.

———. *Department of Defense Appropriations Act, 1970.* 91st Cong., 1st sess., H.R. 15090, P.L. 91-171, December 29, 1969.

———. *Second Supplemental Appropriations Act, 1970.* 91st Cong., 2nd sess., H.R. 17399, P.L. 91-305, July 6, 1970.

———. *Armed Forces Appropriation Authorization, 1971.* 91st Cong., 2nd sess., H.R. 17123, P.L. 91-441, October 7, 1970.

———. *Military Construction and Reserve Facilities Authorization Acts, 1971.* 91st Cong., 2nd sess., H.R. 17604, P.L. 91-511, October 26, 1970.

———. *Independent Offices and Department of Housing and Urban Development Appropriation Act, 1971.* 91st Cong., 2nd sess., H.R. 19830, P.L. 91-556, December 17, 1970.

———. *Foreign Assistance and Related Programs Appropriation Act, 1971.* 91st Cong., 2nd sess., H.R. 17867, P.L. 91-619, December 31, 1970.

———. *Special Foreign Assistance Act of 1971.* 91st Cong., 2nd sess., H.R. 19911, P.L. 91-652, January 5, 1971.

———. *Supplemental Appropriations Act, 1971.* 91st Cong., 2nd sess., H.R. 19928, P.L. 91-665, January 8, 1971.

———. *Department of Defense Appropriations Act, 1971.* 91st Cong., 2nd sess., H.R. 19590, P.L. 91-668, January 11, 1971.

———. *Foreign Military Sales Act, Amendments.* 91st Cong., 2nd sess., H.R. 15628, P.L. 91-672, January 12, 1971.

———. *Department of Labor Supplemental Appropriation.* 92nd Cong., 1st sess., H.J. Res. 465, P.L. 92-4, March 17, 1971.

———. *Supplemental Appropriations, 1971.* 92nd Cong., 1st sess., H.J. Res. 567, P.L. 92-11, April 30, 1971.

———. *Second Supplemental Appropriations Act, 1971.* 92nd Cong., 1st sess., H.R. 8190, P.L. 92-18, May 25, 1971.

———. *Department of Labor Supplemental Appropriation, 1972.* 92nd Cong., 1st sess., H.J. Res. 915, P.L. 92-141, October 15, 1971.

———. *Armed Forces Appropriation Authorization, 1972.* 92nd Cong., 1st sess., H.R. 8687, P.L. 92-156, November 17, 1971.

———. *Supplemental Appropriations Act, 1972.* 92nd Cong., 1st sess., H.R. 11955, P.L. 92-184, December 15, 1971.

———. *Department of Defenses Appropriation Act, 1972.* 92nd Cong., 1st sess., H.R. 11731, P.L. 92-204, December 18, 1971.

———. *Urgent Supplemental Appropriations, 1972.* 92nd Cong., 2nd sess., H.J. Res. 1097, P.L. 92-256, March 21, 1972.

———. *Second Supplemental Appropriations Act, 1972.* 92nd Cong., 2nd sess., H.R. 14582, P.L. 92-306, May 27, 1972.

———. *Armed Forces Appropriation Authorization, 1973.* 92nd Cong., 2nd sess., H.R. 15495, P.L. 92-436, September 26, 1972.

———. *Department of Defenses Appropriation Act, 1973.* 92nd Cong., 2nd sess., H.R. 16593, P.L. 92-570, October 26, 1972.

————. *Supplemental Appropriations, 1973.* 93rd Cong., 1st sess., H.J. Res. 496, P.L. 93-25, April 26, 1973.

————. *Second Supplemental Appropriations Act, 1973.* 93rd Cong., 1st sess., H.R. 9055, P.L. 93-50, July 1, 1973.

————. *Continuing Appropriations, 1974.* 93rd Cong., 1st sess., H.J. Res. 636, P.L. 93-52, July 1, 1973.

————. *War Powers Resolution.* 93rd Cong., 1st sess., H.J. Res. 542, P.L. 93-148, November 7, 1973.

————. *Department of Defense Appropriation Authorization Act, 1974.* 93rd Cong., 1st sess., H.R. 9286, P.L. 93-155, November 16, 1973.

————. *Foreign Assistance Act of 1973.* 93rd Cong., 1st sess. S. 1443, P.L. 93-189, December 17, 1973.

————. *Emergency Security Assistance Act of 1973.* 93rd Cong., 1st sess., H.R. 11088, P.L. 93-199, December 26, 1973.

————. *Department of Defenses Appropriation Act, 1974.* 93rd Cong., 2nd sess., H.R. 11575, P.L. 93-238, January 2, 1974.

————. *Foreign Assistance and Related Programs Appropriation Act, 1974.* 93rd Cong., 2nd sess., H.R. 11771, P.L. 93-240, January 2, 1974.

————. *Supplemental Appropriations Act, 1974.* 93rd Cong., 2nd sess., H.R. 11576, P.L. 93-245, January 3, 1974.

————. *Veterans Administration Supplemental Appropriation.* 93rd Cong., 2nd sess., H.J. Res. 941, P.L. 93-261, April 11, 1974.

————. *Second Supplemental Appropriations Act, 1974.* 93rd Cong., 2nd sess., H.R. 14013, P.L. 93-305, June 8, 1974.

————. *Department of Defense Supplemental Appropriation Authorization Act, 1974.* 93rd Cong., 2nd sess., H.R. 12565, P.L. 93-307, 8 June 1974.

————. *Continuing Appropriations, 1975.* 93rd Cong., 2nd sess., H.J. Res. 1062, P.L. 93-324, June 30, 1974.

————. *Department of Defense Appropriation Authorization Act, 1975.* 93rd Cong., 2nd sess., H.R. 14592, P.L. 93-365, August 5, 1974.

————. *Department of Defenses Appropriation Act, 1975.* 93rd Cong., 2nd sess., H.R. 16243, P.L. 93-437, October 8, 1974.

————. *Foreign Assistance Act of 1974.* 93rd Cong., 2nd sess., S. 3394, P.L. 93-559, December 30, 1974.

————. *Supplemental Appropriations, 1975.* 93rd Cong., 2nd sess., H.J. Res. 1180, P.L. 93-624, January 1975.

————. *Veterans Administration; Federal Election Commission Additional Appropriations.* 94th Cong., 1st sess., H.J. Res. 375, P.L. 94-17, April 24, 1975.

————. *The Indochina Migration and Refugee Assistance Act of 1975.* 94th Cong., 1st sess., H.R. 6755, P.L. 94-23, May 23, 1975.

————. *Cambodian and Vietnamese Refugees. Special Assistance Appropriation.* 94th Cong., 1st sess., H.R. 6894, P.L. 94-24, May 23, 1975.

————. *Second Supplemental Appropriations Act, 1975.* 94th Cong., 1st sess., H.R. 5899, P.L. 94-32, June 12, 1975.

Newspapers and Periodicals

Baldwin, Hanson, W. "75,000 More G.I.'s Going to Vietnam." *New York Times*, October 4, 1966, 1.

Broder, David, S. "Republicans Seek Domestic Cutback Before A Tax Rise." *New York Times*, March 27, 1966, 1.

"G.O.P. Says Johnson Deceives on War." *New York Times*, September 21, 1966, 5.

"Johnson Juggles, But It Isn't Easy." *New York Times*, December 11, 1966, 240.

"Johnson to Seek Up to $10 Billion More for Vietnam." *Wall Street Journal*, December 7, 1966, 3.

Le Breton, Edmund. "GOP Leaders Warn against Any Tax Boost." *Washington Post*, December 22 1965, A2.

Norris, John, G. "Senators Back Military on Spending." *Washington Post*, August 21, 1966, A19.

Wicker, Tom. "Johnson Is Beset By Tax Rise Issue." *New York Times*, December 20, 1965, 1.

THE GLOBAL WAR ON TERROR (GWOT)

Books

Fletcher, Charles, Pamela W. Forsyth, Michael C. Frieders, and others. *COST User's Guide: Using the Contingency Operations Support Tool (COST) to Estimate the Costs of Contingency Operations*. Alexandria: Institute for Defense Analysis, 2004.

Government Publications

Congressional Budget Office. *Federal Funding for Homeland Security: An Update*. Washington, DC: GPO, 2005.

Congressional Research Service. *Availability of Army Funds Without Immediate Supplemental*, CRS Memorandum, by Stephen Daggett. Washington, DC: GPO, 2003.

Congressional Research Service. *Combating Terrorism: 2001 Congressional Debate on Emergency Supplemental Allocations*, CRS RL31187, by Amy Belasco and Larry Nowles. Washington, DC: GPO, 2002.

Congressional Research Service, *Combating Terrorism: First Emergency Supplemental Appropriations – Distribution of Funds to Departments and Agencies*, RL31173, by James R. Riehl. Washington, DC: GPO, 2003.

Congressional Research Service. *Supplemental Appropriations for FY2002: Combating Terrorism and Other Issues*, CRS RL31406, by Amy Belasco and Larry Nowles. Washington, DC: GPO, 2002.

Government Accountability Office. *Combating Terrorism: Determining and Reporting Federal Funding Data*, GAO-06-161. Washington, DC: GPO, 2006.

Government Accountability Office. *Fiscal Year 2004 Costs for the Global War on Terrorism Will Exceed Supplemental, Requiring DOD to Shift Funds from Other Uses*, GAO-04-915. Washington, DC: GPO, 2004.

Government Accountability Office. *Global War on Terrorism: DoD Should Consider All Funds Requested for the War When Determining Needs and Covering Expenses*, GAO-05-767. Washington, DC: GPO, 2005.

Government Accountability Office. Report to Senate. Committee on Appropriations. Subcommittee on Defense. *Tracking of Emergency Response Funds for the War on Terrorism*, GAO-03-346. Washington, DC: GPO, 2003.

Riehl, James, R. 2003. See Congressional Research Service. 2003.

U.S. Department of Defense. Office of the Chairman of the Joint Chiefs of Staff.Directorate for Force Structure, Resources and Assessments (J8). Program and Budget Analysis Division (PBAD). Unpublished Unclassified Working Papers. September 9, 2003.

U.S. Department of Defense. Office of the Chairman of the Joint Chiefs of Staff."Posture Statement of the Chairman of the Joint Chiefs of Staff, General Peter Pace." Prepared for: Congress. Senate. Committee on Armed Services. 109th Cong., 2nd sess., February 7, 2006.

U.S. Department of Defense. Office of the Under Secretary of Defense (Comptroller). *FY 2004 Supplemental Request for Operation Iraqi Freedom (OIF), Operation Enduring Freedom (OEF), Operation Noble Eagle (ONE)*. [Washington, DC]: U.S. Department of Defense, 2003.

U.S. Department of Defense. Office of the Under Secretary of Defense (Comptroller). *Defense Emergency Response Fund FY2002 Execution Report*. Unpublished Briefing Papers.September, 2002.

U.S. President. Speech. "George W. Bush Address to a Joint Session of Congress." U.S. Capitol, Washington, DC, September 20, 2001.

U.S. President. Speech. "George W. Bush State of the Union Address." U.S. Capitol, Washington, DC, January 29, 2002.

Zakheim, Dov. "Transcript of Under Secretary of Defense (Comptroller) Press Conference/Briefing." Department of Defense, Washington, DC, April 16, 2003). Available at http://www.defenselink.mil/transcripts/2003/tr20030416-0111.html.

Zakheim, Dov. "Transcript of Under Secretary of Defense (Comptroller) Press Conference/Briefing." Department of Defense, Washington, DC, (3 February 2003): Available at http://www.defenselink.mil/transcripts/2003/t02032003_t0203budget.html.

Journals

Matthews, William. "Shadow Budget." *Armed Forces Journal*. (April 2006): 10.

Legislation and Related Documents

Hearings, Debates, and Committee Reports

U.S. Congress. House. Committee on Appropriations. Subcommittee on Defense. FY *2004 Appropriations: Hearing before the Committee on Appropriations, Subcommittee on Defense*. 108th Cong., 1st sess., March 27, 2003.

U.S. Congress. Senate. Committee on Armed Services. *Posture Hearing FY2006 Budget: Defense*.109th Cong., 1st sess., February 17, 2005.

Public Laws

U.S. Congress. *2001 Emergency Supplemental Appropriations Act for Recovery from and Response to Terrorist Attacks on the United States*. 107th Cong., 1st sess., H.R. 2888, P.L. 107-38, September 18, 2001.

U.S. Congress. *Making Further Continuing Appropriations for the Fiscal Year 2002, and for Other Purposes*. H.J. Res. 68, P.L. 107–48, October 12, 2001.

U.S. Congress. *Foreign Operations, Export Financing, and Related Programs Appropriations Act, 2002*. 107th Cong., 2nd sess., H.R. 2506, P.L. 107–115, January 10, 2002.

U.S. Congress. *Department of Defense and Emergency Supplemental Appropriations for Recovery From and Response to Terrorist Attacks on the United States, 2002.* 107th Cong., 2nd sess., H.R. 3338, P.L. 107–117, January 10, 2002.

U.S. Congress. *2002 Supplemental Appropriations Act for Further Recovery From and Response to Terrorist Attacks on the United States.* 107th Cong., 2nd sess., H.R. 4775, P.L. 107-206, August 2, 2002.

U.S. Congress. *Afghanistan Freedom Support Act of 2002.* 107th Cong., 2nd sess., P.L. 107-327, December 4, 2002.

U.S. Congress. *Consolidated Appropriations Resolution, 2003.* 108th Cong., 1st sess., H.J. Res. 2, P.L. 108–7, February 20, 2003.

U.S. Congress. *An Act Making Emergency Wartime Supplemental Appropriations for the Fiscal Year 2003, and for Other Purposes.* 108th Cong., 1st sess., H.R. 1559, P.L. 108-11, April 16, 2003.

U.S. Congress. *Department of Defense Appropriation Act, 2004.* 108th Cong., 1st sess., H.R. 2658, P.L. 108-87, September 30, 2003.

U.S. Congress. *An Act Making emergency supplemental appropriations for defense and for the reconstruction of Iraq and Afghanistan for the fiscal year ending September 30, 2004, and for other purposes.* 108th Cong., 1st sess., H.R. 3289, P.L. 108-106, November 6, 2003.

U.S. Congress. Consolidated Appropriations Act, 2004." 108th Cong., 1st sess., H.R. 2673, P.L. 108-199, January 23, 2004.

U.S. Congress. *Department of Defense Appropriation Act, 2005.* 108th Cong., 2nd sess., H.R. 4613, P.L. 108-287, August 5, 2004.

U.S. Congress. *Consolidated Appropriations Act, 2005.* 108th Cong., 2nd sess., H.R. 4818, P.L. 108–447, December 8, 2004.

U.S. Congress. *An Act Making emergency supplemental appropriations for defense the Global War on Terror, and Tsunami Relief, for the fiscal year ending September 30, 2005, and for other purposes.* 109th Cong., 1st sess., H.R. 1268, P.L. 109-13, May 11, 2005.

U.S. Congress. *Making Continuing Appropriations for the Fiscal Year 2006, and for Other Purposes.* 109th Cong., 1st sess., H.J. Res. 68, P.L. 109-77, September 30, 2005.

Newspapers and Periodicals

Zakheim, Dov. "Time Is Running Out On Supplemental Budget." *The Hill,* July 17, 2002.

Other Documents

Congressional Quarterly.Budget Tracker News. *CQ Almanac Backgrounder: Fiscal 2003 Iraq Supplemental Appropriations.*Washington, DC: Congressional Quarterly, 2004.

Index

About the Author

RICHARD M. MILLER, JR., is a serving officer in the U.S. Navy with extensive operational experience and background in budget issues who most recently worked as a resource manager and congressional analyst for the Chairman of the Joint Chiefs of Staff. A distinguished graduate of the National War College and the Naval War College, Commander Miller is the winner of the B. Franklin Reinauer Defense Economics Prize. In addition, he was a Federal Executive Fellow at the Institute for the Study of Conflict, Ideology, and Policy at Boston University.